For the spectator, the recreational skater, or the aspiring world champion, *The Illustrated Encyclopedia of Ice Skating* is the first comprehensive guide to the rules, background and practice of every skating discipline and sport.

Illustrated with hundreds of clear diagrams and photographs, this definitive work of reference provides all the facts on figure skating, pair skating, ice dancing, touring and speed skating, together with a full explanation of every ice rink sport: curling, *Eisschiessen,* bandy and ice hockey, complete with up-to-date information on rule changes and judging procedures.

The rules, equipment, competition requirements, development, practice and skating moves of each sport and discipline are given in detail. The contribution of skating stars — Sonja Henie, Dick Button, the Protopopovs, Rodnina and Zaitsev, John Curry, Gordie Howe and Bobby Hull — is presented in an informed and lively manner.

An extensive reference section includes a three-language glossary of skating terms, and a complete list of world and Olympic champions.

Anyone who has ever enjoyed the spectacle of ice dancing, marveled at the perfect symmetry of pair skaters, wondered at the grace of a figure skater or the energy of a hockey player will gain new insight and information.

MARK HELLER is the wintersports correspondent for *The Guardian.* The contributors to *The Illustrated Encyclopedia of Ice Skating* are all leading skating authorities in their own skating discipline or sport: sports journalists, international competitors, television commentators and members of skating associations and governing bodies.

The Illustrated Encyclopedia of
ICE SKATING

The Illustrated Encyclopedia of ICE SKATING

Edited by

MARK HELLER

PADDINGTON PRESS LTD

NEW YORK & LONDON

Library of Congress Cataloging in Publication Data
Main entry under title:
The Illustrated encyclopedia of ice skating.
Bibliography: p. 211
Includes index.
1. Skating—Dictionaries. I. Heller, Mark F.
GV849.I44 796.9'1'03 79-14633
ISBN 0 448 22427 5 (U.S. and Canada only)
ISBN 0 7092 0325 X

Filmset in England by SX Composing Ltd., Rayleigh, Essex
Printed and bound in the United States
Designed by Sandra Shafee

In the United States
PADDINGTON PRESS
Distributed by
GROSSET & DUNLAP

In the United Kingdom
PADDINGTON PRESS

In Canada
Distributed by
RANDOM HOUSE OF CANADA LTD.

In Southern Africa
Distributed by
ERNEST STANTON (PUBLISHERS) (PTY.) LTD.

In Australia and New Zealand
Distributed by
A.H. & A.W. REED

CONTENTS

CONTRIBUTORS

SANDRA STEVENSON is the skating correspondent for *The Guardian* and is a frequent contributor to *Skate*, an international publication. A skater since childhood, for several years she made her living by appearing in ice shows. She now travels all over the world, reporting on major international championships.

DOUG GILBERT is a sports writer for the *Montreal Gazette* with a special interest in ice hockey, and has been closely associated with the North American game for many years.

ALAN WEEKS is the B.B.C.'s leading television commentator on skating and ice hockey. He was the secretary of Brighton Tigers ice hockey team, and his efforts helped make this team the leader in the European league. He is a director of the Sports Aid Foundation which sponsors young athletes.

DR. KURT OPPELT was the Austrian, European, world and Olympic champion in pair skating for 1956. He is now the director of Pennsylvania State University Ice Skating School and has been a coach and instructor for many years. He is the chairman of the Ice Skating Institute of America Committee for Handicapped Programs and is a pioneer in the development of teaching methods for disabled skaters.

ROBIN WELSH is the secretary of The Royal Caledonian Curling Club, the mother club of curling in the world, and secretary of the International Curling Federation. He is the author of *Beginner's Guide to Curling*, and edits *The Scottish Curler*, a curling magazine.

NIGEL BROWN has competed in international pair skating competitions and represented Switzerland in three world championships in ice dancing, after introducing the discipline to the Alps. A noted skating authority, he is the author of a complete history of skating.

ERNEST MATTHEWS has had a lifelong association with skating, in particular, speed skating. He is active in skating associations and is an Honorary Life Member of the International Speed Skating Association and the International Skating Union (ISU).

CLAUS DEUTELMOSER is a journalist specializing in wintersports and has been a distinguished competitor in *Eisschiessen*.

HARRY L.J. KOLKS is the editor of the Dutch skating journal, *Skaatskronik*, and is closely connected with the development of skating sports in the Netherlands.

BORIS KHAVINE is a leading Soviet sports writer and skating authority.

FRANK NOVOSAD is a Canadian sports journalist with a special interest in the relationship between skating and music.

FOREWORD

SKATING IS A PLEASURE that knows no social bounds and has a history as old as the human race. From Glasgow to Los Angeles, Alaska to Omsk, indoor and outdoor ice rinks are crowded with ordinary people, young and old, skating in pairs, in groups or alone, for no other reason than enjoyment. The basic fun of sliding – on snow or ice – has been with us since prehistoric times. The first true skates were made for pleasure – the fact that they proved useful for transport over frozen lakes and rivers was an added bonus.

Nowadays, everyone can appreciate the athleticism and artistry of world class competitive skating, thanks to television. Figure skating, pair skating, ice hockey, speed skating and ice dancing have become compulsive viewing for millions who live far from any form of ice.

This encyclopedia is the first to include the entire spectrum of ice rink activities. The contributors are some of the most literate and experienced observers of the ice rink sports – in some cases they are themselves former world class or Olympic competitors. They explain the rules, practice and development of such diverse sports as bandy, curling, ice hockey, speed skating, *Eisschiessen* and figure skating, with the aid of hundreds of diagrams and photographs. A three-language glossary explains technical terms and a complete register of Olympic and world championship results is provided.

The result is a complete source book for anyone interested in skating either as a participant or a spectator: from recreational skaters who barely know the basic moves and aspiring world champions, to armchair experts who would like to know just what did happen in that split-second flash of limbs and skates. It is hoped that the information provided by this book will enhance and complement the spectacle of competitive performance while giving greater insight into the technicalities of the sports.

The compilation of this book would have been impossible without the wholehearted cooperation of the national and international governing bodies of each skating sport. My thanks are due to Beat Häsler, Director of the International Skating Union, Ernest Matthews of the International Speed Skating Association, Harry L.J. Kolks, editor of *Skaatskronik*, the Dutch skating journal, and to all the dozens of people who patiently answered my questions. Above all, my thanks are due to the contributors who were mercifully tolerant of my desire for a standard style and format. Last but not least, my thanks to Elizabeth Wilhide, my editor at Paddington Press who helped to turn the manuscript into a readable book.

MARK HELLER
London, 1979

The Illustrated Encyclopedia of
ICE SKATING

INTRODUCING

SKATING

I

THE DEVELOPMENT OF SKATING

Ice skating was born as a means of transportation over frozen lakes and rivers of northern Europe. Numerous archeological finds seem to indicate that some form of skating was a widespread winter activity more than four thousand years ago. The earliest skates were fashioned from the metacarpal bones of oxen, deer and sheep. They were about a foot (30cm) long and had a hole drilled at each end through which were threaded the leather thongs that bound them to the skater's feet. They may have been derived from sled runners; by tying the runners to his feet, Neolithic man could become his own sled. By comparison with modern skates, they were sliders rather than skates. Because they were flat-bottomed it was not possible to get any forward thrust from a sideways stroke; the "skater" had to carry a staff with a pointed end which was used to push, guide the slide and to brake. Experiments carried out in the 1890s by Herbert Fowler using replicas of these ancient bone skates did discover that a considerable degree of push was possible by taking off from the point of the skate.

What are believed to be the oldest known skates are a pair of bone skates, 11 inches long (28cm) found in a Swiss lake and thought to be about four thousand years old. They are now in the Stadtbibliothek in Bern, Switzerland.

Bone skates were used for thousands of years until about A.D. 200 when iron implements began to be used in Scandinavia. Thick iron blades were set into a wooden plate which was strapped to the foot. The Scandinavian sagas contain many references to sliding on ice. Runic poetry also refers repeatedly to sliding on ice and implies that it is one of the essential accomplishments of a nobleman or a warrior. The Younger Edda refers in *Saxo Grammaticus* to a certain Oller as being "such a cunning wizard [at skating]." Bishop Percy's translations of runic poetry include a number of epic poems in which sliding over ice is listed among the eight or nine boasted skills.

Whether these references do describe skating on short skates over ice is open to some doubt. Skating might have been confused with skiing – a well-established skill for Norsemen – references suffering in translation owing to a widespread contemporary ignorance of anything to do with skiing outside of Scandinavia. The prob-

Medieval skating scene at St. George's Gate, Antwerp, Belgium, showing early skating games and contemporary skates.

lem is further complicated by the known existence of a special type of skate, known as a snow skate, about 24inches long (60cm) which was used for moving over frozen snow too hard for ordinary skis.

The earliest "modern" iron skates appeared in Holland some time before the fourteenth century, when an iron blade was slotted into the sole of a wooden clog. It was this invention which led directly to the discovery of the "Dutch Roll" – the simplest skating step – which is still used by all skaters at some time and is the main step used by speed skaters. The Dutch Roll uses the inside edges of the skates to push diagonally backward while gliding forward on the outside edge of the other skate. This was only possible with a hard and sharp iron blade. The Dutch Roll transformed skating from uncontrolled crude sliding to controlled and powerful gliding.

The earliest known pictorial record of modern skating is the woodcut illustration for Brugmann's book, *Vita Lijdwine*, dated 1498, the history of a young Dutch girl, Liedwi, who was knocked down by another skater and broke a rib. She never recovered from the accident and retreated to a convent to spend her life in religious work. The accident is said to have happened in 1396 when Liedwi was sixteen. In the background of the fallen Liedwi is the picture of a skater unmistakably performing what we know as the Dutch Roll. After her death Liedwi was adopted as the patron saint of skaters.

According to accounts of the Battle of the River Ij in 1572 against the army of Don Frederick, Dutch army troops wearing skates crossed the river and took the Spaniards by surprise. Don Frederick subsequently ordered several thousand pairs for his own troops and attempted to teach them to skate. It seems that this scheme failed and Don Frederick was never able to make military use of the skates.

By the middle of the seventeenth century skating had become a popular sport in the Low Countries. Speed races on the frozen canals were a regular feature of village life while the aristocracy enjoyed themselves in elementary figure skating and graceful promenading on skates. From the Low Countries skating was introduced into Britain at the time of the Restoration by Charles II and his retinue who had learned the art while in exile in Holland. However skating in some form has been known in Britain considerably longer. It is mentioned in Fitzstephen's *Description of the most noble City of London* written in 1180 and translated by Stow in the sixteenth century – by which time skating was well-known and Stow would not have been misled by references to an activity he could not understand. By the time of the great frost of 1662/3, skating had become popular and was a much-practiced sport. London may still have been unaccustomed to the activity for skating is mentioned by Pepys in his entry for December 1, 1662 and also by Evelyn that same winter as something of a novelty. Both also refer to skating on the Thames during the frost of 1683.

Possibly owing to a succession of hard winters, skating was accepted in England as a serious pastime. A repertoire of movements was first described in print by a Scotsman, Robert Jones, in his *Treatise of Skating* published in 1772, thought to be the first published book on skating. Scotland can boast a further skating first. The world's first skating club was founded in Edinburgh in 1784, according to the earliest surviving records, though the club probably dates back much earlier.

In France, in the early nineteenth century, a group of poets, artists, writers and priests who took up skating extended the original British repertoire of established skating movements by inventing pirouettes, steps and a jump. One of them, J. Garcin, author of *Le Vrai Patineur* (1813) gave skating a language of its own. This French group, known as the "Gilets Rouges" because they wore red vests, laid especial emphasis on graceful carriage of the body while skating. They introduced an aesthetic into skating performance.

With the invention of the all-metal skates by E.V. Bushnell in America towards the middle of the nineteenth century, a new wave of enthusiasm for skating spread through many countries. Bushnell's invention signaled the beginning of a general improvement in the skate. With firm fastening uniting skate and boot it was possible to twist and turn and to attempt extravagant movements, enabling skating to make a great technical leap forward.

Britain, and later Vienna, became centers of this important evolution. In Britain, the Victorian skater whose inventive genius was considerable, concentrated on cutting new figures and turns that today form the basis of skating art. Then in 1864, Jackson Haines, a North American ballet master who had adapted dance movements to skating, arrived in

Young boy skating in the English style. A woodcut from an English children's book, *circa* 1830.

Europe. Unable to introduce his new principles to British skating – Victorian austerity allowed no frivolity – he went to Stockholm and from there embarked in 1868 upon a triumphant tour of continental Europe. He finally settled in Vienna where his ideas that skating figures should be interpreted to music were most welcomed.

There were now two opposing schools of thought. The English practiced skating as a science, as something to do. The Viennese, under the influence of Jackson Haines, practiced it as a spectacle, as something to see. For over a quarter of a century a conflict of ideas divided the skaters of the world. But in the end the Viennese school had triumphed in continental Europe by the close of the century.

During this time, skating was instrumental in creating the wintersports holiday. Enthusiastic British skaters who found their own skating season too short and too unpredictable set off to Switzerland to skate on the frozen lakes of the Alps, St. Moritz and Davos and discovered all the other pleasures of a winter alpine landscape. These early holidaymakers were

An inventive approach to pair skating. A lithograph by Vernet from *Le Bon Genre de Paris*, 1810

the first to encourage the creation of natural ice rinks. They made skating the most important of all the wintersports.

But not every Briton went abroad to skate. In the Fen country of England speed skating became a sport of the people. Races were organized for cash prizes and this, and the heavy betting on the results, inspired some dubious practices and threatened to destroy the original high ideals of the sport. In 1879 a number of British skaters met to discuss how best to restore the sporting spirit to skating. The result was the founding of the National Skating Association of Great Britain, the first skating federation in the world. At first the Association recognized only speed skating but in 1881 it also took figure skating under its wing.

About 1870 a new form of skating appeared in the Fen district and in Lincolnshire. It was the first ice rink skating game: bandy, a kind of field hockey on ice which eventually became modern ice hockey. Whether or not it was in fact invented in England as early as the eighteenth century is still under debate.

In July 1892 the International Skating Union (ISU) was founded to protect the interests of skating and to organize international competitions. The founder countries were Holland, Great Britain,

Young Swiss pair skaters at the turn of the century brave the snow at a skating rink in the Alps.

Germany and Austria together, Sweden and Hungary. The first world championship took place in St. Petersburg (Leningrad) in 1896. The competition was divided into two sections corresponding to the English and the Viennese schools – "figuring" as it was then called – and a free program of the competitor's own devising, skated to music. The winner was Gilbert Fuchs of Germany who became the first world champion. From then on skating was enriched by a number of talented performers, many of them the inventors of new movements, like Ulrich Salchow of Sweden who won the first Olympic skating competition, ten world championships, nine European titles and thirty-eight gold medals and invented the Salchow jump.

The earliest international skating competitions were monopolized by men. Then in 1902 a young English woman, Madge Syers-Cave, entered the world championships and finished second to the great Salchow. In 1906 the first women's world championship was held in Davos and was won by Madge Syers-Cave. Jenny Herz of Vienna, who came second, also made history by being the first woman to execute the sitting spin invented by Jackson Haines.

Women skaters now had to be recognized as the equals of men in technique.

This brought about another medium of expression to the art – pair skating. In 1908 the first world pairs championships were held in St. Petersburg and won by Anna Hübler and Heinrich Burger of Germany.

Music soon began to be used as an accompaniment to exhibition performances and in competition programs. Lily Kronberger of Hungary took a brass band to Vienna for the world championships of 1911 to accompany her interpretation of the *Pas des Patineurs*. But this was exceptionally sophisticated for its time. For the most part music was merely a pleasant background; there was no attempt to fit the skating figures to music.

Skating was looked upon not as an athletic sport but as an art, a lyrical expression of poetry in motion. Then Sonja Henie, an eleven-year-old girl competitor in the 1924 winter Olympic games at Chamonix changed the entire face of the sport. The appearance of a child in the adult-oriented world of competitive skat-

Beatrice Loughran, an early "fancy" skater, pirouettes at Lake Placid, New York.

The famous Norwegian figure skating champion, Sonja Henie, shown after winning her third Olympic gold medal at Garmisch-Partenkirchen in 1929.

ing was in itself a sensation, but Sonja Henie rammed home the potentialities of youth by injecting an athletic tone into her performance. She did not win this contest, her first international competition, but the talent she showed started a new trend. She went on to dominate women's skating for a decade, winning ten world titles and six European and three Olympic gold medals. She became one of the most famous celebrities in the world of sport and made skating known and appreciated throughout the world. Apart from remodeling women's skating she refashioned it as well. The athletic element she introduced into skating could not be performed wearing ankle-length skirts and wide hats. Sonja Henie brought in the short skirt that enabled women skaters to indulge in any movement unhampered. Last but not least Sonja Henie, for the first time in skating history, drew crowds that packed the ice-rinks and stadiums for her freestyle skating exhibitions, and changed skating from a participator sport for the few into a spectator attraction for all. Retiring from amateur competition, she went to the United States to skate in a new way, becoming a professional show girl on ice and establishing the "ice show" as a permanent theatrical entertainment.

The Sonja Henie era brought a fresh wave of enthusiasm for skating. Artificial ice rinks, not by any means a new invention, mushroomed in the principal cities of the world and made year-round skating for everyone a possibility. It also allowed aspiring skaters to train for twelve months in the year. The standards now being set in international competitions require such dedication. It is estimated that some twenty thousand hours of training are needed to produce a world champion and not less than ten thousand to make a high-grade senior for a national event.

By 1935 skating began to develop along highly scientific lines under the influence of the modern English school. The scientific approach applied by British skaters in the nineteenth century to figure skating was not applied to free skating. A cold, almost soulless, technique produced a mechanical skater, powerful and reliable but showing little individual personal expression. Cecilia Colledge of Great Britain, world champion in 1937, exemplified the view that full representation of the difficult art of skating could be achieved only by perfect technique and that this could be acquired only by concentrating on it to the exclusion of everything else. The aim of technical perfection laid a solid foundation on which wider development of the art was able to take place.

After World War II, skating was to undergo a spectacular upheaval. A "new look" from America revolutionized the art. But before it burst upon the skating world a new heroine passed by. Barbara Ann Scott of Canada, champion of the world in 1947 and 1948, brought skating onto the front pages of the newspapers by her charm, her radiant grace, and her incomparable talent. Like Sonja Henie, her name echoed in the remotest parts of the world where wintersports had never been heard of.

The athletic element that Sonja Henie had initiated manifested itself in a particular vigorous manner with the spectacular arrival in international competition of the U.S. national champion Richard Button in 1947. He thundered onto the ice arena with a display of power skating. Using the ice surface to the full to gather as much speed as possible for takeoff, and cramming every ounce of muscle into the effort, he jumped barrier-high, making

Dick Button executes one of his phenomenal leaps after winning his second Olympic gold medal at Oslo in 1949.

phenomenal leaps. He was the first skater to execute a double Axel in competition (two and a half turns in the air) and he carried off the world championship for five successive years (1948–52).

Skating now went on a jumping spree and an exaggerated forced athleticism invaded the more elegant forms of the sport. Jumping appeared for a time to be for many people the sole object of skating. Women embraced the jumping craze as enthusiastically as the men. Jeannette Altwegg of Great Britain, Jacqueline du Bief of France, world champions in 1951 and 1952 respectively, followed in the wake of Button. Later Carol Heiss, a young American already in the world's elite by the time she was thirteen, executed leaps that rivaled those of any of the men.

Skating jumps reached a high standard of excellence. Ten years after Button's retirement, Donald Jackson of Canada in the 1962 world championships in Prague, executed the first triple jump, a triple Lutz, and he then went on to perform a triple Salchow and a triple loop. During the world championships of Munich in 1974 the U.S. men's champion, Gordie McKellan, achieved in an exhibition display a triple Axel (three and a half turns in the air) and the Innsbruck Olympics in 1976 saw the first somersalt.

Button's influence was also felt in pair skating, but here the athletic element was more gracefully incorporated into the routines. Lifts, double and triple, some of them strangely beautiful in their floating grace, were introduced. And it was in pair skating that artistry first returned to skating. The world champion Russian pair, Ludmilla Belousova and Oleg Protopopov, showed the beauty and elegance of a glide blended with outstanding athletic feats, the whole immaculately performed to music. The artist had rejoined the athlete.

This development was not restricted to pair skating. The unforgettable performances of John Curry of Great Britain who won the European, world and Olympic titles in 1976 with a display of ballet on ice, in terms of athletic virtuosity and breathtaking artistry, raised to the level of art by the interpretation of an imaginative musical score, set an entirely new horizon for both men and women skaters.

The world championships of 1968, won for the fourth time by the Protopopovs, marked an end of an era in skating. For seventy-two years the skating of scientific figures had been reckoned the most important side of the art, although for nearly two decades freestyle skating had surpassed the figure branch in skill and artistry. Championship scoring allocated marks between the two branches of the sport in the proportion of sixty to figure skating against only forty to freestyle. After the 1968 championships the injustice of this was recognized, and in 1969 the two branches were given equal weight and marks allocated between them on a fifty-fifty basis.

In 1973 a further change was made. A short program comprising prescribed free skating movements was introduced to the competition. Marks were reallocated in the proportion of forty to the figures, twenty for the short program and forty for the freestyle performance. This was still found to be out of line with the realities of modern skating, so in 1976 the figure section suffered a further depreciation to the benefit of the freestyle performance: figures thirty, short program twenty, freestyle fifty.

Inevitably, when reviewing the history and development of a sport such as skating, attention must be focused on landmarks in the area of the competitive disciplines. It is these landmarks that receive public attention and acclaim, and they exert a far-reaching influence on public participation in the sport. Strangely, this influence will only be seen in the corners of public ice rinks where solitary skaters practice the performance of school figures with iron concentration. The rest of the rink will be filled with skaters and would-be skaters of all ages and abilities, scraping round and round the area of the rink. Apparently aimless, obviously enthusiastic, they chase no medals, no qualifications, no records, but only enjoyment. This can be seen even more clearly on any winter's day when the weather has been severe, the snow absent, the days clear and sunny, and the ponds, lakes and canals in Holland, England, Scotland or North America are frozen. Chairs are still used as a prop for the novice; courting couples, young or old, still skate gracefully arm-in-arm doing the ancient Dutch Roll; improvised games of ice hockey are played in every corner and speed skaters with their long, flowing steps and graceful crossover turns circuit the edges of the ice. Girls giggle, young men make a joke of their clumsiness and perhaps, in some quiet secluded corner, it might even be possible to glimpse an elderly gentleman performing curious, jerky arabesques about an orange resting on the ice to mark his center. If Liedwi or the red-vested gentlemen or even the Breughels could be miraculously recreated on such a day, they would feel completely at home.

The exceptionally severe winter of 1963, which froze Lake Zurich for only the third time this century, demonstrated how universally popular skating still is for recreational pleasure. That winter saw

Recreational skating in Central Park, New York City, 1862.

Outdoor skating in the middle of New York City at the Rockefeller Center skating rink.

literally hundreds of thousands of skaters out on the lake from dawn to dusk.

At three years old it is fun to tumble and slide; at seventy-three, skating is delightful exercise that can provide unparalleled pleasure which otherwise old age seems to preclude. For the more experienced and expert performer, skating offers an infinitely wide variety – speed, for the speed skater is the fastest self-propelled person in the world; art, for skating can provide consummate expression of movement and musical interpretation; competitive excitement in the fastest team game in the world, ice hockey. And for the contemplative, when the still waters of pond or canal are frozen, it is the lowlander's answer to the great pleasure of the cross-country skier. It is a family recreation and a solitary skill at one and the same time.

There are six skating disciplines: singles skating comprising figures and individual freestyle, pair skating, ice dancing, touring skating and speed skating. For any skater, figure skating is the best single approach. Many novice skaters, aspiring to speed skating or ice hockey, often do not realize that a mastery of figure skating and the elementary freestyle figures is the basis for fast, controlled skating.

Figure skating is a strict science and in championships precision counts like gold. But cutting figures with skates is not only for the competition-minded; it is an absorbing recreation for the enthusiast. When a skater can trace a circle on both feet and join two of them together to form a figure eight, it is the first achievement in the art of skating. There are forty-one variations of the figure eight and about a quarter of this number are within the capabilities of most skaters. In every country there are tests or examinations based on a progressive mastery of a set number of figures. Most big city rinks hold special dance sessions when the surface is cleared for a quarter of an hour, two or three times during a public session.

Freestyle skating is the discipline in which all enthusiastic singles novices would like to excel. While many gymnastic demonstrations are beyond the capabilities of the average skater, most can learn to spin, to execute some of the simpler jumps and combinations. And on this simple basis even pair skating can become more than a sedate promenade round the ice rink. But it all starts and finishes with figure skating, and when the rigors of ice hockey and long distance touring have become too much for elderly heart and lungs, it is to recreational figure skating that the devoted, lifelong skater returns.

2

SKATING AND THE ARTS

Sport and art are uneasy companions. For the entire history of western civilization the artist has expressed both public and private disdain for the muscular attributes and supposedly diminished mentality of people who engage in performance competition. That skating, probably the most artistic, graceful and skilled of all competitive sporting activities, should be lumped together with football, boxing and athletics might well seem strange in the age of John Curry and the Protopopovs. But it is a fact and cannot be omitted in the consideration of the history of either art or sport.

Skating, as a winter recreation, has been a popular pastime since the early middle ages. It was not until the late nineteenth century that it was ever considered a competitive sport. The only competitions were speed contests held at the annual winter carnivals on the frozen canals of Holland – and these were folk festivals rather than real skating competitions. This was a period of more than four hundred years during which the arts – notably painting – went through a great evolution from the primitive representations of religious or political experiences and myths, through a period of accurate contemporary reproduction of the scenes and moods of everyday life to emerge eventually as the portrayers of abstract and intellectual concepts.

Few artists – musicians or painters – enjoyed any great financial stability. For them, possibly even more than for the poorest peasant, winter was a time of survival, a time of great physical discomfort and deprivation which did little to stimulate artistic creation. The outside world was cruel, crude, ugly and dangerous. In Europe the "peasant" was actively feared; and not without reason, for it was in this section of the community that many of the revolts, massacres, pillages and plagues originated. Europe of the Hundred Years War, the Thirty Years War, and the plagues and pestilences which destroyed nine-tenths of the population lived two very different lives – the protected colony of court and church followers, the few wealthy merchants and war lords – and the others. It was among the privileged group that art flourished. Here artists and musicians made their income with the portrayal of idyllic country scenes, comfortable family life, complacent public officers and the illustration of the great scenes of military glory and divine mythology.

Literature, as far as recreational activities were concerned, contented itself with the recording of the facts either in the form of diaries, such as those of Pepys and Evelyn (the first to record skating in England and to use the modern word "skate") or as social histories, recording for posterity the life and times of others – the great and the low.

It was not until the mid-eighteenth century that skating received any noteworthy literary attention. This did not take the form of a romantic description of the art or the experience of skating, but rather the recording of what could today be described as the metaphysical implications of the act of skating. Klopstock, the German poet (1724–1803) concerned himself almost entirely with folkloristic recreations and great Nordic classical odes and saw in skating an essentially rustic tradition, a physical attribute like those praised in the Norse chronicles.

Goethe (1749–1832) made only one reference to skating, which he was very fond of and is said to have practiced whenever conditions permitted. This was in his autobiography, *Aus meinem Leben.* Here he specifically refers to skating as a vehicle to the many revelations he had when studying and enjoying nature.

A contemporary of Goethe, Wordsworth, who learned to skate while at school in Hawkshead in the Lake District, practiced skating throughout his life and devoted one entire poem *Nothing* to the almost mystical effect of skating, in particular the performance of circles and pirouettes. Later, in *The Prelude – Childhood Part I,* he recalls with dramatic vividness the excitement of skating in the evening after school had finished:

. . . and in the frosty season
All shod with steel
We hissed along the polished ice in games . . .

There have been a number of poems written about skaters and skating, mostly by what can be described as minor poets. Constance Carrier – *Black Water and Bright Air*; Tagliabue – *Fast*; Winifred Welles – *River Skater*; even Rudyard Kipling wrote a lesser known poem entitled *Skating.* The most recent contribution to a surprisingly long list is David Daiches' *To Kate, Skating better than her date.* Most concordances list such poems under "skating" or "winter scenes."

Prose has treated skating less well. Apart from a large number of contemporary accounts of skating in the Netherlands in the seventeenth and eighteenth centuries and a number of Dutch children's stories of the middle and late nineteenth century, only two major literary works have, even in passing, concerned themselves with skating. Possibly the most famous account is that of an outing by Anna Karenina to a public skating rink in Moscow in the novel by Tolstoy of the same name. More recently, H.E. Bates' novel *Love for Lydia* uses a skating scene as a significant episode. Lydia is taken skating by her young admirer, Christopher Blake; the experience proves to be the key to her own self-discovery. This novel, dramatized on television, enabled the director and cameramen to produce one of the very few really beautiful and expressive passages of film showing recreation skating outside the confines of the modern skating hippodrome.

So far there has been no work of fiction based on skating or with skaters as the central figures, though doubtless, as in the

Hunters in the Snow **by Pieter Brueghel the Elder (1525–1569).**

case of skiing, the competition skating rink will soon feature in some action-packed story to be filmed for television. This would serve admirably as a vehicle for the skating talents of some future world or Olympic skating star.

Examples of paintings of skating are even more hard to find. The best known paintings of skaters are in the works of Pieter Brueghel the Elder (*circa* 1525–1569). Every winter scene he painted is a veritable catalog of ice activities. Best known of all these scenes is *Hunters in the Snow* in the Vienna Kunsthistorisches Museum. In the middle ground there are children playing snake, a man rather unceremoniously hauling his recalcitrant wife along by the hand, a male figure practicing the Dutch Roll, three men playing a game of bandy, three other men engaged in *Eisschiessen*, the forerunner of curling, and two boys playing with tops – a favorite children's ice pastime for the tops spin much better on the smooth ice surface; all that is missing is a decorous couple skating together in harmony. Many of the same activities can be seen in *Winter Landscape with Birdtrap* in the Delporte Collection in Brussels. Here the skating takes place on a frozen canal. The *Numbering of the People at Bethlehem* in the Brussels Museum of Fine Art, has some wonderful detail of contemporary skates and also shows a popular children's game – pushing along the ice in a basket with the aid of two sticks. The *Adoration of the*

The Reverend Walker **by Raeburn.**

Magi, another winter scene, also shows the customary winter ice pleasures.

This form of genre painting – winter landscapes of the Netherlands – became a popular room decoration and there are a large number of such scenes, notably by van der Meer and Avercamp which all bear a superficial resemblance to the Brueghel skating scenes, although they were painted much later. None quite capture the inimitable winter atmosphere of Brueghel's work and Avercamp in particular, seems to have created one particular scene of skaters on a pond or wide canal which he used time and again, rather in the manner of a journeyman painter who furnished wall covering to ordered size and subject.

There appear to have been no skating pictures between the mid-seventeenth century and the early nineteenth century, with the exception of the outstanding portrait by Raeburn of the Reverend Walker. Of all skating pictures, though this pretends to be nothing more than a portrait, this painting succeeds in conveying the very essence of the early English school of figure skating. The bearing and demeanor of the black, serious figure, the strictly disciplined arms and body posture and the obvious competence and love of the art, convey more of the spirit of skating than any picture before or since.

Rather surprisingly, the French Impressionists, although regular visitors to several of the Paris skating rinks, do not appear to have shown any interest in the sport. Only Manet produced two pictures of skaters at the rink in the Rue Blanche, of which only one survives and is now hung in the Fogg Gallery in Cambridge, Massachusetts. This picture conveys little of the sport but does show the fashionable attraction it held in the late nineteenth century.

By the end of the nineteenth century, photography was beginning to record everyday activities and, by the time skating had moved from being a free, winter recreation to a major competitive exhibition in closed rinks, photography had completely supplanted painting for such fleeting and continuously moving spectacles as the freestyle program of a world champion singles skater.

Ballet, now becoming a major inspiration for the freestyle skater, has only ever produced one skating ballet – *Les Patineurs*, choreographed by Frederick Ashton to the music of Meyerbeer from *Le Prophete* and *L'Etoile*, arranged by Constant Lambert. It is, in some way, ironic that John Curry is now working on a skating version of this very ballet; the wheel has come full circle.

3

BASIC EQUIPMENT

ICE RINKS

Ice surfaces for skating can be divided into three distinct periods or ages. All forms of ice activities originated on natural ice surfaces resulting from the freezing of ponds, lakes, canals, rivers and flooded fields. The hard winters of what is known as the little ice age, which lasted from the early fifteenth century until the end of the nineteenth century, made the annual reappearance of considerable areas of ice a regular winter feature and enabled skating to take place from late December until early March. The surfaces, as anyone who has skated on any frozen pond of lake would know, were extremely variable. Given perfect freezing weather with no snow falls, little wind and very low temperatures, the surface could be like a mirror. On the other hand, particularly on larger areas, lakes and large ponds, intermittent snowfall, winds and water currents could leave a sheet of ice lying in waves, with frozen lumpy joins where two adjacent areas had collided and frozen together. Snow mixed with the freezing water could result in a knobbly, fruit-and-nut cake kind of ice which can shake and rattle legs and feet so much that any prolonged skating becomes a true burden.

We know from contemporary accounts that on occasion great efforts were needed to clear the snow from a chosen canal or lake to permit a curling match or a speed skating meet. There is no mention of artificial surfaces being prepared by flooding suitable areas of flat grassland, but it seems likely that this was first practiced in Paris in the late eighteenth century and continued to be done until the advent of manmade ice.

With the arrival of relatively easy winter travel coinciding with a distinct amelioration of the winter weather in the nonalpine countries, the main skating activity shifted from Holland and the British Fen country to the Alps. The earliest wintersports holidays, notably to St. Moritz and Davos, and later to Chamonix, Grindelwald, Gstaad and Villars, revolved around ice rink sports. St. Moritz enthusiasts first skated on the Lake of St. Moritz and later on prepared flat ground next to the Palace and Kulm Hotels. The first special stadium for skating was built at Davos as the lake was too distant for convenience. The Davos Ice Rink was to remain the largest outdoor natural ice rink in the world; it was large enough to house a full 500-meter speed rink, two ice hockey rinks, a curling rink and a special figure skating practice rink. The grandstand housed changing rooms, a restaurant and, most importantly, a balcony on which the ice rink band sat and played marches and waltzes for the skaters.

Ice preparation took place in the late evening after all the skaters had gone home and in the early, pre-dawn hours before even the hardiest figure skaters appeared. First the ice was swept, originally by hand by lines of men with long-handled brooms, sweeping in circles in front of them and later by farm tractors pushing scrapers and snow plows. The ice was watered by a whole array of portable hoses and then polished and scraped to provide a completely true surface.

Frequently, after heavy snowfalls, the rink might be closed for days on end while mountains of snow were swept aside and piled in great ten-foot high walls, which later became part of the grandstand seating for competitions. Similar activity went on in every single wintersports resort.

The end of the great outdoor rinks was inevitable. After the Second World War, although attempts were initially made to recreate these magnificent ice-dromes, labor became not only scarce but prohibitively expensive. At the same time, a succession of disastrous winters with high temperatures and heavy snowfalls resulted in a number of important events being canceled. In addition, the level of competition had become very high and the difference in performance ability too close, so that variations due to weather and human labor in the ice surface resulted in unfair handicaps for some and equally unfair

Outdoor ice rinks at Seefeld in the Austrian Tyrol.

An advertisement for the Central Park Skate Emporium in 1840 boasts, "Everything in the Skating line (except ponds) to suit everybody."

advantages for others.

The demands made by film and the newly arrived television crews added their own burden to the already hard-pressed ice rink owners. Finally, the ISU decreed that all skating competitions were to be held on artificial ice rinks. The ice hockey authorities had already deemed that indoor arenas were guaranteed of good gate money. Even the speed skaters succumbed as the provision of artificially refrigerated speed rinks became a reality.

What is perhaps surprising is that it had taken so long. As early as 1850 Ferdinand Carré had patented a system using sulphuric acid gas for creating artificial ice. This had been successfully used in Paris for a small ice rink. The actual production of artificial cold was much older. William Cullen had discovered a system of evaporating a vapor to freeze water in 1748 at the University of Glasgow. Jacob Perkins discovered a method of using a volatile liquid in a closed system by compressing and expanding it in 1834, and in 1844 John Gorrie, in Florida, used compressed air to cool yellow fever and malaria patients. In the same year, James Harrison used compressed air to refrigerate meat in Australia and later modified his system to use other gases more suitable for use on board ship for transporting frozen carcasses of meat. In 1859, Carré first used ammonia gas dissolved in water for the same purpose.

In 1876, the first artificial ice rink in the world was opened in London, the Glaciarium. The reason this enterprise remained a mere curiosity was the fact that there was ample natural ice to be found in the winter and the machinery used for artificial ice was not sufficiently efficient to be used in the summer. But by 1939, there were very few towns in the western world that did not possess an artificial ice rink although there were very few rinks that operated in the summer. After 1949, there were few ice rinks which did not open for at least ten months every year.

REFRIGERATION SYSTEMS

Two systems are used today. The first, the familiar freon compression system which figures in most domestic refrigerators and uses a synthetic halogenated hydrocarbon gas specifically tailored for cooling is rarely found in large commercial ice rinks, although it is the method used for stage presentations such as *Holiday on Ice*, where the area is comparatively small and the

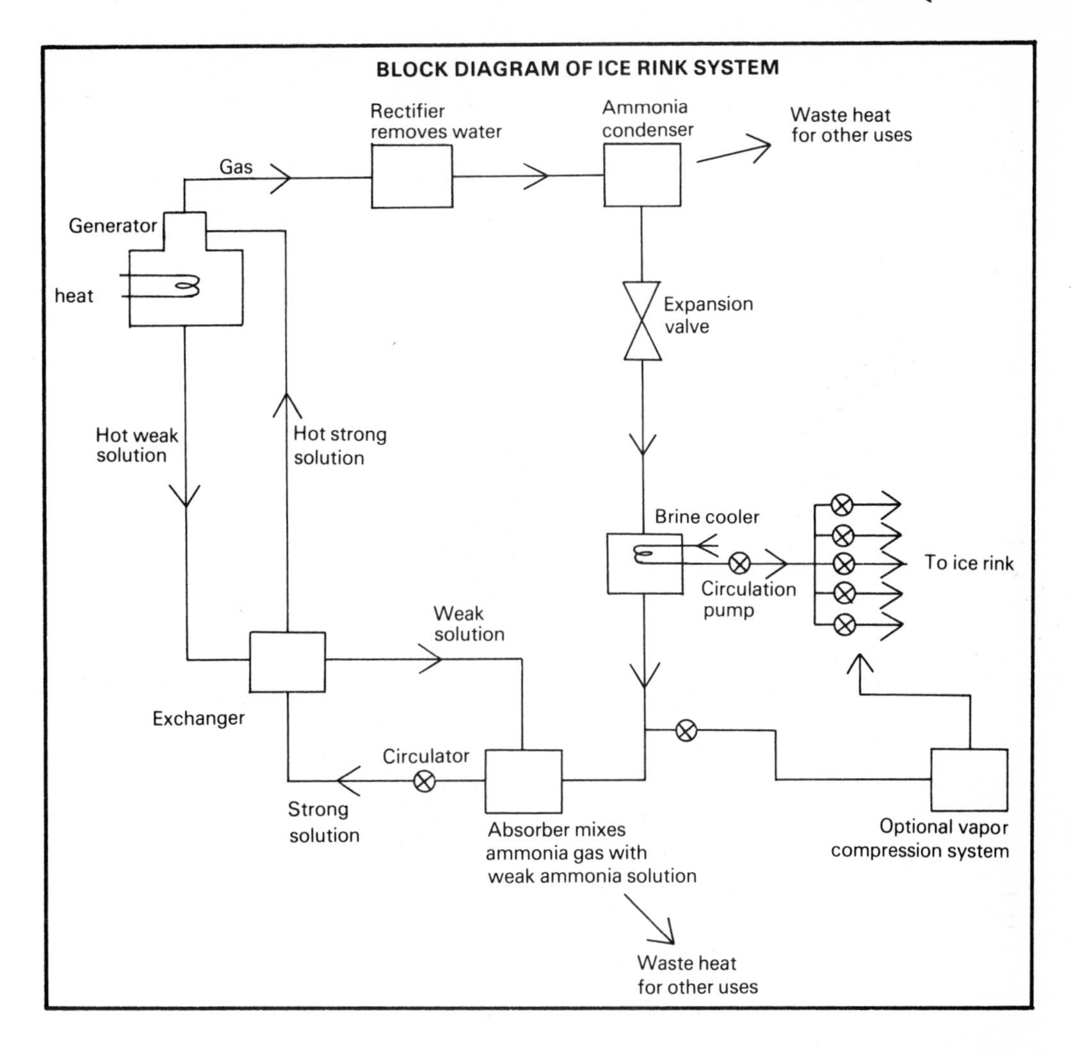

usage limited. Although the freons are nontoxic, they are not suitable for freezing larger areas for technical reasons.

The systems universally used by large ice rink installations, and refrigerated bob runs and ski jumps, are the ammonia anhydride systems. The principle (and this applies equally to the freon systems) is extremely simple. Any gaseous substance, when compressed produces a great deal of heat. When this gas, now usually in the form of a liquid which boils at well below normal temperatures, is released and permitted to expand it becomes extremely cold. In fact, it reclaims the heat it produced on being compressed and by this action refrigerates the area surrounding it. If this cold gas is made to cool a carrier, such as "brine" (nowadays a solution of calcium chloride in water), the brine can be circulated in pipes which, in turn, can be made to freeze a thin layer of water.

In the ammonia anhydride process, ammonia gas, the best heat vehicle after

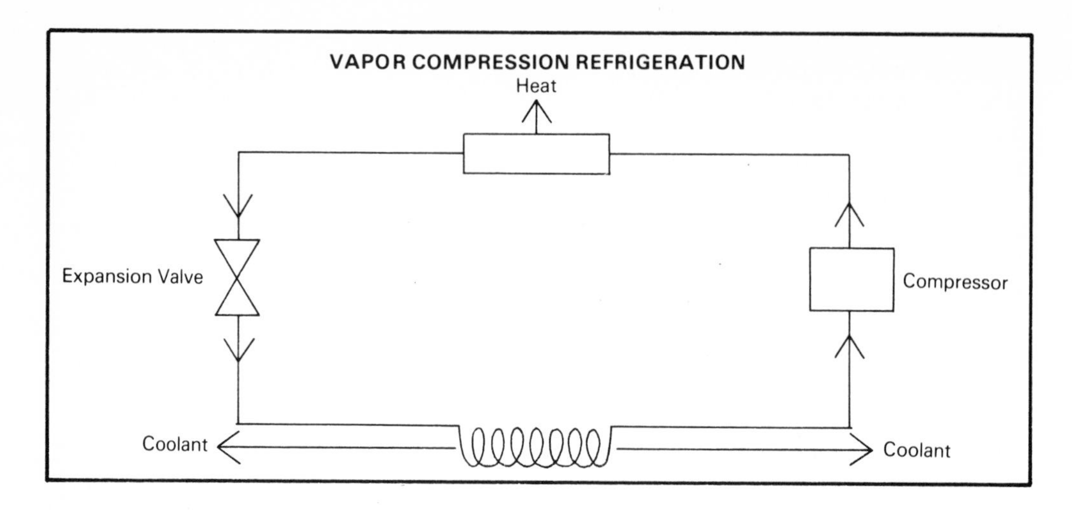

water, is compressed and then allowed to expand. This process can be done in one of two ways. The dry gas can be compressed by means of special pumps and then allowed to expand into a vessel containing coiled pipes carrying brine, and then recompressed; or the compression can be made to take place by dissolving the ammonia in water. Water will dissolve about one thousand times its volume of ammonia gas and having dissolved the gas, the resulting ammonia liquid will take up very much less space than the gas which has been dissolved. It is, in fact, "compressed." The ammonia gas is released by heating, dried, and collected in a strong vessel where it occupies a small volume; the heat drives the gas off under pressure thus achieving the effect of a mechanical compressor. This compressed gas is then expanded in the normal manner and cools the brine pipes, which freezes the ice surface. By varying the speed of decompression and the circulation of brine, it is possible to regulate the freezing temperature very accurately. It is also possible to vary the area to be frozen and to adapt the system to hot or cold outside temperatures. In addition, considerable waste heat is produced and this can, in turn, be usefully employed to heat buildings, swimming pools and the like. This system is known as the ammonia anhydride absorption system. The simple compression system using mechanical compression of either ammonia gas or freon is known as vapor compression refrigeration.

There is one further advantage of using the ammonia process; ammonia gas can be varied in temperature from −104°F to +104°F (−40°C to +40°C) and in this manner it is possible to melt off the accumulated ice very quickly before equally quickly refreezing it.

In practice, in some very large ice rinks – the new Garmisch–Partenkirchen rinks, for example – both the compression system and the absorption system is used, either separately or in tandem. The waste heat operates a large swimming pool, the heating of a very large building complex including a restaurant, gymnasium and swimming pool, as well as the seating accommodation of three international size rinks.

The construction of the actual rink is a

matter of the individual judgment of the engineers concerned, but in general it consists of a concrete foundation, well-drained and capable of disposing of the full complement of water resulting from the melting of the ice sheet. This concrete shell is lined with a suitable heatshield and the hairpin tubes to carry the brine are laid on this, usually embedded in sand. The brine heater pipes require careful designing so that the temperature of the brine reaching the ice area is constant over the entire surface; it is usual to divide the rink into separate areas which can if necessary be frozen at different temperatures.

The brine is circulated by pump and is carefully monitored for composition. Current thought indicates the use of calcium chloride solution of a specific gravity of 1.5 at a pressure of about 30 pounds per square inch. The addition of anti-corrosion chemicals is usually advisable.

Various ice sports require different ice temperatures, so that the quality and friability of the ice suits each purpose. Curling rinks are usually kept at an ice temperature of 10°F (−11 to −12°C); speed skating at 4.5°F (−15°C); ice hockey at 10°F (−12°C), figure skating at 12°F (−10 to −11°C) and recreational skating at an average of 9.5°F (−12.5°C). By dividing up the ice surface, it is perfectly possible to have one end or one side of the rink suitable for curling and the rest for figure skating, or one end devoted to figure skating can have two or three patches at figure skating temperature while the rest of the rink is at recreational temperatures. It takes about twenty minutes to resurface part of a rink. To bring the ice from rough freezing (that is after flooding and freezing) to "patch" condition takes about one hour. For competitions it is possible to run the refrigeration at optimum output and to refreeze every figure skating patch after each competitor without too much delay.

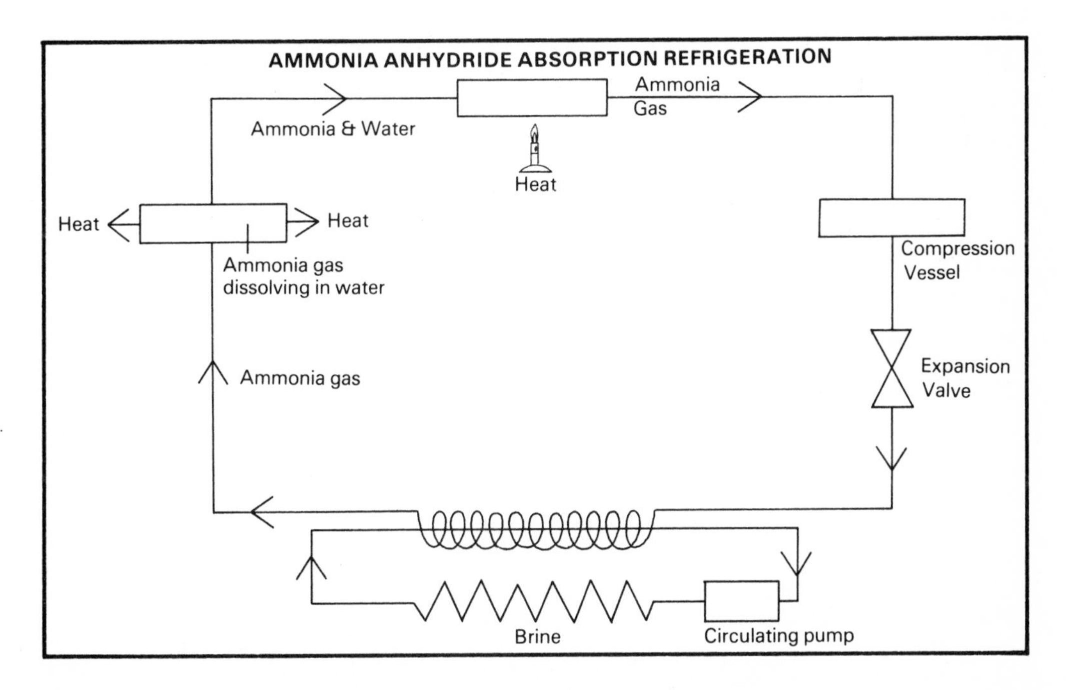

For special purposes the ice can be dyed. Some judges prefer the compulsory figures to be skated on blue or pale grey ice, because this makes the tracings show up better. A number of attempts have been made in ice hockey to dye the ice so that the puck shows up better on television. So far, however, a dead white color has proved to be much the best.

It may seem a travesty to bring an outdoor sport into the realm of the indoor gymnasium, but if it had not been for the development of the artificial ice rink it would not have been possible for televisation of the great competitions – and without television, skating might well still be a rather curious recreation carried out in the dead of winter on some hidden pond.

DRESS

Unlike skiing, skating has not developed a specialized fashion industry and despite the fact that clothes play an important part in the presentation of skating programs, the provision of suitable dress for skaters remains something of a cottage industry.

Beginners normally wear slacks, a sweater and gloves to prevent ice burns in case of falls. The women progress to matching skirt and pants sold in the shops that are always attached to the ice rinks. These are worn over ballet tights. Once the men develop some expertise they adopt the all-in-one "monkey suit" made of stretch material while the women require a considerable wardrobe of dresses.

Because of the expense of hand-tailored garments, the mothers of growing skaters rapidly acquire the skills of a seamstress. A top-level champion will need a number of outfits for figures, a more flamboyant dress for the short program, and a flashy costume for the long program. She will also need practice outfits and exhibition dresses. Just like world fashion, ice rink fashion changes; fads spread like wildfire among the skaters and the design of a world champion's dress will quickly be adopted and copied by other aspiring skaters.

However the demand for special skating

Clothes should be warm for outdoor skating; lightweight for indoor wear. Special skating costumes are often made of stretch fabric. Women wear short skirts and opaque tights.

outfits (and speed skaters fare even worse) is very limited. Even the largest sport outfitters and sports fashion houses can only provide a very limited choice of garments and, so far, no Teddy Tingling or Bogner has appeared on the scene with easily identifiable costumes worn by performers at world and Olympic championships.

SKATES

The demand for skates and boots is much greater and a very specialized and profitable industry has grown up around the manufacture of blades.

The beginner needs only one pair of cheap blades and boots which can be attached by the expert in the skate shop on the rink. A champion, however, will have a special pair of skates for figures and a different set for free skating. The reason is that the blades for figures are ground less sharply than for free skating and the free skating blade has an enormous "master" toe where the lower toe of the toe rake at the front of the blade has been enlarged. It would be quite dangerous for a beginner to skate on these skates, because he or she would keep tripping over the toe. The big toe is used as an aid in jumping and in spinning. The championship skater may also have a special pair of skates for loop figures in which the toe has been removed. If the singles skater also does some ice dancing, he or she will have yet another pair for this branch of the sport. In addition to the skates, the skater must also purchase some skate guards to slip over the blades when walking around the rink. When watching a championship, you will notice that the competitors will come to the edge of the ice, take off their guards, and step onto the ice. When they have finished skating, they will replace the guards before stepping off the ice.

There have been a number of comic incidents through the years, where champions have forgotten to remove the guards and fallen flat on their faces across the ice. The guards stay on until the skater reaches the dressing room. The blades are then wiped dry and left to warm up to room temperature so that water ceases to condense on the cold metal. Vaseline is sometimes used to prevent the edges of the blades from rusting. Skates must not be left to warm up on radiators because too rapid a change of temperature could cause them to warp.

Because of the strong support that boots must provide, breaking them in often results in blisters. A new pair of boots should not be worn for more than ten minutes at any one time. Experienced skaters often wear their new boots (not yet attached to the blades) around the house until they have moulded themselves to the shape of the foot. Others find that wetting the inside of the boots helps them to settle to the shape of the foot. Men's boots are generally black and women's white.

When lacing the boot up the laces should be pulled very tightly over the foot part of the boot, a knot tied where the foot bends into the leg, but the lacing on the part of the boot that covers the leg should not be too tight because this can stop circulation. The lace must then be knotted and tucked firmly into the boot. Accidents can happen if the lace is improperly secured and comes loose during a program and trips the skater.

Skates used to be metal blades which were strapped on over boots, as worn by these Dutch children.

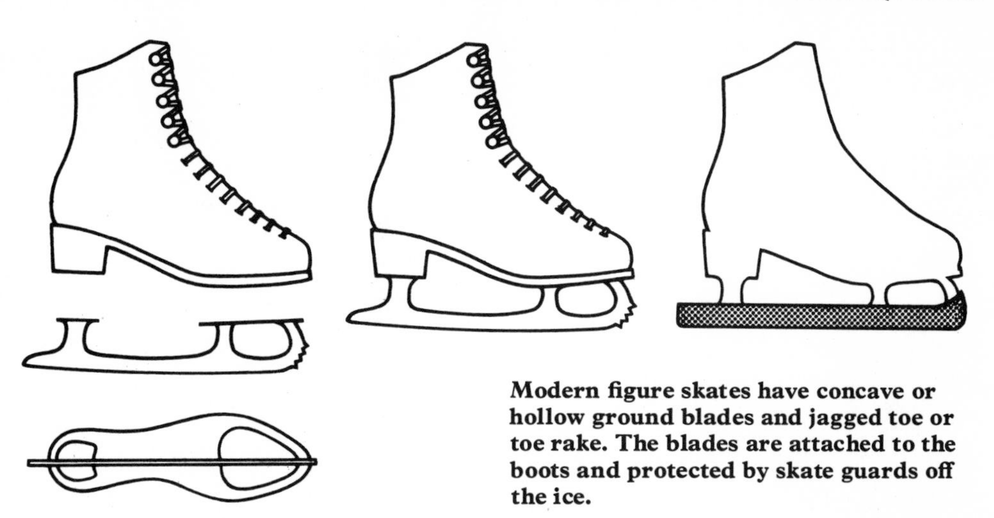

Modern figure skates have concave or hollow ground blades and jagged toe or toe rake. The blades are attached to the boots and protected by skate guards off the ice.

To attach the blade to the boot, the blade is lined up slightly to the inside of the center of the boot, a couple of screws put in and then the skater goes onto the ice to "feel" if the position is correct. Sometimes the blade has to be moved several times to find the correct placing.

Boot covers are thick pieces of material worn over the boot to keep the foot warm when skating outdoors, or during practice sessions in the dank, cold, empty ice rinks. Warm-up leggings of gaily colored, knitted wool, like those worn by ballet dancers during practice sessions, can also be made so they cover the top of the foot.

The blades have to be reground from time to time. A skater learns to tell when the edges of the skates are getting blunt because there is a feeling of slipping sideways. Free skating blades need to be reground more often than figure blades. This process is always a traumatic experience for skaters who know that their blades and therefore their skating can be ruined if the grinding is done sloppily or by someone who is not an expert. Five factors affect how often blades need to be reground: the skater's weight, the quality of the blades, the depth of the hollow in the cross section of the blade, how often the skates are used and how the blades are treated off the ice. Generally, blades will need regrinding if they do not take a sliver from a fingernail, or if nicks can be felt in the edge of the blade.

SKATING

DISCIPLINES

4

SINGLES SKATING

For most people, figure skating is a rewarding, pleasant leisure time amusement that can be pursued into old age. For a few, however, it is a fiercely competitive sport whose participants have spent their childhood training from five to eight hours a day so that at the peak of their athletic ability they can disguise muscle-straining, adrenaline-producing, split-second timed movements with apparent ease and grace, with the ultimate aim of winning an Olympic medal.

Between these two extremes lie the great mass of girls and boys, women and men, members of a thousand different skating clubs throughout the world who compete among themselves, club against club, region against region, for the pleasure of skating and the hope, eventually, to represent their country in the great international championships.

Singles contests in present-day competitive skating comprise three divisions: school figures; a short program of seven compulsory, set, free skating moves; and the free skating program which is sometimes referred to as the long program. These divisions account respectively for thirty, twenty and fifty percent of the total marks. Free skating, with the spins and jumps that thrill television viewers, is today the dominant section of the sport, but this has been so only in very recent years.

When the first international championship was held in 1891 in Hamburg, it consisted solely of school figures. The next year a free skating section was added which counted for forty percent of the total marks. This sixty-forty split remained in effect until the autumn of 1968 when it was changed to fifty-fifty. A minor change had been made earlier in the school figures section, so that instead of skating all six figures from both right and left starts, the starting foot was drawn and alternated. There had been a clamor for many years to reduce the percentage of marks given to figures. Free skating had come a long way from the time when a skater would merely try a few half-turn and single-revolution jumps, some footwork, a spiral or two (skating's equivalent to ballet's arabesques), and a spreadeagle (in which the skater glides along with both feet on the ice pointing 180° away from each other).

However, progress in free skating has always had its critics. When Theresa Weld from the United States showed a modest Salchow jump in the 1920 summer Olympics, she was told officially that jumping was unfeminine and that she would be penalized if she continued to flaunt public opinion. When Karli Schaeffer did the first "blur" spin in which the Austrian went so fast that his image blurred, critics said it was circus-like and not "skating."

Nevertheless, free skating did become more athletic. Cecilia Colledge of Britain became the first woman to demonstrate a double rotation jump (two complete turns in the air) in her efforts to depose Sonja Henie. (Miss Henie's highlights in her competitive days were two Axel jumps in a row. She did show double jumps in her films, however.)

After World War II, Dick Button of the United States amazed everyone by jumping higher than the rink barrier and presenting moves never seen before such as the double Axel (two and a half complete turns in the air), the flying camel (a jump into a spin on the back outside edge in an arabesque position) and later the first triple jump in which three complete 360° turns are made in the air before touching down.

Button's competitors, of course, had to strive to keep up with him, and skaters found themselves spending ever-increasing amounts of their practice time learning such moves. Nowadays a top male competitor must have at least three different triple jumps in his free skating program and at least one should be in combination with another jump.

In 1962 Don Jackson of Canada accomplished the first triple Lutz in a world championship. In 1978 another Canadian, Vern Taylor, took progress a little further by presenting a triple Axel in which the

Peggy Fleming, figure skating champion and Olympic gold medalist, performs a routine at Rockefeller Center skating rink in New York City, 1969.

skater turns three and a half times in the air. Undoubtedly the first quadruple jump will be seen in the near future.

The athletic progress of the women has also increased tremendously. In 1972 Sonja Morgenstern of East Germany became the first woman to present a triple jump (a Salchow) in a world championship. While winning the 1977 world championship, Linda Fratianne, the U.S. title holder, presented two different triples. In the European championship in 1978, Denise Biellmann of Switzerland accomplished the first triple Lutz in women's international competition. The young Russian, Elena Vodorezova, currently accomplishes three different triples, one done in combination.

When the percentage of marks given for free skating was increased to fifty, everyone thought that the free skating would decide the title. This was not so. Trixie Schuba, of Austria, won the 1972 Olympic gold medal even though she was placed only seventh in the free skating. She held onto first place through a phenomenon known as "spread." In judging figures, the judges use most of the point-range available. The best skater may get a 5.0 or 5.1 and the worst, perhaps, 1.9. In free skating, however, judges tend to mark within a very restricted range. The best skater may get the maximum mark, 6.0, while the worst will rarely get less than 4.6. So there is the possibility for a good figure skater to gain such a lead that the good free skater will find it impossible to surmount the difference.

When the authorities realized that the fifty-fifty split was not producing the effect hoped for, they went one step further and in the autumn of 1972, the percentage marks for figure skating were reduced to forty and only three, instead of six figures, had to be skated. The free skating was also reduced, accounting now for only forty percent. A new section, the short program of compulsory free skating moves, was introduced. Separate medals were awarded for figures and for the combined free skating divisions.

Still the ISU found itself without the spectacular free skaters as overall champions. (In 1975 the men's world champion, Sergei Volkov, U.S.S.R., was placed only sixth in the combined free skating sections.) Just before the 1976 Olympics the ISU further reduced the figure skating percentage to thirty and at the same time increased to fifty the percentage of marks for the long program of free skating. In 1978, the ISU was considering proposals to eliminate school figures entirely or to make them a completely separate championship.

For those who are successful, that medal or world championship title can be turned into a financially very agreeable ice show contract. Numerous touring shows star men and women whose championship exploits have whetted the appetites of potential audiences.

Women skaters have until now made the most out of these deals. Although "Charlotte" starred in the first skating film, *The Frozen Warning* in 1917, it was Sonja Henie who convinced Hollywood that an Olympic gold medal could be translated into cold cash at the box office. In all Miss Henie made twelve films which were shown around the world. They not only made a vast amount of money for Miss Henie but they resulted in a boom in artificial ice rink production to cater for the millions of mothers who sought to have their daughters grow up to be another Sonja. At her death in 1969, Miss Henie was reputed to be worth over forty-seven million dollars from her films and her own ice show.

Sonja Henie practices for one of her skating films, *My Lucky Star*.

Inspired by Miss Henie's success, ice show promoters made incredible offers to other Olympic gold medalists, but none was able to duplicate Sonja's appeal. Britain's only winter Olympic figure skating gold medalist, Jeannette Altwegg, created quite a stir when she turned down a generous offer and went to work in a Pestalozzi village orphanage for a nominal salary.

The promoters grew less enthusiastic, but recently skaters have again been commanding fantastic salaries. Peggy Fleming, the American 1968 Olympic gold medalist, has equaled Miss Henie's success in a different medium. Her five, hour-long television specials have been bought by almost every country including Russia and China.

Sometimes it was more profitable to have failed. When Janet Lynn fell in the 1972 Olympics, television audiences loved the blonde American even more for being so fallible and smiling through her tears. That popularity convinced Ice Follies to make her the world's most highly paid woman athlete, promising Ms. Lynn one and a half million dollars over a three-year period.

Dorothy Hamill, the 1976 Olympic gold medalist, also signed a profitable ice show contract, but found it easier to earn more money by endorsing products – expensive dolls and shampoo.

John Curry also won an Olympic gold medal in 1976, but turned down commercial offers to promote his own idea of what an ice show should be. Despite initial difficulties, he started "Theater on Ice" – a small company demonstrating the art of skating in a form similar to ballet, on stage. A success in England, it gained even greater popularity in the United States.

SCHOOL FIGURES

The blade of each skate is one-eighth inch (31–32mm) thick and is hollow ground, that is the center of the blade is scooped out, so that just the outer portions on each side of each blade touch the ice when the skater stands straight up on the ice on two feet. If he leans to the right only one of the two edges on each foot is in contact with the ice, the outside edge of the right foot and the inside edge of the left foot. If the skater leans the other way, to the left, then the outside edge of his left foot and the inside edge of his right foot are the only edges in contact with the ice. The length of the blade is curved in an arc whose radius is approximately seven feet (2.14m). Because of these construction features, if the skater pushes off on one foot, on either the outside or inside edge, forward or backward, he will trace a circle whose radius, if he holds the edge firmly, is approximately seven feet.

It is on this fact that figure skating is based. All forty-one ISU figure eights are

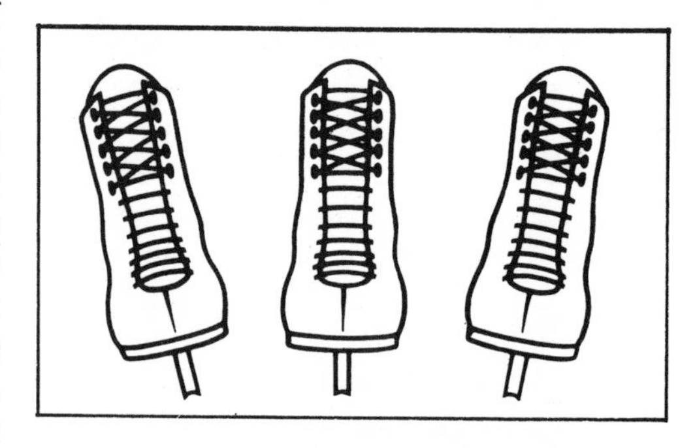

Skating on either the inside or outside edge will produce a curved line.

The circles that make up the basic figure eights are lined up on long and short axes. The long axis divides each circle in half, and the short axis runs between each two circles. Each circle is begun where the axes cross.

variants of circles made from the eight basic edges – right forward outside (**rfo**), right forward inside (**rfi**), left forward outside (**lfo**), left forward inside (**lfi**), right backward outside (**rbo**), right backward inside (**rbi**), left backward outside (**lbo**), and left backward inside (**lbi**).

Figures one, two, three and four are circles done first on one foot. Then after returning exactly to where the skater started, another circle is done on the same edge on the foot. When the skater has returned again to his starting point, called the center, he then repeats the maneuver a second and then a third time. Figure one is the forward outside eight, figure two the forward inside eight, figure three the backward outside eight, and figure four the backward inside eight. The skater must work to make sure both circles are of equal size, that the circles are lined up (that one is not displaced to one side of the other), that

The curve eight is two circles performed on the same edge of each foot – here the right forward outside for one circle and the left forward outside for the second.

the second and third tracings left when the blade glides over the ice are exactly superimposed upon the initial tracing, and that the weight has been correctly held. One slightly wrong placement as the hips and shoulders move round can result in a wobble, producing that dreaded bogeyman of figure skaters, a "flat." Flats occur when both edges of a skate touch the ice at the same time, leaving a double line on the ice.

Before World War II, judges would rely on style for their assessment of the merit of a figure and immediately after the skater had completed the figure, would hold up their marks which were normally much higher than nowadays. (The Norwegian judge gave Sonja Henie the maximum mark of six for both her loop figures at her last appearance as an amateur skater.) Today, however, judges will walk around a figure to check its symmetry and then get down on their hands and knees, sometimes even lie down, to search for those telltale flats, before deciding on the mark.

After learning the four basic figure eights, the skater is taught to incorporate deliberate changes of edge. Figure **5a** (the figures are commonly known by their numbers in the rule book) starts with the skater pushing off on a right forward outside edge. When half the circle has been accomplished, he changes to the inside edge and executes a full circle. When he has returned to the point at which the change took place he pushes off on a left forward inside edge, does a half circle, changes to the outside edge, completes the circle and arrives back at the initial start and repeats twice. Figure **5b** is the same figure but with the start made on the left outside forward edge. This change of edge figure consists of three circles, unlike the two of the basic

In the backward outside curve eight, the first circle is on the right backward outside, and the second on the left backward outside.

figure eights. Figures **6a** and **6b** are the equivalent changes of edge done backward. At first the skater makes wild 'S' changes, but he must learn to effect the change in the length of his blade.

A more complicated figure involving changes of edge is the one-foot eight. **24a** and **b** are the forward one-foot eights and **25a** and **b** are the backward one-foot eights. (**a** indicates a right-foot start, **b** the left foot initial start.) In both cases a whole circle is effected before the change of edge and a whole circle is completed after the change, so that two complete circles are done on one foot. The other foot is then put on the ice and it, too, draws two complete circles. As usual the figure is repeated twice, so that there are six tracings of each circle.

One hundred and eighty degree turns on one foot are also employed in figures. The easiest is a three-turn in which something that resembles a three is traced on the ice. A three-turn is a one-foot turn in which the foot turns from one edge in one direction to the opposite edge in the other direction, using the natural flow of rotations. There are eight sorts of three-turns corresponding to the eight edges. The simplest is the right forward outside to right backward inside three. (The others are **rfi** to **rbo**; **rbo** to **rfi**; **rbi** to **rfo**; **lfo** to **lbi**; **lfi** to **lbo**; **lbo** to **lfi**; **lbi** to **lfo**.)

All eight three-turns are incorporated into a variety of figures and performed halfway round the circles. Double threes are also brought into play in the more advanced figures. In these, one three is done a third of the way through the figure and a second three is done at the two-thirds point. Threes, double threes, and brackets are all combined with changes of edge and one-foot eights.

A bracket turn is also a one-foot turn from one edge in one direction to the opposite edge in the other direction, but it employs the counter-to-normal rotational direction and a tracing resembling a bracket is left on the ice. There are also rocker and counter turns which are one-foot turns from one edge in one direction to the same edge in the opposite direction. The rocker uses the normal flow of rotation, while the counter is opposed to the normal flow. The rocker or counter is used where the change of edge would have taken place in a three-circle figure.

Also included in the figures are loops done inside a circle. There are eight kinds of brackets, eight kinds of rockers, eight kinds of counters and eight kinds of loops, all corresponding to the eight different edges.

The nine most difficult figures have been divided into three groups and on the eve of an international event, one of these groups is drawn for each of the singles events. The foot on which the first and third figure shall be commenced is also drawn. (The second figure is started from the other foot.)

Groups

A **21** (inside rockers)
36 (forward paragraph double threes)
31 (back change loops)
B **20** (outside rockers)
41 (back paragraph brackets)
38 (forward paragraph loops)
C **22** (outside counters)
40 (forward paragraph brackets)
39 (back paragraph loops)

So that the same group will not be drawn for a world championship two years in succession, the group which was drawn for last year's world championship is not included in the draw for the next world championship, or for any other senior contest that season.

As it is necessary to study the tracing left by the skate in order to judge how well a figure has been cut, figures cannot be

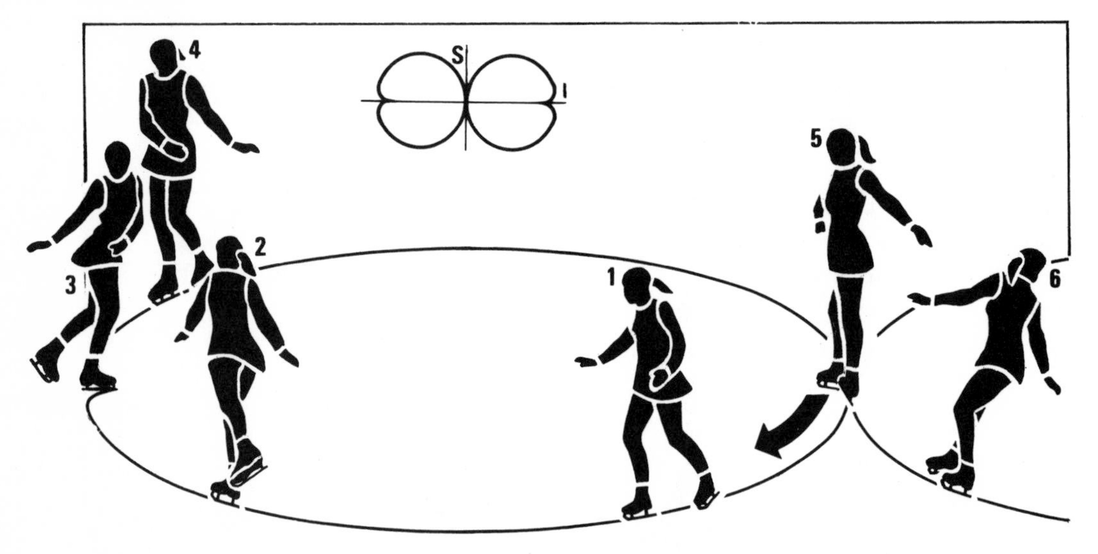

The three turn involves a change of direction on the same foot – here from right forward outside to right backward inside. The tracing resembles a number three.

The bracket is the opposite of the three turn. The skater skates out of the circle, changes edge, and goes on to complete the circle.

In double threes, the skater makes two turns into the circle at one-third and two-thirds of the way around.

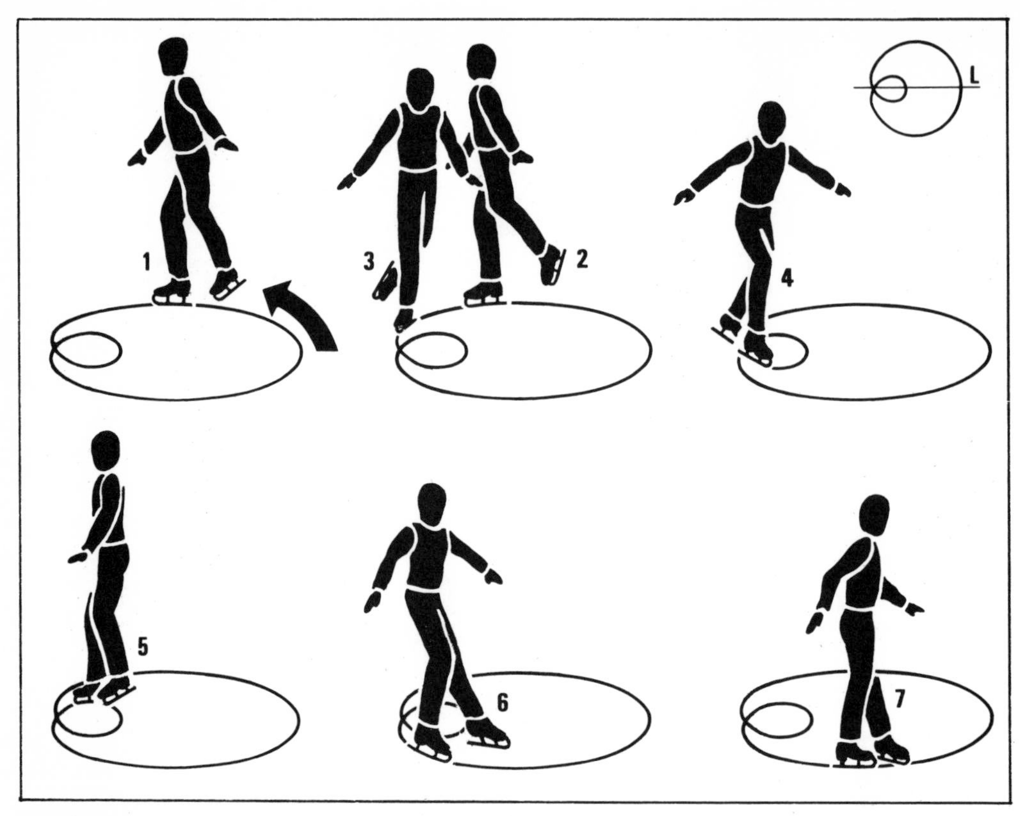

Loops are smaller than other figures. The skater turns into the circle to make a small loop, changing to the same edge of the other foot to complete the circle.

taught or practiced in a public skating session. The skater must hire a "patch" of newly made ice. The patch is generally big enough to allow the skater to draw a three-circled figure. A more experienced skater may hire two adjacent patches, sufficient for an hour's intensive practice. The hire of patches is one of a competitive skater's major expenses because a champion needs at least four hours' practice on the patch every day. Only the skater and his coach are allowed on the patch.

There are often patch sessions in the very early hours of the morning. Since intense concentration is needed to master figures, spectators at a patch session will encounter a cathedral-like hush. The skaters move at a very slow pace and often a gloomy mist rises from the ice.

To do well in figures, a skater seems to need qualities which are exactly the opposite of those demanded of a good free skater. He must be introverted instead of extroverted; he must be extremely unflappable instead of full of emotion; he must love solitary achievement instead of feasting on the excitement of the crowd; and he must be continually holding back every muscle instead of throwing himself into moves.

Rarely has an outstanding figure skater not had trouble with the free skating and

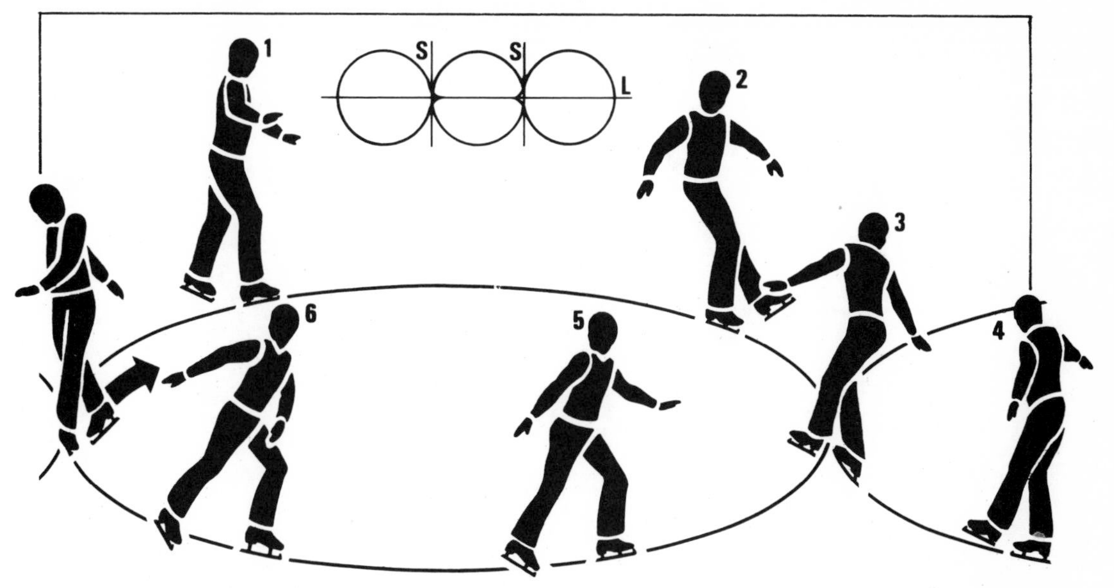

The rocker involves a sharp outward turn on one foot from a forward to a backward direction, or vice versa.

The counter involves a sharp inward turn on one foot from forward to backward, or vice versa.

vice versa. Karen Iten of Switzerland, for example, won a silver medal for the figures in the 1975 world championship but was placed last in the free skating.

In addition to the forty-one figures, there is a whole series of even more complicated

The compulsory figures arena is a basic rectangular rink where the judges and the referee watch the performance of the figures and examine the tracings.

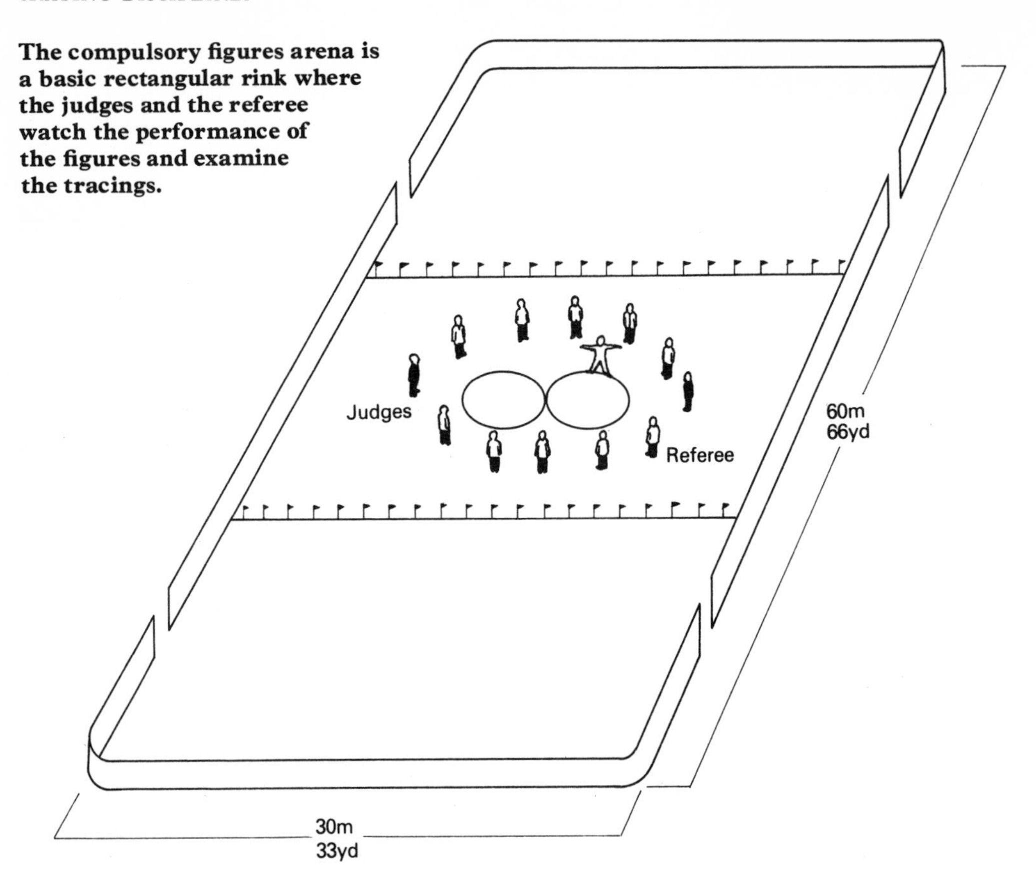

eights such as rocker-bracket-rocker, counter–three, and change edge double loop, which were devised by T.D. Richardson and incorporated into Gold Star figure tests in Britain. Unfortunately Captain Richardson got these figures accepted at a time when figures were becoming less and less popular and it seems unlikely that anyone will ever apply to take any of these tests.

FREESTYLE SKATING

THE SHORT PROGRAM

As in the case of the figures, there are four groups of set moves, but unlike figures, the group to be skated is drawn a year in advance. The skater must choreograph the seven moves to music and perform them in less than two minutes. There is no minimum time set but it is unlikely that the skater could accomplish all seven moves in less than a minute and a half. (Men and women have to skate the same moves.)

The seven moves consist of two solo jumps (such as the double Axel and double

Lutz); a combination of two double jumps or a triple and a double with one of the jumps specified; three spins, including a specified jump into a spin and a change-foot spin; and a set of footwork in a specified pattern, straightline, serpentine or circular.

Unlike the figures, which are each awarded one mark, the short program is given two marks. To begin with, the division of the two marks, for technical merit and artistic impression, was the same as for the long program. At the 1975 ISU Congress, however, this was changed to "required elements" and "presentation," with specific amounts being set for the failure of each of the seven required moves to come out of the required elements marks. It is conceivable that a skater could leave out all the moves but still skate well at speed, utilizing the ice surface, and without upsetting the harmonious composition of the program, so that the required elements mark would be very low and the presentation mark very high.

An omission of either jump in the combination means 0.8 must be taken off from the required element mark. A fault on this move is penalized by a deduction of 0.4 to 0.7. An omission of the solo jump or of a spin combination must result in 0.6 being taken from the required elements mark. A

For free skating, the whole ice arena is used and judges watch the performance from a position behind the barrier.

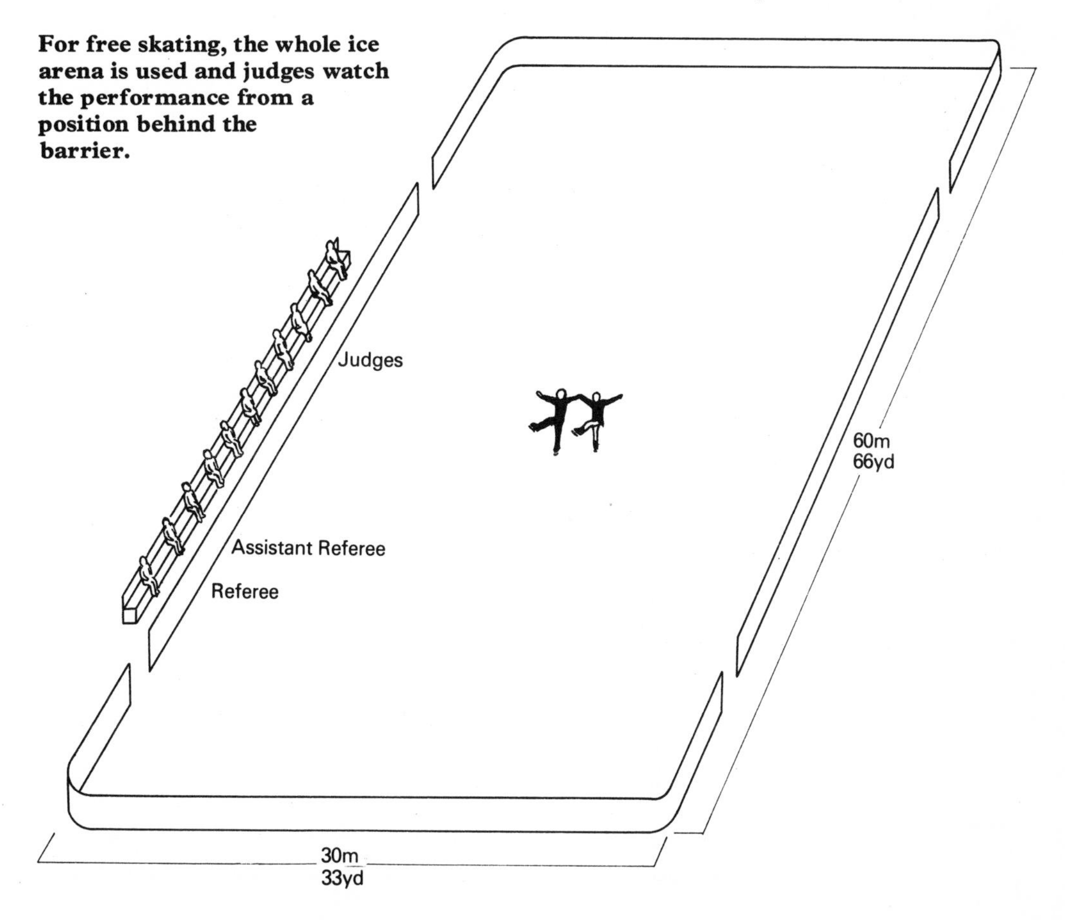

Toller Cranston achieves a perfection of line during the performance of a routine.

fault on these moves is penalized by deducting 0.3 to 0.5. If any of the other moves are omitted 0.4 is deducted. A fault costs from 0.2 to 0.3.

Although this section counts for only twenty percent of the total marks, a fall can be disastrous for a champion. Unlike the long program where falls are common and are no barrier to winning an event, a fall in the short program can cost a title.

THE LONG PROGRAM

Women have four minutes and men five in which they can skate anything in a choreographed program of their own making, to music of their own choice. They have a ten second leeway. If they exceed this, the referee blows his whistle and the judges stop watching the performance. If they skate for less than three or four minutes and fifty seconds, the referee informs the judges and the skater is slightly penalized.

This is the most exciting part of the event and judges frequently gave sixes, the maximum mark, for a superb performance. Because many sixes were given out, the ISU has now specified that top marks are won only for a perfectly faultless showing.

It is in this section that completely new moves are presented. In 1962 Don Jackson of Canada demonstrated the world's first triple Lutz, a move that he had only accomplished a few times in practice and which was not repeated until twelve years later. Christine Errath of East Germany won the 1974 world title after falling in an attempt to be the first woman to execute a triple toe loop in a world championship. Gordon McKellen of the U.S. was the first man to try (unsuccessfully) a triple Axel in a world championship (in 1974).

Provided the skater gets up immediately and carries on, falls are penalized only slightly. About 0.2 is taken off from only one of the marks, that for artistic impression. Even that is not always done. At the Sapporo Olympics, the Swedish judge gave Janet Lynn six for artistic impression even though she fell on a jump sit spin.

SPINS

In recent years jumping has become the prime object of free skating, although the short program has convinced skaters they

In the long program, skaters have a chance to demonstrate their style and artistry in an original choreographed program, skated to music of their own choice.

do have to work on their spins and footwork as well. Spins can be done in almost any position. The novice skater learns to do a one-foot stand spin and then progresses to learn spins in arabesque and sit positions. Learning to spin involves a process in which the mind has to adapt itself to ignoring impulses that come from the inner ear indicating giddiness. This is not difficult, but whenever a spin is tried with the head in a different position the process has to be learnt all over again.

Having learned the three basic spins the skater must learn a "back" spin in which he changes foot so that instead of spinning on a backward inside edge on the front part of his blade with the lower toe of the toe rake anchoring him, he spins on the backward outside edge of his "poor" foot. All spins have to be practiced so that they can be centered – so they stick to one spot.

A man will normally have very few spins in his long program and they will almost certainly be either the flying camel that Dick Button invented, or a jump into a change foot spin. He may also include a very fast, or blur, spin or a crossfoot spin.

A woman will have more spins, the most popular of which is the layback in which the back is bent to achieve a beautiful position.

Spins can be done in many positions. Upright spins are the easiest. In this one-foot upright spin, the tracing foot is the left foot.

The two-foot upright spin is a basic beginner's spin. The skater must learn to keep the spin centered before attempting to increase speed.

There are also some lovely spins in which the blade of the free foot is caught with a hand and pulled up to meet the head or higher so that the leg goes almost into split position.

The basic spins are done using the big toe pick on the bottom of the skate's toe rake and the front part of the blade, using either the "flat" (i.e. both edges) or the backward inside edge. Very few skaters are able to spin on the forward outside edge, which enables them to achieve a particularly good position in the camel spin.

Spins are also done changing foot and in this case, although the skater starts spinning on a backward inside edge, when he changes foot he then spins on a backward outside edge. These spins are called "back spins" although in both cases the skater is in fact spinning backwards. The name refers to the edge used. The "back" spins, like the flying camel in which the skater does not merely change foot but "flies" into a back spin, are very difficult and are part of every top-level skater's program.

Most spins are named after the position the skater strives for while spinning, such as the "upright spin," the "sit spin" and the "camel spin" which is done in an arabesque position and is called a camel spin on account of the hump which beginners always end up with when attempting this move. The camel spin is called the parallel spin in some parts of Britain, because the body and free leg are parallel to the ice. The sit spin is also called the Jackson Haines spin after its originator. The layback spin is named after the required "back-bend" position, as is the case of the cross-foot spin, the only two-foot spin in a skater's repertoire. A windmill spin is a camel spin in which the skater waves his limbs first skyward and then toward the ice and is also known as the "illusion spin." The Grafstrom spin is similar to the camel spin only the body, instead of becoming completely horizontal to the ice, is merely slightly forward and the tracing knee is bent and the free leg raised.

Of course, there are also spins in which the skater assumes first one position and

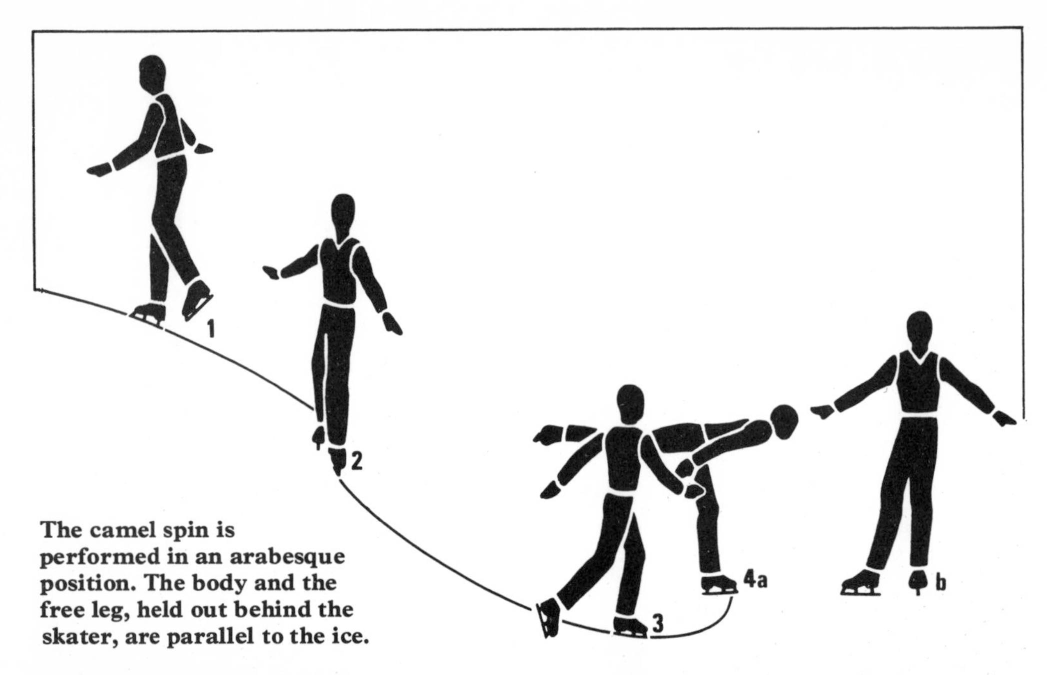

The camel spin is performed in an arabesque position. The body and the free leg, held out behind the skater, are parallel to the ice.

Toller Cranston, Canadian figure skating champion, demonstrates expressive arm and hand movements.

then another. Fashion changes spins. If a world champion does one spin particularly well then it becomes popular, as with Dianne de Leeuw who adapted a "lean-over" camel spin from roller skating in which the head, body and free leg twist to face the roof instead of the ice. Some spins go out of popularity, like the "broken leg" spin, a sit spin where the free leg, instead of being out in front of the body, is placed to the side and bent.

Currently a very popular spin is the "Hamill" camel, invented by the 1976 world championship gold medalist, Dorothy Hamill, in which the skater goes from a back camel and leans back until

The sit spin is made on the forward part of one skate. Acceleration is achieved by folding the arms and crossing the free foot in front of the tracing foot.

The three jump consists of a half turn in the air so the skater lands facing the direction from which he started.

finishing in a back sit spin.

There are also a number of spins in which the skater catches the skate of the free foot and pulls the free leg into various positions, as, for example, in the catch-foot touch head spin and the "pull-up" camel where the free leg is raised high into the air so that the skater almost achieves the "splits" while spinning.

JUMPS

In every top-level program six double jumps will be seen. The novice skater learns to do these as single jumps, that is with only one 360° turn in the air, but by the time he reaches junior competition level he must be able to do them as doubles (two complete 360° turns in the air).

The simplest is the toe loop, which is also called a cherry flip. The skater takes off from a backward outside edge, digs in the toe of his other foot to help give height and lands on the backward outside edge of the takeoff foot. A Lutz has exactly the same takeoff but it is far more difficult, because instead of turning in the normal rotational direction (if you were taking off from the right back outside edge your normal flow of rotation would be anti-clockwise), the turn is counter-rotational and the landing is on the back outside edge of the foot with which you toed on the takeoff.

It is sometimes possible to recognize a Lutz long before the skater has taken off because he often telegraphs the move by racing around the rink and taking a very long backward outside edge in which he repeatedly looks over his shoulder.

Similar to these two jumps but without the toe assist on the takeoff, is the loop jump. In this the skater does a loop in the air taking off from a backward outside edge and landing on the same backward outside edge.

The Salchow is also a basic jump. In this the skater takes off from the backward inside edge of one foot and lands on the backward outside edge of the other foot. This jump can also be done with a toe assist and is then called a toe Salchow or flip.

The king of all jumps is the Axel. Because the skater takes off forward on an outside edge, an added half-turn must be executed so that a single Axel consists of a 540° turn in the air and a double Axel a 900°

A figure skater practices her jumps at a natural ice rink in Switzerland.

turn. The landing is made on the back outside edge of the other foot.

Triple toe loops and triple Salchows are common in a world championship. A few competitors will try triple loops and triple Lutzes. No doubt soon someone will try a quadruple jump.

There are also position jumps, Russian

The Salchow is a basic jump where the skater takes off on one foot, makes one

splits, and stags, in which the aim is not to achieve rotation but to get height to display a good position. These jumps are called by the position the skater achieves in the air and he can adopt one of several methods of takeoff. The landing is usually forward on the toe of one foot and the forward inside edge of the other foot.

In addition to the basic six jumps and the position jumps, there are other jumps

The loop jump begins with a movement similar to a bracket, done on two feet. The skater makes one complete rotation in the air.

complete rotation in the air, and lands on the other foot.

which are performed less often. In a world-class competition you will occasionally see a skater do several single rotation jumps in a row. These will probably be "walleys" which are very difficult. The takeoff is from a backward inside edge and the direction of rotation is against the normal with the landing on the back outside edge of the takeoff foot.

Most jumps are landed on the backward outside edge because this is best for stability and for letting the skater check the rotation. Some jumps are landed on a backward inside edge (the half loop, one-foot Salchow, and one-foot Axel, for example) but these are almost always used in combinations so that the skater takes off again as soon as he has landed, generally into a normal Salchow jump. The half loop consists of a back outside takeoff with the landing made on the backward inside edge of the other foot. The one-foot Salchow, as its name implies, takes off from a backward inside edge and lands on the same edge on the same foot. The one-foot Axel takes off from a forward outside edge and lands on the backward inside edge of the same foot.

Another jump seen only rarely is the inside Axel. The takeoff is from a forward inside edge and the landing is on the backward outside edge of the same foot.

CHAMPIONSHIP FIGURES & JUMPS

SCHOOL FIGURES

There are three groups of figures, each consisting of three of the most difficult variations on the basic figure eight from the ISU schedule. The groups are the same for men and for women. On the eve of the competition, separate draws are made for men and for women to decide which group will be skated. The figures in these groups are:

1 inside rockers, forward paragraph double threes and back change loops;
2 outside rockers, back paragraph brac-

kets and forward paragraph loops;

3 outside counters, forward paragraph brackets and back paragraph loops;

Draws are also made for the foot on which the first figure will be skated. The second figure is then started on the other foot and the third on the drawn foot.

A draw is also made for the order in which the skaters will skate the first figure. In the case of an international event, a draw is first made to see which country will draw first. The number of competitors is divided by three (the number of figures) so that the skaters who draw to skate in the first third of the competition, the first figure, skate the second figure last. The skater who skates the second figure first is a third of the way down the drawn list of the competitors for the first figure. Similarly those skaters who skate the second figure in the first third are placed at the end of the list for the third figure, which commences with the skater who is two-thirds the way down the list for the first figure.

For school figures the judges mark each figure with just one mark (out of the maximum of six). They take into consideration the geometrical symmetry of the figure – whether the circles are circles, and whether they are lined up with each other; whether the turns or loops are opposite each other; and whether the second and third tracings are superimposed upon the first. The manner and style in which the figure was skated is also taken into consideration. Figures are not done to music.

To bring the three marks down to the required thirty percent of the total, they are divided by a factor of 2.5.

THE SHORT PROGRAM

There are four groups of seven moves. These are identical for men and women, with the exception of movement **e** in group three. A group is drawn during the annual world championship which is the climax of each skating season. That group

comes into effect the following July (most world championships are held in March) and stays in effect throughout the following season for all senior competitions and championships, both national and international. Starting in 1976 only one draw is made for both men and women so that the groups are the same. The ISU also has a set of groups for junior level events which are also announced for a year at a time, though not at the world championships, and which are of a slightly less advanced nature.

The (senior) groups are:

Group 1

1 Double Salchow jump.
2 Double Axel jump.
3 Double flip jump in combination with any double or triple jump.
4 Flying camel spin.
5 Sit spin with a change of foot.
6 A spin in which at least two positions must be used and a change of foot.
7 A straight line step sequence.

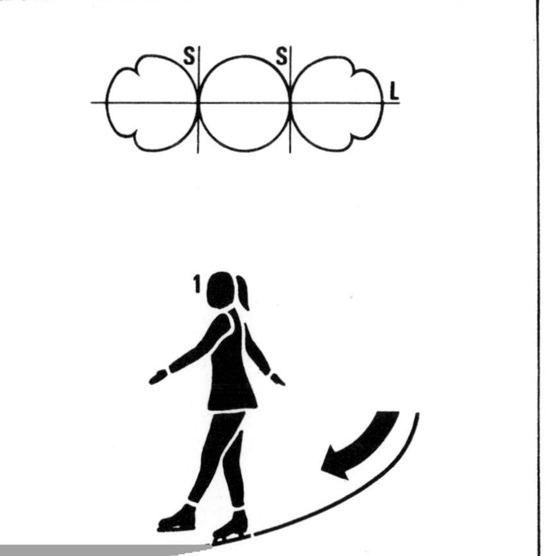

Group 2

1 Double Lutz jump.
2 Double Axel jump.
3 Double loop jump in combination with the same or any other double or triple jump.
4 Flying sit spin.
5 Camel spin with change of foot.
6 A spin in which at least two positions must be used and a change of foot.
7 A circular step sequence.

Group 3

1 Double loop jump.
2 Double Axel jump.
3 A double toe loop in combination with the same jump or any other double or triple jump.
4 Flying sit spin landing on the opposite foot to the one effecting the takeoff.
5 For women – a layback or sideways leaning spin.
For men – a crossfoot spin.
6 A spin in which at least two positions are used and a change of foot.
7 A serpentine pattern of footwork.

Group 4

1 Double flip jump.
2 Double Axel jump.
3 A double loop jump in combination with any other double or triple jump or the same jump repeated.
4 Open Axel into a back sit spin.
5 Camel spin with change of foot.
6 A spin with at least two changes of position and a change of foot.
7 A straight line step sequence.

For the third move in all four groups the prescribed jump may be done before or

Change double threes is an advanced figure based on the three turn, but including changes of edge at the long axis.

after the elected jump. No turn or touch-down of the free foot is allowed between the two jumps. All spins must have a minimum number of six rotations in the prescribed position. In the case of change foot spins at least five rotations must be done on each foot. The change of foot may be done as the easier step-over or as the more difficult jump. Variations in the position of the head, arms and legs, and variations in the speed are permitted but only one change of foot is allowed. Spins must be concluded either by jamming the toe of the free foot into the ice or by taking a backward outside edge on the free foot. A windmill spin is not considered a camel spin. A common fault in the flying sit spin, with the landing on the reverse foot to the takeoff, is the tendency of a skater to do an Axel to a sit spin and not to achieve a sitting position in the air.

These seven moves have to be choreographed by the skaters to music of their own choice. They may be skated in any

The Axel jump has a forward takeoff. The skater must complete one and a half turns in the air before landing on the back outside edge of the other foot.

The Lutz jump includes a difficult counter-rotational turn in the air with a toe-assist takeoff.

order and in any amount of time provided this is less than two minutes. Two marks are given for this category. The first is for "required elements" and the second is for "presentation." As with all marks for figure skating they are both out of a maximum of six with one decimal place being used. There are specific amounts which the judges must take off from the required elements mark if any move is messed up or missed out. Should this mistake not make any difference to the flow and continuity of the program very little will be taken off the presentation mark so these two marks may be greatly varied.

If the jump combination is omitted, 0.8 is taken off. If it is merely flubbed, from 0.4 to 0.5 is taken off, depending on the seriousness of the mistake. If the second move in any of the four groups is omitted, 0.6 must be taken off, 0.3 to 0.5 if a mistake is made while performing it. The same penalty is applied to the sixth move. For any of the other compulsory moves, the penalty for omission is 0.4 and for a mistake 0.2–0.3 is taken off. The compulsory moves are generally referred to as the "short" program. As with the school figures, the two marks for the short program are divided by 2.5 to bring them into line with their allocation of twenty percent of the total.

THE LONG PROGRAM

This third section is worth fifty percent of the total marks. The women have four minutes and the men five minutes to do almost exactly as they please. There is a ten-second leeway either way and in each event a special timekeeper is provided to record when the skater starts moving which, of course, is not necessarily when the music starts, to when he or she stops, which is normally when the music stops. In major events the timekeeper controls an electronic clock which is visible to the public and which counts down the seconds. The skater is penalized if he skates for less than three minutes and fifty seconds for a woman or four minutes and fifty seconds for a man. However if the skater does over four or five minutes and ten seconds then the referee merely blows his whistle and the judges stop considering the performance.

A spiral is a graceful contrast to jumps and spins.

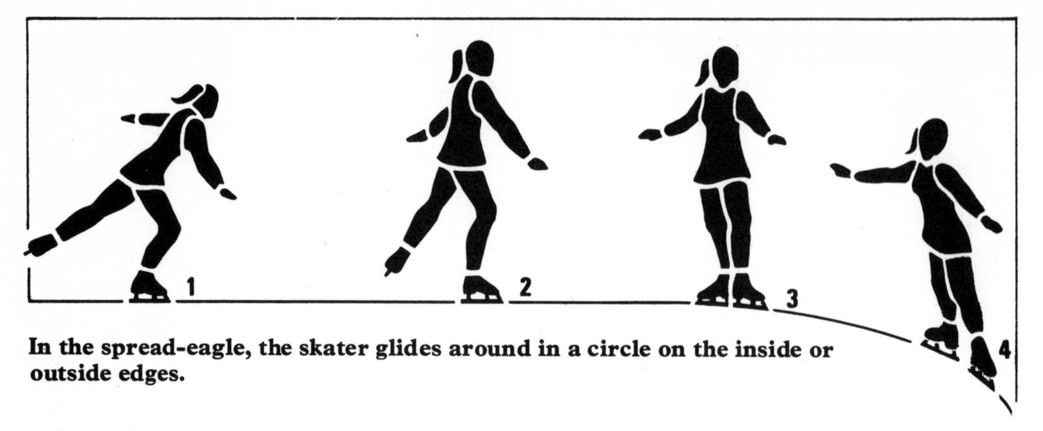

In the spread-eagle, the skater glides around in a circle on the inside or outside edges.

Like the compulsory moves, the free skating is given two separate marks each out of a maximum of six. The first mark is for technical merit and the second is for artistic impression. Considerable thought by the skater and trainer go into selecting the music, which is specially arranged and recorded on a record or tape. Most skaters keep the same free skating routine for two years.

The most important facet of the routine is the number and variety of jumps. Men are judged mostly by their ability to achieve several different kinds of triple jumps in which they spin in the air for 1080° before touching the ice. However spins, particularly jump spins, must also be demonstrated, as must a variety of footwork. Although a few women are able to do a triple jump, the double jumps in their program are the primary measure of their worth. These jumps must be woven artistically into the program to coincide with highlights and the mood of the music.

Pivoting can be done in a forward or backward direction, tracing an ever-decreasing circle.

As well as spins, which women seem to do better than men and the footwork, women include more spirals than men (moves in which the skater moves along the ice in an arabesque position) and variations on the spreadeagle in which the skater moves along on two feet each pointing in opposite directions.

Jumps must have a "clean" takeoff in which the rotation is not begun before the skater becomes airborne. They must also have a clean landing on a definite edge, usually the backward outside edge. A landing on the toe rake may prevent many a fall but it gives itself away with a scratchy sound.

Spins have to be centered – the skater must remain pivoting on one spot. Traveling from the center is common but the penalty, apart from loss of marks, is felt with a resultant lack of stability and speed.

New moves introduced into international championship freestyle programs are often marked down by judges. Just as the first "blur" spin was decried as "too acrobatic," Terry Kubicka (U.S.A.) was accused of employing a move that was not "skating" when he introduced a back somersault into his routine in 1976.

SINGLES SKATING TESTS

Each nation which pursues skating has its own series of tests designed to take the skater from beginner's level through all forty-one school figures and by gradual steps to a free skating goal of a high standard. The ISU also has its own series of tests. Most nations use the tests to determine whether a skater has advanced enough to enter certain of their own championships.

For instance, in Britain (unless you are the reigning junior champion) you must have passed the NSA's intergold test to enter the British senior championships. To enter the junior championships of Britain a singles skater must have passed his silver test as well as be under sixteen by a certain date. To enter for the primary championship of Britain the singles skater must have passed both parts of his intersilver test and be between ten and fourteen.

In North America there are as yet no age restrictions for entry to the three different levels of competition (novice, junior, and senior) but there are test requirements. To enter a senior event the skater must have passed his USFSA (or in Canada, CFSA) gold (or eighth) test; to enter a junior-level event, the skater must have passed his USFSA sixth test (or in Canada, CFSA seventh test); to enter a novice level event the skater must pass the USFSA fourth test or the CFSA fifth test.

In Britain there are also a series of tests in the English style of skating. This form of skating was prevalent in the mid-nineteenth century until the international style came along and almost universally replaced the English style. Just a few enthusiasts keep this interpretation of skating alive today. They can be easily recognized by their stiff stance, their arms almost glued to their sides as they perform figures about a center marked by a ball or orange.

The British test schedule begins with a preliminary test in which forward outside, forward inside and backward outside curves must be demonstrated with a modicum of success. There is also a preliminary free skating test. This was only introduced recently. Judges seem to re-

Judges look for good posture, graceful movements, reasonable speed and correct tracings.

quire the same standard as they used to for the bronze free skating test, which reflects the upgrading of the standard of free skating generally.

The basic figure eights, figures **1, 2, 3** and **4**, have to be mastered for the bronze (third class) figure test as well as the forward changes of edge **5a** and **b**. There is also a bronze test for free skating in which the applicant must skate and interpret music of his own choosing for a period of one and a half minutes. The intersilver (or intermediary second class) figure test consists of the three turn figures **8a** and **b**, **9a** and **b** and the forward one-foot eights, **24a** and **b**.

The figure and free skating parts of the bronze and the intersilver tests may be combined but rarely are, because skaters usually develop free skating skills in advance of their figure skating abilities. It is quite common for a skater to have passed his intersilver free(two minutes free skating) before taking his bronze figures. However he must then work on his figures as he can progress no further. The silver figure test must be passed before the silver free skating test can be attempted.

The silver (or second class) figure test consists of the back change edges, numbers **6a** and **b**; the basic double three figures **10, 11, 12,** and **13**; the basic loop figures **14, 15, 16,** and **17** and the basic bracket figures, **18a** and **b**, and **19a** and **b.** The free skating is for a three-minute period and must include at least two different double jumps and at least three different spins, one of which must be done from a jump.

The intermediate first class (or intergold) test cannot be split into separate figure and free skating tests; both sections must be taken at the same time. The figures consist of the outside counters **22a** and **b**; the inside counters, **23a** and **b**; and the three change threes (also called paragraph threes) **34a** and **b**; **35a** and **b.** The skater must also do the forward and backward change loops **30a** and **b**, **31a** and **b** and **32a** and **b**, the outside change brackets. The free skating is for a three and a half minute period for women and a four minute period for men. Each must do at least three different double jumps and two flying sit spins in addition to other jumps, spins and footwork.

The first class, or gold, test also consists of figure and free skating sections that must be taken together. The figures comprise the outside rockers **20a** and **b**; the inside rockers **21a** and **b**; all double three change double threes (also called paragraph double threes) **36a** and **b**, **37a** and **b**; all the loop change loops (paragraph loops) **38a** and **b**, **39a** and **b**; and all the bracket change brackets (paragraph brackets) **40a** and **b**, **41a** and **b**.

The gold free skating is four minutes for women and five minutes for men, just like an international event. In addition there is a gold star free skating test which few have ever taken. The free skating times are the same as for the gold medal but a minimum mark of 5.5 for both technical merit and artistic impression is required, the equivalent of being placed somewhere in the top ten in the world.

To gain the gold medal, it is necessary to have put in a great deal of training over several years. The youngest-ever British gold medalist was Valda Osbourne, who was later to win the European championship. Ms. Osbourne passed her gold medal test on June 6, 1944 when she was nine years old. In North America the youngest-ever gold medalist was Priscilla Hill, who was nine when she passed her USFSA eighth (gold) test in 1971, beating the previous record set by Carol Heiss (U.S.A.) and Barbara Ann Scott (Canada), both of whom went on to win Olympic gold medals.

The NSA in Britain and the ISIA (Ice Skating Institute of America) have also devised a series of simple tests for children to encourage them to learn basic moves and to prepare them for the regular schedule of tests.

COMPETITION JUDGING

Figure skating is not a sport in which stop-watches, tape-measures, or the number of goals scored determine the outcome. Human judgment is the sole factor controlling the result. An odd numbered panel of from three to nine amateur officials vote independently and the winner is selected by a majority.

There are no licensing, age or physical specifications for a judge, although the adoption of certain requirements in all three fields is under consideration at the moment by the ISU.

The practice of selecting and training judges varies considerably from country to country, but everywhere it is necessary to have worked long and hard before you can hope for the plum assignment of International Judge with its travel privileges and prestige value.

The United States and Canada use clinics and trial judging to determine the skill of a potential judge, although the applicants need never to have actually skated. Starting at the lowest level of competition, a "trial" judge behaves just as an actual judge would, although his marks are not made public nor are they used in determining the results of the competition. If the trial judge's marks agree with those of the actual judges, considered to be the experts, on several different occasions, he becomes a judge at that level and may proceed to trial judge at the next level.

In Britain there are no trial judging procedures, but to judge at a certain standard a judge must have reached the same standard as a skater. To be an international championship judge he must have obtained the gold medal first class test in that branch of skating.

Nevertheless, because the technical aspects of the free skating section of the sport have advanced tremendously in the last few decades, a gold medal won in the 1930s, when many of today's moves were not even conceived, does not automatically qualify the holder to differentiate between, say, a split triple twist and a double, something which can be lost in the blink of an eyelid.

After a scandal a couple of years ago regarding the eyesight of one judge, a physical examination of each official by the ISU was suggested but this policy has yet to be implemented. East Germany has further proposed that the judges' ages be confined to a range of twenty-five to fifty-five when, presumably, alertness is at its height. Judges tend to be quite old but this is mainly because they are amateur and in the West it is generally not until a person is well advanced in his career that he can take the time off for the travel a judge must do. To prevent problems of this nature, the ISU has set up a judging seminar which has taken place every year since 1973 after the world championships.

International championships have been held indoors since 1967 but this is not a requirement for lesser events and even indoor rinks, if unheated, can cause extreme discomfort. Skaters are on the ice for a maximum of five minutes but the judges will be there for hours. There is no record of a judge having sacrificed his life for skating, but Mr. J. Machado of Canada came close. He was taken off the ice suffering from pneumonia after spending six hours judging the men's figures in a blizzard during the 1936 Olympics. Because of the hardship, women were not allowed to officiate in international championships until Mollie Phillips of Wales persuaded the ISU to lift the ban in 1947.

An international championship judges' panel consists of nine members, six of whom represent the countries placed highest in that event in the previous year, and three of whom are drawn out of the hat from the other countries competing. Separate panels judge the women, men, pairs and ice dancing. For the purpose of selecting Olympic judges, the previous event is considered to be the previous world championship. Also on the ice with the referee, assistant referee and nine judges, is a substitute. His marks are not made public nor are they used to compute the results unless illness should occur, or one of the nine fails to show up for one of the sections.

The referee can question any of the marks and usually brings all the judges together after a discrepancy of more than one whole point. He will ask those who gave the lowest mark and the highest mark for an explanation but no action is taken

The free skater is evaluated on technical merit – the difficulty of the program, height of jumps, smoothness of landings – and artistic impression – the ability to interpret the music.

during the event. If the referee does not feel that sufficient explanation was given he will report the occurrence to the ISU who will determine whether a case for suspension can be made. This of course is done with the best intentions but unfortunately it tends to inhibit the timid judge who then spends his time trying to outguess what his colleagues are thinking, so that he can award the same marks.

There is just as much pressure on the judges as on the skaters. They know that their performance is being taken apart by millions of television viewers most of whom know nothing of the technicalities of the sport and none of whom the judge can reach with his explanations.

The ruling of one judge per country came into effect after Sonja Henie won her first world title in a very controversial manner. Up to 1927 one judge per skating club was allowed which in this event meant three Norwegians, an Austrian and a German. Fourteen-year-old Sonja was skating on her home rink supported by fourteen thousand spectators including the Norwegian royal family. Understandably, the Norwegians voted for Sonja and not for the rather staid Herma Szabo Plank, who had held the title since the championship was reinstated in 1922 after World War I.

After the first skater has performed at the beginning of each section the referee has the option of drawing the judges together and letting them know the panel's highest and lowest marks and the average before they are made public. The judges are then given the option of changing these marks. Since it is only the position in which each judge places a skater that affects the results, and not the actual marks given, this procedure merely has the effect of allowing a judge who has geared his marks too low a chance to change (so that he is not booed at by the crowd continually throughout the event). One who has started marking too high gets a chance to avoid being boxed into a position in which he would like to give the last skater a higher mark than the rest but cannot since he has already awarded the highest mark possible.

Once an event is under way the referee will occasionally call the panel together after the marks have been made public. This is called a "huddle." It usually occurs if two of the judges are more than one whole point apart. The referee will ask for an explanation from both the highest and the

Dorothy Hamill, United States figure skating champion, wins the short program event in the 1976 Olympics at Innsbruck.

lowest scorers, but will take no action. The judges are not allowed to change their marks at this time. If the referee feels that the explanation was not sufficient he will make a written report on the incident to the ISU who will request a written explanation from the judge. Though the ISU has no power over the initial selection of an International Judge, it does have the power to suspend them from international participation for a period from one year to life. Increasingly the ISU is becoming militant in matters of national bias.

It is almost impossible for a judge to be free from national bias. It is extremely difficult for him to mark his own contestants down since he knows his national association is unlikely to choose him to go abroad again if he does not support his own candidate. Also he is more familiar with that skater's program and knows just how good that skater can be. In an unprecedented decision, the ISU banned all judges from the U.S.S.R. from international championships in the 1977–78 season. The reason they gave was that they were tired of suspending Soviet judges for national bias, only to have them replaced by others who duplicated their actions.

In addition some decisions are almost impossible to make. Arguments are still being made over whether the technical skills of Marika Kilius and Hans-Jürgen Bäumler of West Germany should have overcome the exceptional grace of the Protopopovs of the U.S.S.R in the mid-1960s. Today, it is a matter of taste whether you prefer the perfect balletic line of John Curry of Britain, the superbly innovative entertainment of Toller Cranston of Canada, the high jumping of Yuri Ovchinnikov of the U.S.S.R, or the more conventional Vladimir Kovalev, also of the U.S.S.R. Pity the judges. Whichever way they vote someone will think they are wrong.

5

PAIR SKATING

Pair skating is considered by many experts to be the pinnacle of achievement in the artistry of skating. This opinion is shared by the audiences of millions that television brings to these events. It is not difficult to see why this should be – pair skating at championship level brings together the most impressive elements of individual skating, the familiar moves of ice dancing, a whole list of special combination figures peculiar to pair skating and, for emotional and artistic enjoyment, the familiar and always captivating sight of man and woman in perfect harmony of movement and grace. It is an unbeatable combination.

Pair skating first appeared at the end of the 1880s. It was in Vienna in 1888 when the first public exhibition of "mixed pair" skating took place. At this time it was not uncommon for pairs of men or pairs of women to skate and for this reason the term "mixed" was used for what is now the classical pairing. The unisex pair competitions did not prove to be very popular and it is the mixed pair skating that has survived to this day. It has become an unstated convention that "pair skating" always implies a mixed pair. However in the United States there are still a few minor level competitions for pairs of women.

In the beginning, the technique of artistic pair skating was extremely primitive. The skaters, holding hands, merely carried out the elements of individual skating. Individual skaters came together to make up the pairs. It is occasionally argued that pair skaters are the failures of singles skating because they do not have to do the compulsory school figures and their routine formerly only consisted of free skating. It may, of course, be true in the odd case that a successful pairs skater had, in fact, turned to this discipline because of failure at school figures, but the skills required are so high that such a skater would be unlikely to be successful in pairs. It was far more common for ice dancers to be failed pair skaters, though this too, and notably in the United States, is no longer the case.

Since the late 1960s pair skating competitions have contained a compulsory section. By this date pair skating had become so complicated that it became harder and harder for the judges to differentiate between the pairs. One year it was decreed that, in the world championship, the pairs should skate their programs for the judges so that the judges could tabulate what each pair was doing. After twenty-four hours, when the judges had had plenty of

The sedate style of a pair of English skaters in 1908.

time to decide who was doing the most difficult moves, the pairs were required to repeat their performances and on this occasion the judges gave out their marks.

Naturally some skaters became upset because they had skated well on one evening and less well the following evening, and the judges were confused as to whether they should give credit for the previous showing.

Eventually a separate section was set up in which six basic pair skating movements were required. With all the pairs now doing exactly the same thing, it was easier for the judges to separate them into approximate categories and made judging the subsequent free skating a little easier.

The first pairs competition took place in 1891 and caused immense interest. This new form of skating seemed closely allied to dancing and made skating seem more spectacular and more emotional. Nevertheless, pairs skating was not included in the world skating championships which started in 1896. It was not until 1908, in St. Petersburg, that the first world championship title was awarded for pair skating. As the technique of pair skating at that time differed only marginally from singles skating, Austria, Germany and Great Britain, the leading singles skating nations, were successful.

The first winter Olympic title for pairs skating was awarded in 1908 at the fourth Olympic games when the skating competitions took place in the Prince's Skating Hall in London.

Anna Hübler, twenty-three years old, and Heinrich Burger, twenty-six, from Germany were the first world and Olympic pairs skating champions. The husband-and-wife teams of Phyllis and James Johnson of Great Britain and Ludovika and Walter Jakobsson of Finland were their greatest rivals. In the following years each of these pairs won the world championship more than once. It is interesting to note that the Finnish couple still figured among the medals after World War I.

Ludovika and Walter Jakobsson were the really noteworthy skaters of this epoch, winning their first world championship in 1911. The German girl, Ludovika Eilers, was then twenty-six and Walter Jakobsson twenty-nine; a year later they were married and Ludovika changed both her name and her nationality. They won the world championship again in 1914 and in 1923 and the Olympic gold medal in 1920. In 1924 they won the silver medal in the Olympics.

The mid-1920s saw the Austrians winning victory after victory in the international pairs competitions with a fresh and very delicate technique. Without unduly complicating their program they were able to achieve very high marks purely on the basis of their exceptional mastery of the medium.

The Viennese Engelmann family was outstanding. Eduard Engelmann was one of the leading figure skaters of Europe at the end of the 1880s. His daughter Helene Engelmann, skating with Karl Mejstrik, was pairs champion in 1913 and repeated her world championship success partnered by Alfred Berger in 1922 and 1924. It was also with Berger that she won the Olympic title in 1924 at Chamonix.

Herma Jaross-Szabo is unique in skating history. Having achieved world status as a pairs skater, she proceeded to do equally well as a singles skater, winning the Olympic figures championship in 1924 and women's world figure championship from 1922 to 1926. In 1927 Sonja Henie stole her world title away and Herma disappeared entirely from the skating scene.

From the beginning of the 1920s there

Ludmilla Belousova and Oleg Protopopov of the Soviet Union create a sensation and win a gold medal at Innsbruck in 1964.

was evidence among the world's best pairs of the first tendency to complicate their programs, a tendency that became most marked by the end of the 1920s when the technique of pairs skating divorced itself increasingly from the conventional singles skating figures. This contributed greatly to raising the value of the programs skated by the leading pairs. The program of the French married couple, Andrée and Pierre Brunet and the Hungarian married couple, Emilia Rotter and Laszlo Szollas were notable for their previously unseen figures and the perfection of their programs. These two couples between them won eight world championships: the French in 1926, 1928, 1930 and 1932; the Hungarians in 1931, 1933, 1934 and 1935. The French couple however beat their rivals by winning the Olympic gold in 1928 and

Perfect symmetry and harmony of movement raise pair skating to the level of artistry.

1932, while the Hungarians only managed the bronze.

The real impact of the new approaches to pairs skating was most strikingly shown by the German pair, Maxi Herber and Ernst Baier. After their Olympic victory in 1936, they won every world championship before World War II. The Herber/Baier couple were given every opportunity the Third Reich could provide. A top-level composer was commissioned to write a piece to suit their skating so that every note complemented them. Hitler was among the many government officials who witnessed them receive their Olympic gold medals in Garmisch in 1936.

After a seven-year gap, due to the war, when the figure skating championships began again, the lead fell to countries who never before had shone in the world of ice skating – the United States and Canada. The reason is not hard to find. During those seven years the rinks of Europe were closed, there was little competition available and still less opportunity for training The young generation who should have been ready for world class competition in 1947 had had virtually no exposure to the sport and the European nations had to start virtually from scratch. If, for the preceding fifty years, overseas skaters had had to take second place, the situation was completely reversed in the late forties and fifties when European skaters looked for a reassessment of their position. The once-famous pairs of France and Finland had no international success and the Austrian dominance in the figure skating world dimmed. The world championships in 1947 and 1948 were surprisingly won by a Belgian pair, Micheline Lannoy and Pierre Baugnier and they won the Olympic pairs championship in 1948 as well.

At this time the technical arsenal of the

pairs skaters had reached a formidable size. In fact, the general level of skating had greatly improved in the previous fifty years and the moves previously reserved for the élite came into general use. The leading pairs were given high marks for complicated figures which were the specialty of singles skaters, but an impeccable execution was also required.

It was here that the Canadians triumphed. Between 1954 and 1962 they failed to win only once, in the winter of 1956. This series of Canadian victories was started by Frances Dafoe and Norris Bowden in 1954 and 1955; Barbara Wagner and Robert Paul won the world championship from 1957 to 1960 and also the Olympic pairs championship in 1960 but ceded the world championship in 1962 to Maria and Otto Jelinek.

The Jelinek family had escaped from Czechoslovakia just before the war when the children were still small, and settled in Canada. At the world championships of 1962 in Prague the Jelineks were in some doubt as to how they would be received in their homeland now that they were Canadians. They need not have worried; they were greeted with rapturous enthusiasm.

After this run of Canadian victories, the title passed to the impressive German pair Marika Kilius and Hans-Jürgen Bäumler, until the appearance on the victory rostrum of the first Russian pair, Belousova/Protopopov, at the winter Olympics in Innsbruck in 1964.

The gold medal performance at Innsbruck, awarded to Ludmilla Belousova and Oleg Protopopov was the sensation of these winter Olympics and proved to be a well-deserved victory. During the following four years they won every single pairs championship. It was not an easy path to victory. Their first win came at the mature ages of twenty-eight and thirty-one. Nor was it a straightforward victory. They won by a narrow margin and the final result was controversial. The deciding vote was given by Dr. Suzanne Francis of Canada against the Germans, Marika Kilius and Hans-Jürgen Bäumler. She had actually put the Canadian team first, then the Protopopovs, then Kilius/Bäumler.

The world championships followed the Olympics a few weeks later. Dr. Francis was scheduled to judge this event also, which was held in Dortmund. However there was so much bad feeling that Dr. Francis was sent a telegram telling her that the German Federation could not guarantee her safety and asking her not to come. In her absence, Kilius/Bäumler retained their world title. The German couple, however, later were required to return their Olympic silver medals. The Russians had protested against an advertisement in the Olympic program for a record of Marika singing. The International Olympic Committee (IOC) upheld the Russian claim that this made Marika a professional and demanded the return of the medals. The ISU disagreed however with the IOC and did not follow their example. Kilius/Bäumler then retired, leaving the field open to the Protopopovs.

Dr. Francis has remained a controversial judge. In 1976 when the Olympics were again held in Innsbruck she was one of the two judges not to agree that John Curry deserved the gold medal. She put the Canadian champion in first place and she and the Russian judge, who put his own competitor ahead of Curry, were suspended by the ISU for national bias.

Belousova and Protopopov will go into history for having made a completely new statement in the history of pairs skating.

They refused to repeat one figure after another endlessly and by using choreography to its full, they lifted their program to a true work of art. Their sporting career was crowned by the gold medal for pairs skating at the Grenoble Winter Olympics in 1968.

The Protopopovs were beaten in 1969 at the European championships by the far more athletic but infinitely less artistic Irina Rodnina and Alexei Ulanov. At the world championships that year, the Protopopovs had dropped to third place and the following year they could not place high enough in their national championships to get onto the Soviet team. Their era had passed, much to the regret of many skating followers. The Protopopovs continued to compete within the U.S.S.R. and in December 1973 they won a world professional championship in Tokyo. Their popularity continued and two years later they were invited to headline a show at Madison Square Garden to raise funds for the U.S. Olympic effort.

Irina Rodnina and Alexei Ulanov came abruptly to championship honours when still very young. In their very first world championship in Colorado Springs in 1969 they won their first gold medal. It is very rare that the judges rate the performance of newcomers so highly – seniority in skating plays an important role. Rodnina and Ulanov had assimilated the experience and perfection of Belousova and Protopopov, had "created" their own original, more complicated program and they performed it in a more brilliant manner to a faster rhythm. If, for Belousova and Protopopov, lyrical passages are the hallmark, then for their successors it is expressiveness in a major key.

Rodnina and Ulanov won a series of victories between 1969 and 1972, including the gold medal at the Sapporo winter Olympics. The partnership broke up after the 1972 season. Alexei Ulanov had fallen

Irina Rodnina and Alexander Zaitsev of the Soviet Union perform in the pairs short program at the world championships in Tokyo, 1977.

in love with the female half of his and Rodnina's strongest rivals, Ludmilla Smirnova and Andrei Sureikin. Stories from Sapporo circulated the tabloid papers throughout the world, detailing that Rodnina and Ulanov were skating but not talking while Ulanov's eyes strayed continually to Ludmilla. (They shared the same practice sessions.) Immediately the pair event was over, Smirnova/Sureikin were dispatched back to Leningrad, in spite of the fact that the IOC wanted all the medal holders to give an exhibition in the closing ceremony. As soon as Ulanov returned from the Olympics he made his way from his home in Moscow to Leningrad and he and Ludmilla were married. Both original couples came to Calgary for the world championship a few weeks later but Ulanov's heart was obviously not in skating and he dropped Rodnina, who hit her head and had to spend the night in the hospital. Returning to the U.S.S.R., Ulanov started skating with his new wife.

In her biography, Rodnina says that this was the most terrible time of her life. Potential partners were brought from all over the U.S.S.R. A rink in Moscow was closed for a week while these boys auditioned for Rodnina. She accepted Alexander Zaitsev from Leningrad who turned out to be an even better partner than Ulanov.

Zaitsev, with Rodnina, won the European and world championship at his first attempt. Mr. and Mrs. Ulanov were firmly in second place but a long way behind the champions. They drifted off the skating scene while Irina and "Sasha" went on to new heights. In 1978, Irina won her tenth consecutive world title, equaling Sonja Henie's record.

Irina missed the 1979 season because of her pregnancy (she and Sasha were married in 1975). Just before the world championships of that year, she gave birth to a baby boy, but she is expected to return to try and claim her third Olympic gold medal in 1980. She is undoubtedly one of the most significant women in skating.

CHAMPIONSHIP PAIR SKATING

Unlike singles skating or ice dancing, pair skating comprises only two sections: a compulsory moves section in which six moves must be skated in any order and to music of the competitors' own choice in a time span of up to two minutes, worth twenty-five percent of the total marks; and a free section worth seventy-five percent. Although in the free section the skaters may do almost anything they like, certain movements are not permitted. These include circus-like adagio skating in which the man swings the woman continuously

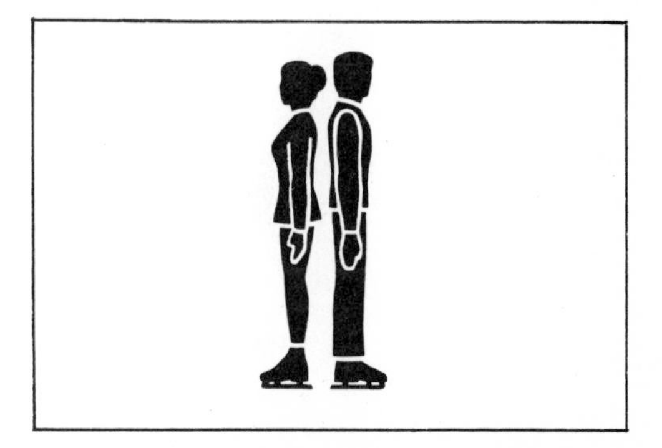

In pair skating, the woman should be shorter than the man to facilitate lifts.

Judges look for a united harmonious performance. Certain restrictions apply concerning lifts and other movements.

around with her head narrowly missing the ice but with no part of her body actually touching the ice. Other moves which are merely feats of strength and have no relation to the pair's skating skill, for example when the man carries the woman around the rink without her turning, are also not permitted.

The pair has from four minutes and fifty seconds to five minutes and ten seconds to show its skill. The program should incorporate a variety of lifts, spins in which the pair spin while holding each other, solo jumps done side by side – either with a mirror effect or a shadow effect depending on whether both partners jump the same way around (shadow) or in different directions (mirror) – solo spins and footwork both while holding and while separated. In all these moves, unison is of paramount importance and you will often see one partner yelling to his or her colleague to come out of a solo spin that instant because that partner had lost his or her speed.

COMPULSORY MOVES

As in singles, compulsory moves receive two marks, one for "required elements" and one for "presentation." There are four groups of these compulsory moves which rotate on a four-yearly cycle. Group A is in operation from the end of July 1979 until the following July; Group B is the specified group for the period July 1980 until the following July; Group C from July 1981; Group D from July 1982 and then back to Group A for the next Olympic season in July 1983 to July 1984.

The groups consist of the following compulsory moves:

Pair skaters begin by practicing skating together side by side to coordinate movements exactly.

Group A

1 Solo double Salchow jumps.

2 Double lasso lift. Both partners commence skating side by side, hand in hand; the woman is then lifted from a forward outside edge and turns two and a half complete rotations before being placed back on the ice on a backward outside edge. The man turns only once while the woman turns over his head two and a half times. The man has his arms extended so that the woman turns high over his head and the woman has her legs out behind her in an almost split position.

3 Backward outside death spiral. While the man goes into a pivot, the woman circles him on a backward outside edge leaning backwards until her head narrowly misses the ice, but with no part of her body actually touching the ice. The hold is hand in hand. Unlike the

Practicing school figures together improves footwork.

The ability to shadow skate – skating in unison without touching – is important.

The waltz hold is a common pair skating hold where the partners face each other in a waltz position.

adagio spins which are not permitted, in the death spiral the woman is skating while being swung around her partner. One fault noticeable in less able pairs is that the man has trouble staying in a pivot position with one leg bent and the other leg extended behind him with its toe anchored to the ice. This move looks extremely dangerous but in fact is not so. Faults are the result of the woman lying on the ice but not for bumping her head as would be imagined.

4 Change foot sit spin done separately.

5 Camel spin. The partners hold each other with the woman's inside arm on the man's inside shoulder and his arm around her back, both in an arabesque position with their outside arms extended in front of them with their hands clasped.

6 Serpentine patterns of steps.

Group B

1 Solo double toe loop jumps.

2 Double hand-to-hand loop lift. The skaters go backward, the man behind the woman, with the man's right hand in the woman's right hand and the left hands together. The woman is then lifted and turned as the man turns a full seven hundred and twenty degrees and she is placed back on the ice on a backward outside edge. The woman has

Spirals can be done side by side or face to face.

Variations of the basic spiral can be developed in practice.

In the death spiral, the woman skates a large circle in a horizontal position.

scope to do what she will with her legs and they can be in an almost split position or stretched in a crossed position.

3 A forward inside death spiral. Similar to the backward outside death spiral, but the woman skates on a forward inside edge instead of a backward outside edge. This move was invented by the famous Russian pair, Ludmilla Belousova and Oleg Protopopov in 1968 and introduced to the West for the first time in 1969. The original backward outside death spiral was invented by a young German girl who won great fame in skating shows and starred in the first skating film. Her name was "Charlotte" – she had dropped her surname earlier.
4 Solo flying camel spins.
5 Pair Grafstrom spins. This is under review at present and likely to be changed.
6 Straight line step sequences.

Group C

1 Solo double loop jumps.
2 One hand lasso lift. This is similar to the double lasso lift but the woman turns three and a half times instead of two and a half times so that she has the time to steady herself to let go of her partner with one of her hands while high above his head and raise her free arm above her head. To keep her up in the air for her extra revolution the man also turns an extra turn so he revolves seven hundred and twenty degrees to her one thousand two hundred and sixty degrees. This lift got its name from the similarity of throwing a lasso to throwing a woman around the man's head.
3 Backward outside death spiral.
4 Solo camel spin with change of foot.
5 Jump into sit spin while holding each other.
6 Circular sequence of steps.

Group D

1 Solo double flip jumps.
2 Overhead one-armed hip Axel lift. In this both skaters go backward while holding outside hands with the man's other arm gripping the woman's inside hip and her hand on his shoulder. The woman then kicks and is lifted backward and cartwheels high over her partner while he turns. He releases his hand while in the air and catches it while descending.
3 Backward inside death spiral. The woman circles around the man, who is in a pivot position, until her head touches the ice while skating on a backward inside edge.
4 Solo change foot sit spin.
5 Catch waist camel spin.
6 Serpentine step sequence.

FREE SKATING

In the free skating some of the compulsory moves are repeated. No program is ever complete without one of the three death spirals mentioned above, although they are sometimes developed so that the woman is lifted off the ice and jumps or is flipped from one death spiral to another. In another variation the man swings the woman while changing the handhold behind his back.

For variety, pair skaters perform some of their program separately. This requires expert coordination and accurate timing.

JUMPS

All pairs strive to do many solo jumps. Irina Rodnina and Alexander Zaitsev introduced side-by-side double Axels and a few pairs now present side-by-side triple jumps. Also recently introduced are the twist lifts in which the man throws the woman into the air while she twists and then catches her before she lands on the ice. In a double twist lift, the woman turns seven hundred and twenty degrees. In a triple twist lift which is only done by a very small number of mostly Russian and East German pairs, the woman turns one thousand and eighty degrees. There is also a split double twist lift in which the woman achieves a split position before twisting.

The three jump lift is one of the easiest lifts. The woman springs up into a counterclockwise turn while the man makes a half turn on the ice.

The throw jumps are also a recent innovation. In these the man throws the woman away from him and she lands after rotating. A throw double Axel has the woman rotating five hundred and forty degrees. A throw double Axel adds another three hundred and sixty degrees to that sum. In 1974, Melissa Militano and Johnny Johns of the United States demonstrated the throw triple loop which has since been copied by couples in Eastern Europe. In this the woman is thrown from a backward outside edge and turns three complete revolutions in the air. In 1977, the skating fraternity witnessed the first quadruple twist which was greeted by great controversy. The move was achieved mainly because of the pair's enormous size disparity. Marina Chekasova was a twelve-year-old child and her partner a tall full-grown man. A throw triple Salchow was first tried, unsuccessfully, by the Russian pair, Irina Vorobieva and Alexander Vlasov from Leningrad in 1977. It was first accomplished by the U.S. champions, Tai Babilonia and Randy Gardner, in the summer of the following year.

Above all, pair skating consists of artistry and although couples such as the Protopopovs were eventually eclipsed by younger, more athletic pairs, their superb grace and purity of line placed them in a class which their successors have been completely unable to emulate.

6

ICE DANCING

Dancing on ice bears a close resemblance to ballroom dancing. It made its first appearance in Central Europe in the 1880s, notably in Vienna. When it was first introduced to England it became one of the features of the Edwardian era, particularly at Prince's Skating Club in Knightsbridge, London. At that time, however, it was not a recognized branch of the ice sports, but it was practiced by almost all skaters.

Twice a year waltzing competitions were held, in conjunction with the British figure skating championships and the Instructors' Benefit Carnival. Instructors and leading amateurs took part. Captain and Mrs. T.D. Richardson won these events in 1913 and 1914.

Upon the recommendation of the Figure Skating Committee of the National Skating Association of Great Britain, a committee to study ice dancing was set up in 1933, thereby gaining official recognition. The first British championships were held in 1937 and won by Daphne Wallis and Reginald Wilkie.

A world competition was held in London in 1950. To everyone's amazement an American team won, arousing the ire of the British who demanded a rematch. This was granted and was won by a British pair, but the interest created by this rematch sparked the ISU into allowing the competition which took place the following year to be called a world championship. This was held in Paris on February 27 and 28 and March 1, 1952. The winners were Jean Westwood and Lawrence Demmy of Great Britain and Mr. Demmy is now the Chairman of the Ice Dance Committee of the ISU, the world governing body. The first European championship was held at Bolzano, Italy, between January 29 and 31, 1954, and once again the winners were Jean Westwood and Lawrence Demmy.

The first organized set pattern dance was the "Ten Step," now called the "Swing Fourteenstep." It was invented by Franz Scholler and first performed in Vienna in 1889 when it was known as the "Scholler March." There are now eighteen compulsory set dances recognized by the ISU, the "Swing Fourteenstep" being one of them.

COMPULSORY DANCES

Championships and competitions are composed of three sections – compulsory dances, original set pattern dance and free dancing. In the compulsory dances the steps, timing and movements of each dance must be in accordance with the

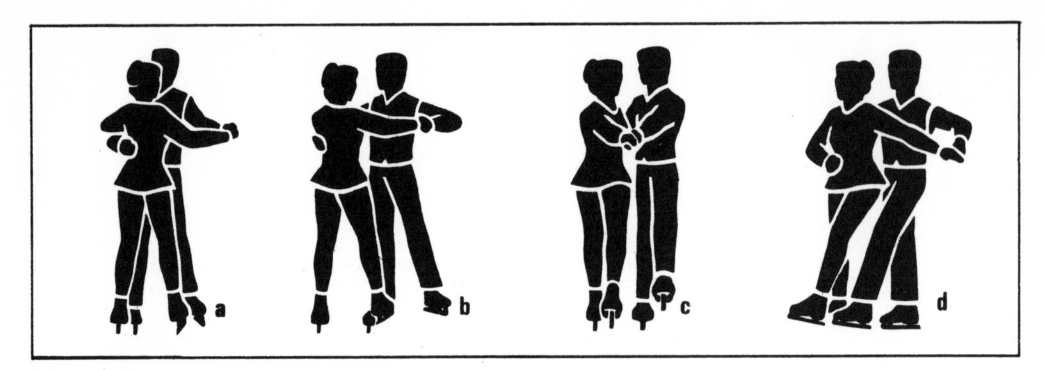

Four dance holds: (a) the waltz hold, (b) the tango hold, (c) the foxtrot hold, (d) the kilian hold.

Free skating steps used in ice dancing include the spiral, a sliding step performed by the woman and a series of kicking hops.

descriptions and diagrams as designated in the official ISU Handbook. Each couple skates three compulsory dances, chosen by a draw on the eve of the championship, and the nine judges each give a mark out of a possible 6.0, using decimal places for intermediate values. The three marks for the three dances are added, then divided by 2.5 to give the couples marks for compulsory dances. The division makes the maximum possible marks thirty percent of the final total.

ORIGINAL SET DANCES

The original set dance is performed to a rhythm determined by the ISU for the second following year and announced not later than May 1. This is not a free dance, and only music with constant and regular tempo may be used. Each couple choose their own music, tempo and composition, and also the steps, connecting steps, turns and rotations – so long as they conform to ISU rules.

The judges give two sets of marks – out of a possible 6.0 – for "composition" (originality, difficulty of performance, variety, correct steps and sequences, correct selection of music to rhythm chosen), and for "presentation" (correct timing to music, movements in rhythm with music, cleanness, sureness, style). These two sets of marks are added together and divided by 2.5 to give marks for the original set dance. This mark amounts to twenty percent of the final total.

FREE DANCING

The free dance has no required sequence of steps, so is a display of the couples' personal ideas in concept and arrangement. The duration of the free dance is four minutes and must consist of a non-repetitive combination of new or known dances. The couples choose their own music, which must be dance music although not necessarily in constant tempo, and there can only be three changes of tune. All steps, turns and changes of position are permitted, plus free skating movements appropriate to the rhythm, character and music of the dance. But the following limitations are imposed: there must be no more than five separations of partners, none of which last more than five seconds or be more than two arms length apart; there must be no more than five arabesques and pivots; spins must not exceed three revolutions; skating on toe picks must not be excessive; steps while skaters make body movements must not exceed two measures of music; five small dance lifts are allowed but the man must not raise his hands above the level of his waistline, and, if turning during the lift, it must not exceed one and a half revolutions; five small jumps are permitted, but the dancer must not turn more than half a revolution; movements standing on, sitting on, or leaning on boots of the partner is not allowed, neither is the holding of skates or lying over the partner's skating leg.

Each judge gives two marks – out of a possible 6.0 – for "technical merit" (diffi-

Ludmilla Pakhoma and Alexander Gorshkov of the Soviet Union in ice dance costume.

The official ISU dance pattern of steps for the foxtrot.

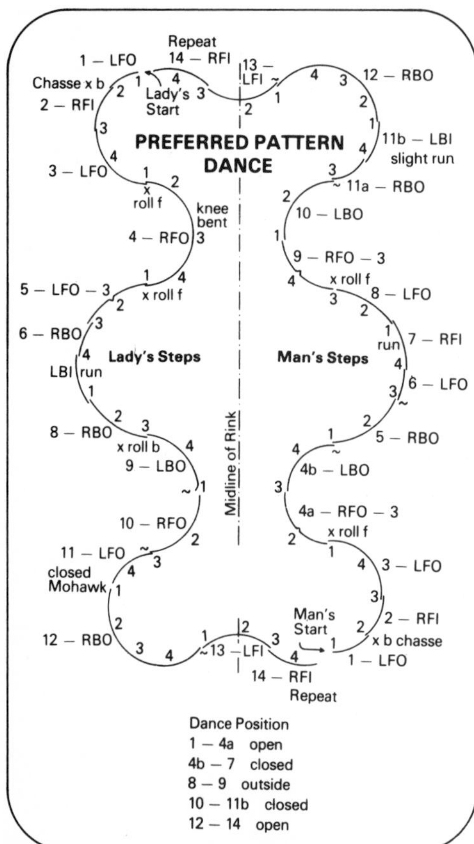

The foxtrot step sequence sets the pattern of the dance which is repeated around the rink.

culty, variety, cleanness, sureness) and "artistic impression" (conformity with music chosen, utilization of space, composition of program, easy movement, sureness in time to music, carriage, originality, expression of character of music). These two marks are added together, and represent fifty percent of the final total. All three sections' marks are added to determine how many marks each judge has awarded each couple.

The championships and competitions are organized by the ISU. The chairman of the Ice Dance Technical Committee is Lawrence Demmy (Great Britain), and his committee members are George Blunun (Canada), Hans Kutschera (Austria) and Emil Skakala (Czechoslovakia).

I count myself lucky to have started reporting international competitions during the Courtney Jones era, for he was the great stylist of his time. European champion five times, world champion four times, he shared those successes with two partners, first June Markham, then Doreen Denny. When they took to the ice the audience knew they were watching something special – they only had to skate around the rink in a Kilian hold during warm up to have everyone applauding.

At that time ballroom dancing was frowned on as an influence on ice dancing, but Courtney had taken lessons on the dance floor, much to his advantage. Nowadays ballroom dancers take an active part in the preparation of their ice counterparts, and in Britain, seminars have been held for both ice and ballroom dancers. Hilary Green and Glyn Watts, former British champions, who won silver medals in the world event in 1974, were trained by Peri Horne and advised by Bill and Bobbie Irvine, former professional ballroom champions. Green/Watts' successors have also consulted ballroom dancing instructors.

Couples are not teamed by any kind of system. In some cases it is almost by accident. Courtney Jones was due to take his gold dance medal, partnered by his trainer Gladys Hogg. But Gladys fell ill before the test and suggested another of her pupils – June Markham – should dance with him, and so brought together new British, European and world champions.

Because his work as a fashion designer occupied the daytime hours, Courtney, with June and then with Doreen, trained at Queen's Ice Club, London for three hours a day, six days a week – between 11 P.M. and 2 A.M. Their dedication was rewarded with world supremacy.

Courtney Jones is now an international judge and officiated at the 1975 world championships. Doreen Denny, who trained the U.S. Olympic bronze medalists, Colleen O'Connor and Jim Milns, is now the U.S. Olympic coach for ice dancing.

MUSIC FOR SKATING

Rhythm is implicit in human movement, and it is from this basic premise that the correlation between music and movement has evolved. Skating as a form of organized movement becomes inevitably a form of dance.

The possibility of skating to music was first realized during the late nineteenth century by the American, Jackson Haines, who transferred his skill as a ballroom dancer to the ice. However, his countrymen found his new style of skating too radical, and in search of a more receptive audience Haines took his creation to Vienna. What better place, after all, to display the sweep and grace of skating than "the home of the waltz?" Haines was a sensation. For his vision, he came to be known as "the father of modern figure skating."

Social dance was the first dance influence on figure skating and then, in 1909, when Serge Diaghilev brought the Russian Ballet to Paris, skating along with all of the arts was swept into a revolution of style and movement. Two of the stars of that first ballet, Anna Pavlova and Vaslav Nijinsky, were household names for the next three decades and by the 1920s and 1930s skaters were bringing these dancers' influences to the ice.

Sonja Henie was the first to present a

skating program taken from Anna Pavlova's famous *Dying Swan*. Both performed their solo variations to Saint-Saëns' work for cello and orchestra from *Carnival of the Animals*. When Sonja Henie retired from amateur competition, she went on to make many films – popular skating musicals which exerted a great influence on her era and those succeeding.

One of Henie's chief rivals, Vivi-Anne Hultén, possessed a less sugared but more aesthetic sense, regarding figure skating as simply ballet on ice. She traveled with her own ballet master and presented interpretations from great Romantic ballets such as *Les Sylphides* and *Swan Lake*. One of Hultén's Canadian exhibitions inspired Mary Rose Thacker (North American champion in 1939 and 1941) to present the first musically choreographed program in a Canadian national championship. Had Hultén attained Olympic and world titles and had she possessed Henie's charisma and acumen for show business, she might have turned skating in a different direction.

These women were performing at a time when skating programs were created without music. A skater would arrive at an event and request a rinkside orchestra to play a waltz or ten-step, to which they would display their variations. The advent of inexpensive records and playing equipment in the 1930s eliminated the need for live musicians at figure skating events. Ice dancing kept the rinkside musicians in existence longer than solo performers but eventually this expensive form of musical accompaniment disappeared. With it, one of the more social aspects of skating also vanished.

Prior to World War II, skaters' attitudes toward music were less cavalier than at present. Carnivals, which were immensely popular, listed the names of the compositions and their creators in program notes. The organization and approach to music was as we see it in the ballet today. Walteufel, Adam, Delibes, Glazunov were favorite composers of the skaters of that era.

Post-World War II developments in figure skating were completely dominated by Dick Button and other North American talents, and the activity became an athletic endeavor. Although there was an undeniable uplift in the technique of skating, the aesthetic aspect suffered. Music began to play more of a background role and, save for the efforts of a few exceptional, artistic individuals, this trend has persisted to the present day.

During the 1950s and 1960s the notable artistic skaters included Jacqueline du Bief, Tenley Albright, Hayes Alan Jenkins and Andrea MacLauglin. These skaters revealed their artistry in competitive programs but exhibitions gave them opportunities to display their other artistic ventures. Famous competitive displays were given by du Bief to Debussy's *Afternoon of a Faun* and Hayes Alan Jenkins presented his suave, quick-footed style to George Gershwin's *Rhapsody in Blue* and Rimsky-Korsakov's *Sheherazade*. Perhaps one of the greatest successes was the program created by Tenley Albright to Richard Strauss's *Der Rosenkavalier*. It was a remarkably conceived and interpreted program. On film it appears strikingly timeless. Albright performed to other such diverse compositions as *Ol' Man River* and Bloch's *Shelomo*.

Although not known as a great competitive skater, Andrea MacLaughlin was famous in North America as an interpretive skater. One of her more famous exhibitions was to Rossini's *Semiramide*.

During the 1960s, music became so

John Curry, world, European and Olympic figure skating champion for 1976, brought the expressiveness of ballet to skating and displayed exceptional musical sensitivity.

strongly identified with certain skaters that no other performers or competitors would approach the work for fear of comparison. The individual who found this right piece of music often experienced lapses in popularity when he or she attempted to interpret another work. Donald Jackson, with his quick-reflexed style, was immediately associated with Bizet's *Carmen* and John Petkevich, with his huge suspend-and-release movement, never succeeded in totally escaping the public's desire to see him skate repeatedly to *España*.

The Soviet pair, Ludmilla and Oleg Protopopov, came onto the skating scene during the 1960s and they brought to the medium exceptional artistry and musical sensitivity. They did not perform a pair routine so much as they created exquisite *pas de deux*. *Liebestraum* by Liszt and the *Moonlight Sonata* by Beethoven were among their famous interpretations and in 1974, several years after they had retired and when their technique was waning, they appeared at a world professional championship with a beautiful version of *The Dying Swan*.

During the last two decades there have

been technically talented women skaters but few striking individuals in terms of artistry. Janet Lynn was the exception. Through her teacher, Slavka Kohout, she became an ethereal interpreter of the Impressionists Debussy and Ravel.

Recently, men have been the adventurers. Toller Cranston and John Curry were and still are the leaders of today's artistic skating. Cranston has brought to the medium a flamboyant style typified by the program he exhibited to *The Sabre Dance* from Khachaturian's *Gayne Ballet* and (although it was not well received competitively) his adventurous study to excerpts from Prokofiev's *Cinderella*.

During his amateur career John Curry experimented with several unusual pieces of music including Stravinsky's *Rite of Spring* but his recognition came with a clearly ballet-derived program to selections from *Don Quixote* by Minkus. Since his Olympic and world wins in 1976, Curry has gone on to develop a Theater of Skating where he performs many works created by famous dance choreographers including Twyla Tharp, Kenneth MacMillan and John Butler. It is with such ventures as Curry's and those initiated by other companies such as Canada Ice Dance Theater that the fullest realization of skating's relationship with music will evolve.

In contemporary amateur skating, the musical development of most interest is being done by the ice dancers. To date, ice dancing has meant "ballroom dancing on ice" but because of the work by the Soviet dancers and two gifted choreographers, Elana Chaikovskja and T.A. Tarasova, ice dancing has taken on a more theatrical appearance. Great skating moments as well as marvelous musical experiences have been given by the Soviet dancers, Ludmilla Pakhomova and Alexandr Gorshkov and Irina Moiseeva and Andrei Minenkov.

Most skaters' awareness of music is elementary. Skating's tie with the concepts of sport has restricted its development as an art form and music has similarly suffered in this relationship.

Because competition demands that skaters make an immediate impression, there has been a reluctance by skating choreographers to be musically adventurous. For competitive programs skaters rarely deviate from the popular Romantic repertoire – Tchaikovsky, Glazunov, Rossini and Bizet – and except in a few cases, exhibitions are done to mundane and repetitious pop tunes.

In the past, several individuals have had music composed specifically for skating (most notably Maxi Herber and Ernst Baier, Patrick Pera and Irina Rodnina and Alexandr Zaitsev) but this is an exciting area yet to be explored.

Skating's particular dynamics, derived from speed and flow, are unique. Its music should have a parallel individuality. Skaters have recognized the correlation of their sport with dance but they have not been able to define the uniqueness of their own type of movement. They have tried primarily to transfer dance styles to the ice rather than develop their own movement form. When a unique style of skating emerges, the fullest realization of the relationship of skating to music will evolve. Perhaps one day we will see dancers performing to music composed for skaters.

7

TOURING SKATING

From time immemorial it has been assumed that skates are as indigenous to the Netherlands as clogs, tulips and windmills – except that skates are older. It used to be said that practically every Dutchman was born on skates. But then those were the days when the whole nation seemed to strap on irons and take to the ice in winter. That set line of mouth, by which the Dutch were supposed to be recognized abroad, was said to be produced on the native ice on the frozen polders where punishing winds blew steadily from the north. And although the Dutch may have been endowed with inborn talent for skating, determined practice behind a chair was still necessary; you pushed one over the ice in front of you until you had acquired the requisite skill and were the equal of your neighbors.

It is a historical fact that skating was part of the Netherlands scene for hundreds of years as an unregulated form of sport, a popular pastime, and an essential activity. There is abundant evidence for this in the dozens of genre paintings from Avercamp to Andreas Schelfhout, and Breitner in the nineteenth century, that are on the museum walls of the world. These paintings record little of the competitive element; it is skating as a pastime that the artists highlight in their matchless chiaroscuro of winter days. The Netherlands do not claim exclusive rights to skating, but it was a pastime in which the entire nation took part, and it is right to say that skating was indigenous and typical – a national property in both senses of the word. Accounts in Dutch literature, for example the nineteenth century diarist Potgieter, fill in the gaps and show just how much ice and skating were part of national life, without distinction of age, sex or social position. In short, for centuries the proper thing to do in Dutch winters was to go skating. And when in Holland something was deemed the proper thing to do, then it was done.

A distinction has to be made between two basic forms of skating. What today is regarded as skating, figure skating, was a minority activity and one more practiced among town folk and the wealthier members of the community in the early sixteenth and seventeenth centuries. The great mass of Dutch people skated on the polders and the canals where distance, speed and endurance were more highly regarded than elegant dress and artistry. This distinction gave birth to what today can loosely be called touring skating – skating distances from one place to another as a matter of recreation in the same way that a skier will tour across country.

Skating on frozen canals in Holland is a traditional winter pastime.

The Netherlands lie behind the North Sea dunes pushed up against tens of thousands of dykes. Hundreds of polders make up a large part of the land surface of the country, like pieces of a jigsaw puzzle. The outlines of the pieces are formed by thousands of miles of inland waterways, canals, drainage channels and moats. As the various states which make up the Netherlands evolved, so did the legal framework within which their people lived. For polder folk the formative laws were those governing the waterways. These laws are very ancient, going back to the thirteenth century. What the Roman roads were for other countries, the waterways were for the Netherlands. They predated the roads by many years and formed the essential communication arteries of the country. It is not surprising that when a severe winter froze the canals they had to be used for transport and communication. Under these circumstances a pair of skates was the equivalent of a bicycle or a two-stroke engine.

People at that time lived farther apart on their homesteads. The horse-drawn barge was not much use when the waterways froze and there was virtually no other means of transport. With simple people and a simple technology and the right weather, skating evolved in the Netherlands of its own accord, without being organized as a sport. It was a popular pastime, a general necessity as far as transport was concerned and an application of exist-

Competitors in Holland's Eleven Towns Tour skate under a canal bridge.

ing technology. Quite large craft on runners were moved by windpower – a kind of ice sailing craft. It was also common practice for skaters to make use of the wind by holding up a bedspread as a sail and reaching frightening speeds in this manner.

As in so many fields, the break in this evolution came with the technological developments of the nineteenth century. Larger waterway craft, better roads, filled-in canals in the cities, increased population, wider trade and better means of transport, all reduced the utilization of that immense water area. In the first half of the century, more canals were actually dug, but increasingly they were intended for larger, faster and more essential traffic. Stretches of water that for centuries had been traversed in winter on skates or sleigh were now kept open. Icebreakers pushed their specially strengthened bows into the skaters' preserves. At the same time, roads came to be more used in winter. Their quality improved until finally modern asphalt surfaces appeared. The nation's youth no longer learned to skate supported on chairs but sat on chairs beside the ice and near the refreshment tents, looking on. By the end of the nineteenth century the national pastime of touring from village to village on skates had become a specialized pursuit of a group. The need went, followed by the general ability. Touring on skates turned into the sport of ice skating and a smaller number of people applied themselves with greater intensity to what had been the practice of a whole nation.

This last statement needs further qualification. It is not the case that today only a few people are actually involved in skating. It remains a national sport in the sense that there are millions of Dutch people who can skate, and millions more who are enthusiastic supporters. They all regard the sport as indigenous and acknowledge it to be very specially Dutch. And in this way, in modern times, two new branches have grown on what had been represented as the dying tree of natural skating.

The tree was dying because there were fewer and fewer occasions for spontaneously donning skates. The old, hard winters that had lasted almost unbroken since the fifteenth century had become rare, newsworthy events so there were scant occasions when young and old, in the countryside, could go out skating from their front door. The two new branches were the organized long and short distance competitions. The former can be seen as a refinement of the old ice touring along the canals, heightened and intensified by the addition of the competitive element. The history of the Elfstedentocht or Eleven Towns Tour provides a good example.

The earliest certain mention of a skating circuit of these towns – Leeuwarden, Sneek, Ijlst, Sloten, Staveren, Hindelopen, Workum, Bolsward, Harlingen, Franeker and Dokkum – was in 1763, when a courtier stated that an event of this kind was held in Friesland. Its existence is further confirmed by reports from subsequent years of such an event. One of the most famous tours took place in 1890 and was won by the equally famous Pim Mulier. Eventually, it was Mulier who, with the Friesian Ice Skating Association, was able to organize a properly regulated tour; the great rush to participate which had been experienced in 1890 was a major factor, but it was not until 1908, after several lingering, uncertain winters, that the competition actually took place. The existing rules of the competition date from 1908. The last Eleven Towns Tour was held in 1963. Since that occasion there has

The rigors of long distance skating are apparent in this view of a stretch of the Eleven Towns Tour.

Spectators line the canal to watch the arrival of the touring skaters.

not been a complete circuit of suitable ice available – although the organizing authorities have enjoyed the cooperation of the provincial and national waterways authorities who, at the onset of severe frost, have always closed their channels to traffic to allow the ice to form. The nostalgia is there, only the climate is not what it was.

Both forms of distance skating are now governed by rules and held over specially marked courses where the competitors could practice before the race. Parallel with this development, and encouraging it, was the establishment late in the nineteenth century of indoor ice rinks in the Netherlands. Applied technology and artificial climates did something to make up for the damage done to traditional skating in the Netherlands resulting from climatic change and industrial advances.

Traditional skating in the Netherlands still inspires widespread interest throughout the country, for pleasure, fitness or for competition. This interest supports and encourages amateurs and professionals alike and explains the great financial efforts made by the Dutch Skating Association and government financial support to keep the sport alive. Holland is still a skating nation, no longer on the local canals but in the ice stadiums. There is no doubt, that given a hard winter (as in 1908, when all the waterways froze over for five months), Dutch youngsters would turn out again to learn skating in the old style, pushing their chairs in front of them over the ice, hanging on to each other's coats, sailing behind a billowing bedspread or gliding at the end of a rope along the rivers and canals. Then the authorities would show their customary understanding and once again set aside stretches of ice for such amusements. But should the youngsters come home in the evening with tingling ears to show their medals awarded them by local organizing committees, their parents will start thinking of distant cheers in international ice stadia around the world.

8

SPEED SKATING

There can be no greater disparity between different branches of the same sport than that between the artistic grace and inventiveness of the figure skater and the lunge and velocity of the speed skater, the fastest self-propelled human being. But it was the speed skater who was the progenitor of the figure skater – by a margin of at least a hundred years.

Speed skating originated on the canals of Holland as a recreation and a means of transport. It is still practiced, when conditions permit, in the form of touring or long-distance skating. The earliest record of touring is of a round trip between two townships in 1676. In the seventeenth century skating spread through Germany, Austria and France. It was thought to have been first introduced into Britain by Frieslanders who came to England to assist in the construction of the canals of the Fens, the low-lying, marshy area between Cambridge and the Wash. Distance or speed skating probably antedated figure skating by a considerable span in Britain, as this form of recreation seems to have been brought in by the returned exiles at the time of the Restoration.

Considering the British reputation for turning recreation into competition, it is not really surprising that the first recorded speed skating competition was on the Fens over a distance of fifteen miles on February 4, 1763. From that date on there is an almost unbroken succession of races recorded in local sporting journals. For the most part these were part of a wager. The winner and runner-up received cash and goods prizes from their patrons and sponsors – a fashion set in the prize fights of the period. A man named Marsh won a top hat and the runner-up a bottle of gin at Carr Mill in Lancashire in 1818, and in 1820 at Clowland the prize was five guineas. In 1825 almost every town and village in the Fens and in the north of England had its champion; sixteen skaters competed at Carter Bridge in 1823 to find the champion of the Fens.

There was a great deal of betting on such races and on special challenges. In January 1821 a Mr. Woodward made a wager of £100 with a Mr. Bland, that Woodward's skater, John Gittam, could skate a straight mile from a flying start, in less than three minutes. John Gittam returned a time of two minutes and fifty-three seconds and Mr. Bland lost. In 1823, Sir C. Boughey, Bart. staged a fashionable winter meet at his estate at Aqualate in Lincolnshire at which a clergyman skated thirty miles in three hours for an undisclosed sum.

Speed skaters compete in the 5,000 meter race at Davos ice rink, Switzerland, 1894.

Skating spread from England to North America, Denmark, Russia, Sweden, and Norway. The first speed skating competition in Norway was held on March 1, 1863, over fifteen hundred Norwegian Ells. Sweden's first competition was in 1882, Finland's 1883 and Russia's (at St. Petersburg) in 1884. The first American championships – over two courses, one of ten and one of twenty miles – was held in 1889 and was won by G.D. Phillips. In 1879 the National Skating Association of Great Britain was formed in Cambridge and the first national championship was held in 1880. It was raced over a course of half a mile and had three turns. These were made round a barrel placed on the ice and the choice of which side to start was decided by the toss of a coin. It was a great advantage to draw the right-hand lane.

At that time the races were held as two-man heats, but no generally accepted distances were laid down. In 1880, the National Skating Association of Great Britain and the Ijsclub of Leeuwarden (Holland) began discussing the organization of an international speed skating competition in Holland. The Dutch were not enthusiastic and, although these discussions led to the formation of the Dutch Skating Association – Nederlandsche Schaatsenrijders Bond – in 1882, whose first secretary was Baron de Salis, it was the Hamburg Skating Club that agreed to stage the competition. There was, however, profound disagreement over the distances to be skated. A succession of mild winters left the arguments on a theoretical level until 1885 when the first international speed skating contest was held. It was under the control of the International Skating Union, and was held in Hamburg on a track 2,800 meters in length. It was won by Axel Paulsen of Norway. The following year saw the championship at Leeuwarden on a track eight hundred meters long and ten meters wide with one turn. This was won by Arie van der Zee, with Pieter Bruisma second. Axel Paulsen and Carl Werner refused to race due to the sharpness of the turns. The following year the race was held in Oslo over three miles and won by Axel Paulsen.

In 1891, the first European championships were announced for speed and figure skating and were the work of the German and Austrian Skating Associations who, acting as a single organization, provided sufficient official backing.

Finally, by the time of the 1889 championships in Amsterdam, standard distances and types of courses had been agreed and speed skating acquired its first set of rules. Four standard distances were to be skated – 500, 1,500, 5,000, and 10,000 meters. The winner was the skater who won over any three distances. The races were to be run in pairs of skaters on a double track.

In 1892, the Dutch called a meeting of all interested associations and clubs to discuss and finalize the layout of skating tracks, the recognition of world records, and – shades of things to come – the position of amateurs versus the sponsored professional competitors. 1892 is the date generally accepted as the official birthdate of the International Skating Union (ISU) which is now in complete control of all speed, figure and ice dance skating in the world. Willem Mulier of Holland was the first president.

Between 1892 and 1928 the rules governing speed skating went through a succession of amendments and refinements but little was changed until after World War II. Then the system of crossing over lanes was altered and, instead of the change from the inner to the outer lane taking place in the middle sixty meters of the straight, the whole length of 111.89 meters straight was used. The start and finish for the 1,000 meters were also moved, the start being set in the middle of one straight and the finish in the middle of the other straight.

In 1970, the 1,000 meters was added to the four existing standard distances as a men's sprint event. It was accepted into the men's Olympic program at Innsbruck in 1976.

TRACK

The standard speed skating track is a two-lane oblong. One circuit is 400 meters. The lanes must be at least 4 meters wide, but preferably 5 meters, and the two 180° turns at either end must have an inner radius of between 25 and 26 meters. The two lanes are marked by colored lines and/or narrow soft snow walls or rubber markers. Starting, finishing and crossover lines are marked by colored lines on the ice.

PAIRING

Pairs who will skate each other are drawn by ballot. The competitors are placed into three groups; the team manager or team leader gives the referee a sealed envelope enclosing a statement showing which of

The international speed skating track is a closed, two-lane circuit 400 meters long.

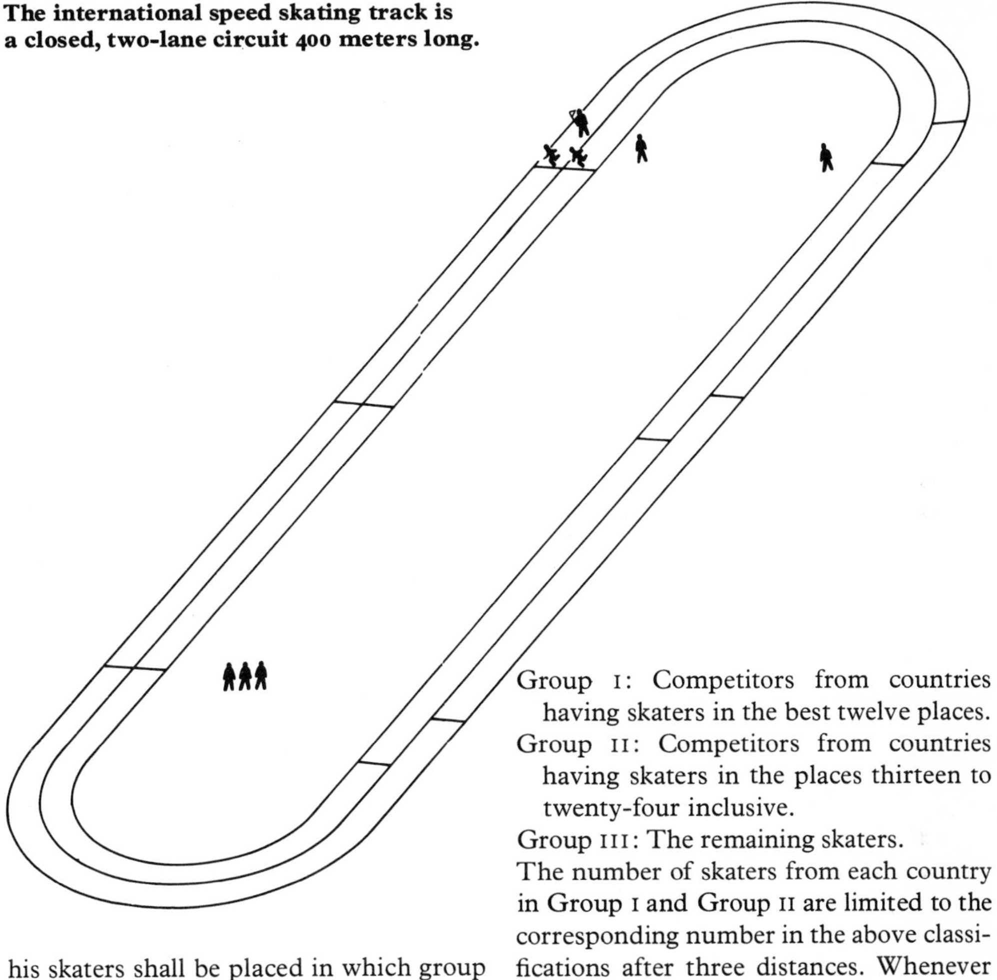

Group I: Competitors from countries having skaters in the best twelve places.
Group II: Competitors from countries having skaters in the places thirteen to twenty-four inclusive.
Group III: The remaining skaters.

The number of skaters from each country in Group I and Group II are limited to the corresponding number in the above classifications after three distances. Whenever possible, skaters from the same country should not be paired against each other.

his skaters shall be placed in which group before the draw is made. If no such statement is presented, the referee places the skaters as he chooses. The 500 meters is drawn first and the first skater drawn in each pair is allocated the inner lane. The 5,000 meters is drawn next. When drawing the 500 meters and the 5,000 meters (500 meters and 1,500 meters for women), the competitors are placed in three groups based on the classification taken from the results of the three distances skated in the same championships the last time they were held.

For the first event of the second day, the 1,500 meters, the skaters are paired according to their time in the 500 meters and the points scored in the 5,000 meters. The best sixteen of the 5,000 meters are paired, but if the best eight skaters on combined points from the 500 meters and 5,000 meters skated on the first day are not in these sixteen then they replace the worst eight in the first selection. The starting order for the final list of pairs is determined

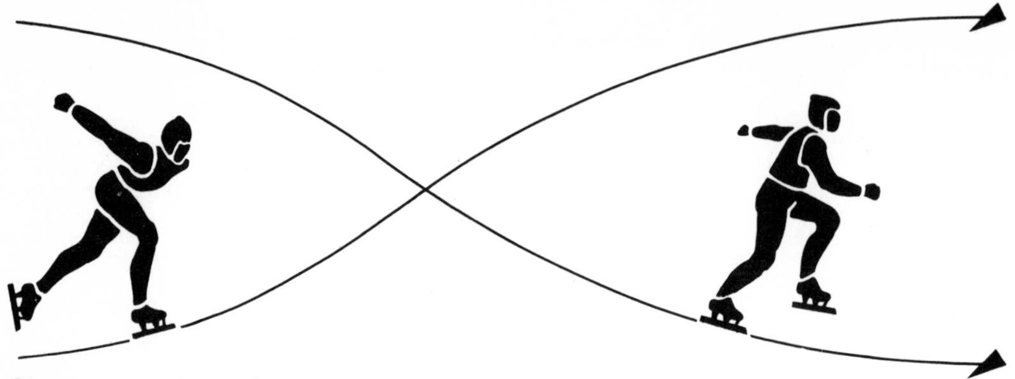

Skaters must change lanes each time they reach the crossing straight section of the track. This gives each skater an equal chance.

by ballot. For participation in the 10,000 meters, the same procedure is followed, using the combined points total for the three distances already raced in order to select only the best sixteen skaters. This ensures that only the best skate all distances, and in particular, take part in the 10,000 meters, always considered to be the most important of the distances. The number participating is limited to the best sixteen skaters.

RULES

Lanes are changed every lap at the crossing line (signaled by the crossing controller), except on the first straight on a 400 meter track when racing the 1,000 meter or the 1,500 meter distances. If they are level when they come out of the bend, the skater on the inner track has to give way to the outer track skater; the reason for this is that the skater on the outer track is fifteen meters in front of the skater on the inner track.

The placing in a competition over the four standard distances is by points which are calculated in the following manner. The time in seconds for all distances is recorded to the third decimal place; the time for the 500 meters is recorded to the nearest one-hundredth of a second and the times for the other distances calculated to one-thousandth of a second. The recorded times are then factorized: time for 1,500 meters is divided by three; time for 5,000 meters is divided by ten; time for 10,000 meters is divided by twenty. The effect of this is to reduce all times to the equivalent of the 500 meters distance.

International championships are run over two days; the prescribed order is the 500 meters on the first morning and the 5,000 meters that same afternoon; the following morning the 1,500 meters is skated and that afternoon the best of sixteen skaters (lowest points for the three events) race for the 10,000 meters. The sprint championships over 500 meters and 1,000 meters are held as a separate competition, also over two days.

Speed skating is unique – in no other athletic competition is the athlete expected to be equally talented in both short and long distance events. No athletic competitor in the track events would even consider having to run, for example, the metric mile and the 10,000 meters, let alone on the same day and, even worse, in a death or glory race against the clock rather than against the field selected in previous heats. For the speed skater this poses considerable problems in training. Although all-year circuit and interval training can be tailored to speed skating needs and specialized weight and endurance training can maintain a peak of physical fitness, only continuous, serious sessions on ice (up to five hours daily) can produce the perfect skating techniques required as well as the essential physical fitness. Before the availability of refrigerated outdoor tracks, serious training had to be limited to the winter months. This did not guarantee regular training sessions. An indoor rink cannot be used for training outdoor speed skaters.

The technique required for the 400 meter rink is based upon the greatest distance to be obtained for each thrust of either leg. The passing of one skate alongside the other is so close that cuts appear on the inside heel of the shoe. The length of the outdoor speed skating blade and the manner in which it is ground, stop the skater from negotiating the turns in an indoor arena and his speed would be far too great for the limited ice surface. The length of an outdoor rink – 111.89 meters – is covered in about eight or nine strides and the outer lane bend, 30 meters in diameter, with eleven or twelve crossovers.

Greater access to suitable training rinks has contributed as much as anything else to the continual bettering of world class performance times. A comparison of Olympic times illustrates this dramatically. In 1924 C. Jewtraw (U.S.A) won the 500 meters in 44.0 seconds; in 1948 F. Helgesen (Norway) won in 43.1 seconds and in 1976 Piet Kleine returned a time of 40.60 seconds. The improvement in the 10,000 meters time are equally impressive. In 1924 J. Skutnabb (Finland) won in 18 minutes 4.8 seconds; in 1948 A. Seyfarth (Sweden) won in 17 minutes 26.3 seconds; and in 1976 Piet Kleine's time was 15 minutes 12.25 seconds.

Although uniform ideal ice conditions, independent of weather and temperature (Olympic tracks must be refrigerated) and improved equipment have played their part, techniques have altered very little from the original Dutch Roll. Serious study of the two phases of the straight skating, the push and the glide, and of the modified step-over push and glide used for skating the turns at either end, has highlighted certain details such as the ideal angle of

Speed skating techniques: (a) the starting position, (b) gliding forward to gain speed, (c) balancing the body over the skating leg, (d) turning corners by means of the crossover.

glide and push and the most economic body and arm movements and positions.

EQUIPMENT

The equipment is simple. The skates, suitable only for speed skating, have long, thin blades set in aluminum supports fastened to the sole of a slight, laced "shoe." The blade itself is ground flat without a "radius" and the laced shoe is tailored to the foot of the skater. The position of the sole and heel plates is located in keeping with the skater's length of leg. The length of the blade is not fixed by rule, but is longer than either ice hockey skates or figure skates; it extends beyond the foot by about one and a half inches at the heel and about two inches at the toe. The rear end is angled sharply towards the foot, while the front end has a slight upward curve. It is extremely difficult to stop on these skates, and it is usual to coast until the speed has been sufficiently reduced to enable the skater to turn around, for nothing must be done that will take the edge off the blade before a race. Even the small amount of ice gathered on the blade is removed at the start.

In the event of a fall, a skater can cut himself with his own skate or be struck by the skate of the other skater in the same pair. If a fall should occur, the skater allows himself to slide clear of the ice until he is stopped by the boundary of the track.

Speed skates have long, thin, aluminum blades fastened to a lightweight boot.

Women have competed ever since the sport was first started, though never against men. For example, in 1805 there was a distance race held in Leeuwarden, Holland, in which one hundred and thirty women took part. Touring skating and the associated town-to-town races were always open to women as well as men. However, as the sport became increasingly organized (by men), the participation of women in such races was considered "unsuitable and immodest."

The record book lists world records for women dated January 26 and 27, 1929, but it was not until 1932 that women skated three events as a demonstration in the Olympics. They had their own world championships from 1936 onward, competing in the 500 meters, 1,000 meters, 3,000 meters and 5,000 meters over two days. But until 1960, women were not permitted to compete in the Olympic winter games. At this championship, the famous Russian skater Lidia Skoblikova competed. She did not compete in the 500 meters, but was fourth in the 1,000 meters and won the 1,500 meters and 3,000 meters. At the games in Innsbruck in 1964, she won three women's events and shared first place as joint winner in the fourth event.

Women now skate four distances: 500 meters, 1,000 meters, 1,500 meters and 3,000 meters. They also skate the 500 meters and 1,000 meters sprint events. Their times compare roughly to those of

A Swiss speed skater displays perfect form.

A competitor in the 1,000 meter event at the United States Olympic speed skating trials.

women track athletes set against men's times. In the 1979 world championships, the 500 meters was won by Sheila Young (U.S.A.) in 42.26 seconds and the 1,500 meters by Sylvia Burka (Canada) in 2 minutes 18.6 seconds. These compare with the men's times of 39.11 seconds and 2 minutes 03.33 seconds for the same distances.

Junior international competitions for boys and girls under twenty enjoy great popularity. The 1975 junior world championship held in Stromsund (Sweden) brought together seventy-two competitors from nineteen countries and the event grows in strength every year.

SHORT-TRACK RACING

Although the international 400-meter track racing produces an annual flurry of media attention on the occasion of a world championship or a winter Olympics, it is only half the speed skating story and possibly the less exciting half at that.

Ever since artificially refrigerated indoor skating halls have attracted the general public, an interest that reached its peak in the 1920s and 1930s at the same time as the roller skating boom, "short-track racing," the official ISU designation, or "indoor racing" as it is more popularly known, has been attracting a steadily increasing public.

TRACK

Short-track racing developed from a fairly chaotic, unstandardized form of circuit racing over various distances on a great variety of shapes and sizes of rinks. Now it is an exciting, internationally recognized branch of the sport, based upon a standard 110-meter track. This size was adopted so that the same track could be used at all ice hockey rinks throughout the world which are 185 feet by 85 feet (56m by 26m) and at all the standard figure skating championship rinks which are 200 feet by 100 feet (60m by 30m). By having a 110-meter track, three tracks can be marked out on the figure skating rink, and two on the hockey rink. In this manner, the number of times the surface has to be remade for a meet is reduced.

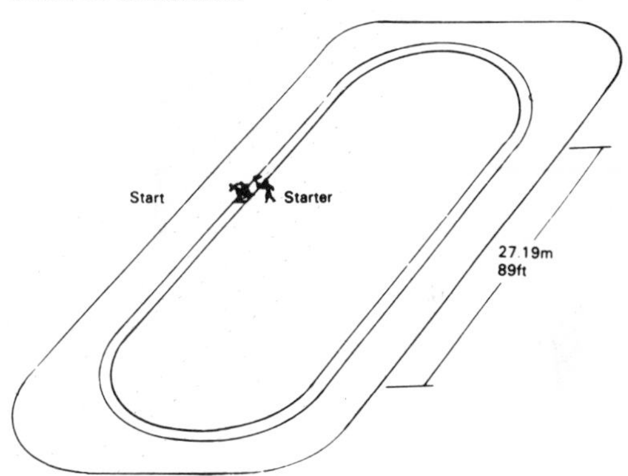

The standard track for short-track racing is 110 meters long.

EQUIPMENT

For this type of speed skating, the skates are very different to those used on the 400-meter tracks. The cups that support the sole plate and the heel are very much higher. This is to ensure that when the skater leans inward on the very small radius bends of the track, the sole of the shoe or the sole plate of the skate do not touch the ice. If this should take place, the

In relay races, the incoming team member is only in the race once he has been touched by the skater who is being replaced. Teams have four members.

skater will fall. The tube that holds the blade of the indoor racing skate is stronger and the blade is thicker in order to withstand the strain when the skater is cornering. The blade is ground to a radius that is almost equal to that used for figure skaters.

RULES

In addition to modified distance races featuring a mass start of four skaters for short distances and six skaters for long distances, short-track racing has taken over the popular and exciting relay races from roller skating.

Relay teams consist of four members and one reserve. The reserve can only take part with the approval of the referee when the referee is satisfied that a member of the team cannot continue due to injury or damage to his skates. The races take place between four teams; each team has one competitor on the track and a further three in the center of the rink, keeping pace with the racers and ready, at any moment, to take over from a team member who falters, falls or is tiring. All four members of the team must take part in the race at some time or another. The relay takes place by a touch on the body (it must be between shoulder and bottom) from the hand of the other member of the team and it must be plainly seen by the judges. A gun is fired to denote that there are three laps still to be skated by the leading team and the last relay must take place before the skater crosses the finish line with two laps still to be skated. The whole event is carried out at a speed equal to a 500 meter sprint. It is on record that the Aldwych Speed Skating Club skated a three-mile relay in 7 minutes 39.4 seconds – a remarkable achievement in such a small area.

The growth in short-track racing began in 1927, in Britain, and by 1933 a National Ice Speed League had been formed. The first British International meet was held in 1948 in Ayr in Scotland. The ISU did not recognize this form of speed skating until 1967 and it was not until 1975 that the ISU Congress in Munich appointed a short-track technical committee to promote a world championship in this discipline. A first step in this direction was taken by the United States International Speed Skating Association who, with the support of the Bicentennial Committee of the State of Illinois, staged a world-class competition in the giant refrigerated rink of the campus of Illinois State University.

Speed skating clothing is warm and streamlined. Skaters starting in the inner lane wear white armbands; those starting in the outer lane wear red ones.

Arms flying, competitors sprint on the final lap of a $\frac{3}{4}$-mile race at a speed skating meet at Lake Placid, New York.

Although the ISU recommends a standard size for indoor ice rinks, measuring 60 meters by 30 meters, which will accommodate all the ice rink disciplines, architects, civil engineers and planners have interpreted the measurements in different ways. Britain has suffered particularly badly in this respect. Quite apart from the loss of the majority of famous rinks to bingo and the property developers, a recent exercise undertaken to list and measure all Britain's rinks, found only four to be of standard size. Consequently speed regulations stipulate only the width of track and the minimum radius of the bends.

In 1978 the first ISU short-track championship was held. This is intended to be the forerunner of the indoor speed skating world championship and took place at Solihull in April. It was attended by skaters from eight nations and three continents – thirty men and twenty-one women. Jim Lynch of Australia was the overall champion, and Sarah Doctor of the U.S.A., the women's champion. The relay was won by Britain for the men in 8 minutes 02.13 seconds for 5,000 meters and the U.S.A. won the women's relay in 5 minutes 18.40 seconds for 3,000 meters.

Speed skating, like every other world championship sport has produced its own legendary competitors. "Turkey" William Smart dominated British speed skating until the mid-1880s by which time he was forty-one and had been unbeaten since 1854. Axel Paulsen of Norway not only gave his name to one of the great figure-skating jumps but also toured the world popularizing speed skating from 1882 to 1884. Clas Thunberg of Finland is ranked with Nurmi as a folk hero, winning no fewer than four golds, one silver and one bronze. Ivar Ballungrund of Norway just beat this record by an additional silver medal. Lidia Skoblikova of Russia is one of the all-time greats, winning six golds in two Olympics, the 1,500 meters and 3,000 meters in Squaw Valley and all four events in Innsbruck in 1964. And then there is Franz Krienbühl of Switzerland who is a bit more than a legend; he started speed skating in the mid-1960s and qualified for the 1968 Olympics at the age of thirty-nine. In the winter of 1975–76 he collected no fewer than nineteen Swiss speed records and went on to the Olympics at Innsbruck where, at the age of forty-seven he came eighth in the world, only 47 seconds behind Piet Kleine, who was then twenty-two. He certainly proves the old adage that it is never too late to learn. For someone who until his mid-thirties preferred Mozart to dawn training sessions, good food to the rigorous diet required of top athletes and had not skated since childhood, this is quite an achievement.

9

TEACHING SKATING TO THE DISABLED

The loss of recreational activities and the consequent lack of social contact is only one of the many deprivations with which the disabled are faced on the return or entry into "normal" life. Historically this problem was deliberately avoided as a result of the age-old custom of quarantining any person who failed to conform to the accepted physical or mental standards. The great increase of disabled veterans following the end of World War I and the increasing successes of the medical profession in rescuing previously hopeless cases provided the initial stimulus to rehabilitate the disabled. Nevertheless, during the 1920s and 1930s, the participation of physically disabled people in everyday activities was unusual and those few who indulged in any form of sport were considered almost eccentric.

However, the end of World War II forced a complete reconsideration of the treatment of disabled people. They were recognized as normal people, who through no fault of their own, and due only to a relatively minor physical disability, were quite unnecessarily being debarred from obvious communal activities. Sport of any kind offers an ideal and obvious escape from this form of mental imprisonment.

Early on, a disabled person must learn to accept those limitations which cannot be changed and to acquire the strength of mind to work to overcome those secondary limitations which can be altered. Rehabilitation, a word with unfortunate connotations, consists basically of the efforts made to regain the utmost use of all available bodily functions. This is the basic ingredient to a road to recovery. It is a journey of self-discovery – a chance to learn physical and psychological strengths.

Repetitive exercising rarely leads to great success and it is for this reason that sport can play a major part. Both skiing and skating, being individual recreational activities with a high degree of challenge and competitiveness, are particularly suitable for serious rehabilitation. In particular, they can do much to fight an inevitable sense of self-pity and prove by positive achievement that disabled people can not only be the equals of competent companions, but that often they can surpass them.

Though wintersports in general might not be the most accessible of activities, skating, now a year-round sport carried out indoors in cities rather than in the winter mountains, is one of the most valuable therapeutic activities. Unlike skiing, skating requires little or no active leg twisting movements and all the normal maneuvers are carried out by means of the curve of the skate aided by an inward or outward lean of foot and leg together with a given minimum of forward speed.

Special prostheses for skating can be designed for all but total bilateral leg amputees. The use of two-foot skates provides satisfactory activity and does not introduce unnecessary limitations. One-footed propulsion is no real handicap and sound central balance over the prosthesis, provided that it is capable of being lifted off the ice, will permit most basic movements and many of the more advanced figures as well. A well-designed prosthesis will permit virtually all skating movements except the most advanced jumps and spins on the absent leg. It is dangerous and wrong to make any limitations to any activity before the impracticability has been proved; the ingenuity and determination of most active disabled people is a constant source of wonder.

The design of sporting prostheses is now a very advanced science and a number of sound and practical varieties are available. Each must be specifically designed for the purpose to which it is to be put. For skating, the most important point to remember is that no ankle flexion is required but a certain degree of resistance to rotation must be available. A knee joint must be capable of being firmly locked in the extended position; a collapse of the lock can lead to a serious and unexpected fall.

Irrespective of the type of prosthesis employed, preliminary exercises are absolutely essential before any attempt is made to move on the ice. In addition to the long list of special exercises for strengthening leg and thigh muscles the following, as applicable, are specially designed for skating:

1 Stand up from a bench without use of the hands, first as a single exercise and then progressively as a sequence movement; standing up and sitting down again.
2 Walk up and down stairs using weight shifts from hip to hip from above thigh and calf, placing the foot flat on the stair at each step.
3 Stretch and bend the leg while sitting on a bench. Weights should be added to the leg gradually.
4 Sit on the floor and get up from this position to a stable standing position.

The actual teaching of skating skills to all kinds of handicapped persons, whatever their disability, must be carried out by specially trained instructors. It is important not to represent skating as a "falling" experience when teaching the disabled to skate – a commonly held view of both skating and skiing. The teaching of falling should be avoided as part of the initial instruction. If a student is taught to fall before being given a proper chance to stand on the surface, he will always seek the "easy way out" and try to sit down, which in many cases should be avoided at all costs. Since falling is usually an unconscious action, it is more important that the instructor should give strong encouragement at such a moment rather than rely on previously taught falling exercises. Such preparation exercises will have been introduced on the gymnasium floor long before any approach to an ice surface has been made.

For all disabled people, the first five or

ten minutes on the ice are the most important of the entire instruction. If they gain control of their body at this point they accomplish a major task which will automatically lead to increased self-confidence and subsequent rapid acquisition of further skating skills.

A successful method of instruction has been found which consists, in essence, of five stages. The first takes place on dry land and consists of teaching balance on skates (finding the balance point), followed by walking steps on the balance point of the skate blade. The step used is that which, on ice, will result in sliding forward or backward, in other words with feet turned outward at an angle to each other for forward and into each other for backward movement. For each step, the leg is lifted upward and outward with the upper body remaining motionless. At the same time the correct position of the arms is taught. These exercises will enable the pupil to move forward, backward and to stop in "snow plow" position, when on the ice.

The second stage consists of the first steps on ice. This is a critical phase for building confidence and dispelling fear of instability. It is essential for the first step onto ice that the skater's center of gravity (or balance) remains directly above the skates and the skater immediately rediscovers the balance point of the skate blade which has been achieved during the dry land exercises. Steps are taken so that the pupil lifts one foot by raising the thigh so that knee and toe of the skate come forward. With each step the skate is replaced on the ice next to the other foot with toes further apart than the heels and the sole parallel to the ice. As a preliminary to the actual steps, the pupil will have experimented sliding the skate forward and backward no more than three inches, during the course of discovering the balance point of the skate blade. Progress from this state should consist of taking steps with a short glide, but on no account to try pushing. Correct stepping will result in forward motion accompanied by a short glide on both feet.

The third stage consists of expanding the individual step to a striking out movement where the individual movements are slower and the distance covered is greater.

The fourth stage consists of introducing steering movements using the natural curve of the skate and the edge of the blade. This will involve a reconsideration of body and arm positions and movements.

The final stage consists of learning the various stopping maneuvers. Three are customarily taught – the snow plow stop with the feet in a V-position, the T-stop where one foot is placed behind the other at right angles and lastly the hockey stop where both feet are parallel and are turned to a right angle to the direction of progress.

Basic instruction does not differ in any marked degree to the customary system of beginners' instruction. It must be stressed that every single case will require individual attention and adaptation and any one stage may prove a major obstacle. Patience and perseverance with no pressure are the clues to successful skating instruction of disabled people.

Blind persons are particularly well suited to enjoy the freedom and movement that skating can provide. Owing to the so-called "navigation phenomenon" of the blind, orientation while skating proves no problem. This inherent ability for navigation, the capability of assimilating a series of postural and positional changes and assembling these signals into a coherent and logical sequence is helped a lot by the need for a constant posture – head and shoulders in a constant relationship and ears at a constant level. Rough ice or sudden interruptions can disturb the navigation. Blind skaters are particularly suited to pair skating or ice dancing. They often require a companion, so the progression to some form of pair skating is an obvious aim.

Teaching paraplegics is comparable in every way to teaching amputees. Feasibility is determined by the availability of a suitable brace, to give rigidity to an affected limb so that it can bear weight. One limb does not have to be involved in active propulsion, but can serve as a support.

Before planning a skating course for any disabled person, a careful analysis of the degree of disability must be made. On the basis of such an investigation the most suitable prosthesis or aid can be designed and adapted and the details of tuition worked out. If this is successful, the degree of satisfaction for both pupil and instructor is immeasurable. Most failures are due to a lack of understanding of the disability in relation to the teaching of skating.

TEACHING SKATING TO THE MENTALLY HANDICAPPED

The teaching of skating to mentally retarded people is fundamentally similar to teaching the physically handicapped. Everything that has been said about the benefits of achievement and of participating in an individual activity in company with other people applies even more strongly. In particular, skating is a valuable family activity and it is not unusual for the skater to become extremely active in teaching family and friends this new activity.

Beside what could be termed the psychological advantages, it has been found that skating increases the concentration of mentally retarded people and they are capable of retaining their skating skills over a long period without practice. Teaching figure skating movements is less successful however, than teaching the tasks involved in an obstacle course, for example. The successful completion of such a course is doubly beneficial. It enables the demonstration of skills in competition and gives great pleasure.

Most mentally retarded people can be taught skating, provided that there is some degree of coordination and experienced teaching is available.

ICE RINK

SPORTS

10

CURLING

The origin of curling is lost in the mists which also shroud the origin of golf, the other great game which Scotland has given to the world. Hardy Scotsmen hurling rocks across a frozen loch in a primeval test of strength and then setting marks on the ice as target areas is as good a theory as any about the beginnings of a game which is now played in fifteen countries.

The Scots claim curling as "their ain game" but there is some doubt whether the game started in Scotland or the low countries. The Dutch argument rests on two winter landscapes by the Flemish painter, Pieter Breughel (1530–1569), *Hunters in the Snow* and *The Bird Trap*, which show a game like curling being played on ice.

One important area of evidence tilts the scale in Scotland's favor – that only in Scotland have ancient curling stones and other relics been unearthed in archeological diggings and recovered from lochs and bogs. It seems likely that Breughel's sportsmen were playing with frozen clods of earth.

Whether curling started in Scotland or not, it is certain that the Scots nurtured and developed the game for centuries – often through long mild spells when no play was possible – and established the rules of curling, which they introduced to many countries.

It is significant that the principal aim of The Royal Caledonian Curling Club (instituted in 1838), the mother club of the game in the world, is: "to unite curlers throughout the world into one brotherhood of the rink and to regulate by rules the ancient Scottish game of curling."

The first landmark in curling histories is the Stirling Stone on which the date 1511 is inscribed. This famous stone, which is on display in the Smith Institute, Stirling, is called a *loofie* – *loof* being the old Scottish word for the palm of the hand – and it has rough finger grips for throwing it down the ice.

The earliest irregular stones were also called *kuting* or quoiting stones and must have been thrown with a quoiting action. They were small, varying in weight from five pounds to twenty-five pounds (2.5kg to 11kg).

Roughly three hundred years ago, the introduction of a rough handle changed the whole character of the game. The handles, of iron, wood or horn, were inserted in the stones by the local blacksmith or by the curlers themselves and curling stones became bigger and bigger, massive blocks of all shapes and sizes jostling for position on

A curling match in progress at a Swiss mountain resort.

the ice. The main advantage of a big stone was that, if a curler could throw it to a counting position, it was difficult for opposing stones to dislodge it.

This strong-arm era of the game culminated with the biggest known stone, the Jubilee Stone, which weighs 117 pounds and is now part of The Royal Caledonian Curling Club museum in Perth Ice Rink. It was taken from the sea at the mouth of the Pease Burn at Cockburnspath in Berwickshire and was laid upside down at the stables in the area so that the running surface would be worn smooth by horses' hooves.

The introduction of a handle to the curling stone was the first major revolution in the game's history. The second, which had even more far-reaching effects, was the rounding of the stone, the first evidence of which occurred towards the end of the eighteenth century.

The rounded stones brought skill and accuracy to the game. They ran consistently on the ice and "wicked" (rebounded) off other stones at predictable angles. Curling changed dramatically from a trial of strength to a test of skill.

More excitement was to follow. While experimenting with the new stones, curlers, reputedly in the Fenwick and Kilmarnock areas of Ayrshire, discovered that, by turning the handle of a stone to the right or left (the "in-turn" and the "out-turn"), they could control the curved path of the stone (the "draw").

This new method, originally called the Fenwick Twist or the Kilmarnock Twist, spread into other Scottish areas at the beginning of the nineteenth century and soon became general practice. The curved line of a running stone, giving the effect of using the bias in bowls, enabled curlers to play the whole range of curling shots with far more accuracy than before and introduced a spectacular new shot – the draw or slow shot round a guard – which had hitherto been impossible or a fluke.

There have been other refinements since the invention of the Twist in Ayrshire. The curling stones used today evolved through many types called by the names of their localities, the most famous being Ailsas, quarried from the small island of Ailsa Craig in the Firth of Clyde which for more than one hundred years has provided stones for the curling world. But the game has remained basically the same since the turning of the handle of a stone, "the birth of the birl," around 1800.

As curling gained in popularity in the nineteenth century, challenge matches were arranged between neighboring parishes and provinces and these confrontations brought into focus the wide disparity in the sizes of stones and discrepancies in the rules which varied throughout the country.

It was reported after the match between Midlothian and Lanarkshire in 1831: "there was a want of cooperation between the players." This was understating the case and the need for national regulations led to the formation of the Grand Caledonian Curling Club in 1838. The Club became The Royal Caledonian Curling Club in 1843, the Royal title being granted after the Earl of Mansfield, then the President, illustrated the game to Queen Victoria on the polished ballroom floor of Scone Palace.

The Royal Club, the headquarters of which have always been in Edinburgh, quickly established itself. The number of member clubs doubled in two years and quadrupled in five years when the membership was 116 clubs. Today, over six hundred Scottish clubs are affiliated and many thousands of clubs overseas are members through their national associations in addition to member clubs in the English and Welsh Curling Associations.

The following brief summaries illustrate the development of the game in the other curling countries in the world:

Canada Canada is easily the biggest curling nation with around 750,000 curlers. Scottish soldiers and fur traders introduced the game after the Siege of Québec in the latter part of the eighteenth century. Curling is widespread in Canada; even small villages have their curling rink. The Royal Montreal Curling Club, founded by Scots in 1807, was the first curling club in Canada and the first sporting club of any kind in the North American continent. The major event is the Canadian Championship ("Macdonald Brier"), started in 1927 and competed for annually by the champions of all the Provinces. Canada dominated the world championship from 1959 to 1972, winning twelve times in fourteen years. Schoolboy and schoolgirl curling is tremendously popular in Canada and other nations are following this lead.

United States Curling is played mainly in the midwest and the east but there are now thirteen state associations and it is felt that the game could become as popular in the United States as in Canada. It is believed that Scots introduced the game in Michigan in 1832. The first United States national championship was held in 1957.

Switzerland Scots started the game in the 1880s in St. Moritz. The Swiss mountain resorts are a winter paradise for visiting curlers. Artificial ice rinks are being built in many areas. There are over seven thousand curlers and the game was given a new impetus by the first victory of the Swiss in the world championship in 1975. The Swiss Curling Association was formed in 1942.

Sweden A Scot introduced the game in 1846 but it is only recently that curling has taken firm root. The growth of interest by young players and the Swedes' competitive attributes are the reasons. Their quality of play was underlined when they won the world championship in 1973. There are about seven thousand curlers and the number is increasing fast. The Swedish Curling Association was instituted in 1916.

Norway A Scottish club played challenge matches to launch Norwegian curling in 1880. Further missionary tours by Scots between 1954 and 1958 helped to spread modern curling. A big indoor ice rink was opened in Asker, Oslo, in 1969, but, unfortunately, was destroyed by fire. There are about fifteen hundred curlers in Norway.

New Zealand Scots started the game over a century ago. The New Zealand curlers, who made their first curling tour to Scotland in February 1973, still play the old-style game – out-of-doors on the dams in Central Otago – but, after their Scottish tour, are talking of building indoor rinks. There are twenty-eight clubs in New Zealand, most of which are bounded by the mountains of Otago, from Ranfurly west to Alexandra, the two main curling centers being Naseby and Oturehua.

France The winter Olympic games in Chamonix in 1924, when a Scottish rink won the curling gold medals for Great

Britain, crystalized the curling interest in France. The French championship was started then. The Haute Savoie area is the stronghold of French curling.

Germany Curling started in 1931 but began to spread after an international tournament in Garmisch-Partenkirchen, Bavaria, in 1961. Now there are thirty clubs and many events in Germany and the quality of play rises each year. The German Curling Association was founded in 1966.

Italy Curling is based mainly in Cortina d'Ampezzo in the Dolomites, site of the 1956 winter Olympics, where a midsummer bonspiel is a feature.

Denmark New clubs are springing up in Denmark. The Danish Curling Association was formed in 1970 with headquarters in Copenhagen. With Italy, Denmark joined the world championship in 1973 to make a line-up of ten nations.

Holland The Dutch Curling Association was formed in 1974, and, in cooperation with Utrecht curling club, launched the international Windmill Cup. There are four major clubs in Holland.

Austria Kitzbühel in the Tyrol is the center of the game in Austria, the Kitzbühel club having been formed in 1955, and other nations are laying plans to start curling.

A curler in the Bernese Oberland demonstrates a sliding delivery.

PRACTICE OF THE GAME

The game of curling is played on a sheet of ice ("rink") by two teams ("rinks") of four players, each player throwing two stones and playing them alternately with his opposite number. Stones weighing around 40 pounds (19.15kg) are thrown 42 yards (38.40m) to circles (the "house") marked on the ice. The object is to count more stones than your opponents nearer the centre of the circles (the "tee"). When all sixteen stones have been played, an "end" is completed and the teams then turn and play the next end down the same sheet of ice in the opposite direction. Games are played by time or by an agreed number of ends and are decided by a majority of shots.

To throw a stone, the curler places his right foot on the "hack" and adopts a sitting position with his left foot comfortably placed slightly ahead of him. He grips the handle of the stone, firmly but not tightly, in his right hand, holding his "broom" in his left hand for balance. He takes aim on the broom held by the captain of the team ("skip") at the other end of the ice, and with a pendulum movement draws the stone back, lifts it off the ice and throws it forward, releasing it with a full follow-through directed at the skip's broom. On the backswing, the curler raises his body, swinging the left leg backward or to the side to balance the weight of the stone on his right side. On delivery, the curler imparts turn to the stone – in-turn or out-turn – which causes the stone to rotate and makes it run in a curve to right or left.

The technique and tactics of modern curling at the top level were introduced by Canadian curlers and have been adopted by almost all curling countries since the world championship, instituted in 1959, brought together the national champions in world competition.

The long-sliding delivery of a curling stone, with its demands on athleticism and balance, popularized the game among the youth of Canada. The "slide" starts in the normal way with the player sitting comfortably on the hack, but as he swings the stone forward, he thrusts strongly with his right leg and slides out on a slippery sole on his left shoe.

In conjunction with the long slide, the Canadians introduced the "take-out" game which places a premium on accuracy and nerve. The policy is to strike out opposing stones and eliminate the possibility of lucky shots off a group of stones by opposing players. A single miss by Team A in the take-out game can be costly as this gives Team B the chance to place a second counting stone in a position square to the first one, making it impossible for Team A to remove both stones at once.

A team which falls behind adopts a new tactic – laying stones short so that, if they are missed by the opposition, slow drawing stones can be played behind the first stones, using them as guards.

There are many variations to this simply-stated definition of the take-out game, to which can be added the strain on the skip as the game nears its climax and he strives to keep the vital last stone at the last end. To achieve this, he must sometimes "blank an end" which means that he must leave no stones in the house, after which the winner of the previous end must start the next end.

The take-out game is only played by top class players or by players aspiring to competitive play. The vast majority of curlers use a standing or short-sliding delivery and play a drawing game in which a number of stones – sometimes all sixteen – are placed in positions in the house.

To throw a stone, curlers place their right foot on the hack and adopt a sitting position with the left foot slightly ahead.

The long-sliding delivery, which is not for curlers of middle age or over, has attracted increasing numbers of youngsters to the curling colors. The explosion of young players in Canadian curling began immediately after the Second World War. Since then, coaching schemes for young curlers have been promoted in many countries.

In former times, the training of young people was the responsibility of the experienced players in a club and often – too often – beginners were handed a broom and left to find their own feet on the ice. Now, youth is being served by curling clinics, national junior events and a world junior championship, sponsored by Uniroyal and inaugurated in Toronto in 1975.

Curling tours, by men's and ladies' teams, are a feature of modern curling. The Royal Caledonian Curling Club sent a Scottish team to Canada in 1902, and, since then, exchange tours of all types have traveled in all directions to spread goodwill. Tours generally last for two or three weeks and lucky members of touring teams have described the curling tour as the experience of a lifetime.

The Royal Caledonian Curling Club also led the way in the establishment of the International Curling Federation. The club called a meeting of curling administrators and personalities from overseas countries in Perth, Scotland, in 1965 and the constitution of the Federation was officially ratified in 1966. Elected representatives from Scotland, Canada, United States, Switzerland, Sweden, Norway, France, Germany, Italy, Denmark, England and Holland annually attend meetings of the Federation – during the week of the world championship – to discuss international rules and administration. The Secretary of the Federation is the Secretary of The Royal Caledonian Curling Club.

EQUIPMENT

The modern curling stone is a work of art, carefully fashioned by craftsmen. It is made of granite of consistent hardness and homogeneous quality and fine grain which will not flake or chip. Rough blocks weighing about 100 pounds (45.36kg) are hewn and matched in color and texture. Each stone is reduced to a size 12 pounds (5.4kg) heavier than the final weight, a hole is bored through the center and the stone is again reduced in weight and ground prior to the formation of a concave cup and circular running rim. After polishing, the stone is completed with the final adjustment of the running rim and the addition of a striking band (the hitting area of the stone). The hole in the center is then countersunk square to receive the iron bolt which holds the handle.

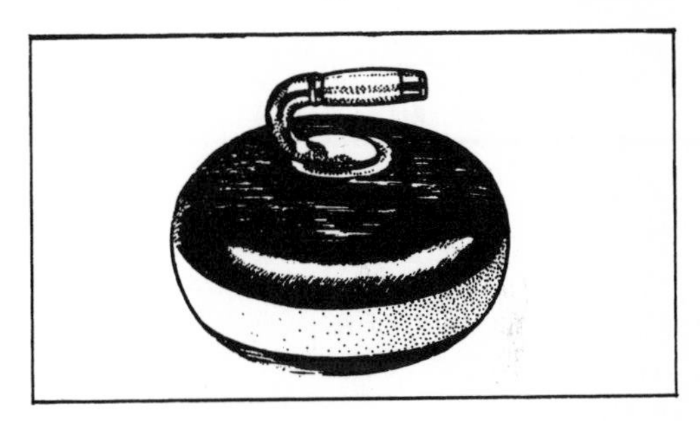

The curling stone has a circular running rim and a curved handle.

In most curling countries, standard sets of stones are provided on ice rinks for the use of curlers. In addition to stones, the paraphernalia of the game includes hacks (for throwing from) and brooms or brushes (for sweeping with).

As its name implies, the hack was originally a cut in the ice into which a

The broom is used to sweep in front of the stone and by the skip to give directions.

curler placed his foot to give him purchase as he threw a stone. Today, the hack is a rubber-covered implement with metal prongs which hold it in place in the ice. The curler places his right foot on it (left foot if he is left-handed) as he delivers his stone on the ice. The sunken hack used in Canada and the United States is a hole cut in the ice and lined with rubber to prevent slipping.

Some curlers still use a crampit, a long iron implement, with spikes on the underside which grip the ice, on which a player stands with both feet, taking a step forward on it as he throws his stone. The crampit, which is unknown overseas except in New Zealand, is now seldom seen in Scotland except at outdoor bonspiels.

A broom or brush is carried by every curler. It is used by the skip of the rink of four players to direct his players, each curler throwing stones in the direction of the skip's broom with the required in-turn or out-turn imparted to the handle of the stone. In addition, the two players not involved in directing or throwing a stone run alongside their side's moving stone to sweep it if called to do so by the skip.

Sweeping is an integral part of curling and a matchwinning feature of the game. It is reckoned that powerful sweepers can bring a stone 12 feet (3.66m) further than an unswept stone on good ice. In addition, sweeping will keep the stone on a straighter path, reducing the amount of its draw, so that a swept stone can be brought past a guarding stone.

Another vitally important piece of a curler's equipment is his footwear. This is a matter of personal choice and depends on what type of curling is played. Most top class players use a sliding delivery which requires a sliding sole on the left foot. Those who play with a standing or short-slide delivery use a less slippery sole and others use a slip-on sole for delivery and then slip it off again for sweeping. Curlers choose their curling shoes or boots carefully to give them the maximum amount of confidence.

RINK PREPARATION

In olden times, Jack Frost was toasted at annual curling suppers as "the curlers' friend – and foe" and the tradition continues today. Long-suffering curlers were totally dependent on the fickle frost and often laid careful plans for the bonspiel only to have their hopes dashed by a sudden thaw.

Today, almost all competitive curling is played in indoor ice rinks but some clubs still maintain outdoor ponds. There is great activity when the thermometer falls and the news comes that the ice is bearing.

Plans are made each year for the biggest bonspiel in the world, the Grand Match of The Royal Caledonian Curling Club. It is often a labor of love as the match is held infrequently; heavy frosts over a long period are required to provide the requisite six inches of black ice on a major Scottish loch.

The Grand Match is a magnificent sight with 2,400 curlers on the same sheet of ice – on Loch Leven, Lake of Menteith or Lindores Loch, whichever freezes first. Two days are required for ice-marking, accomplished by a skilled corps of men

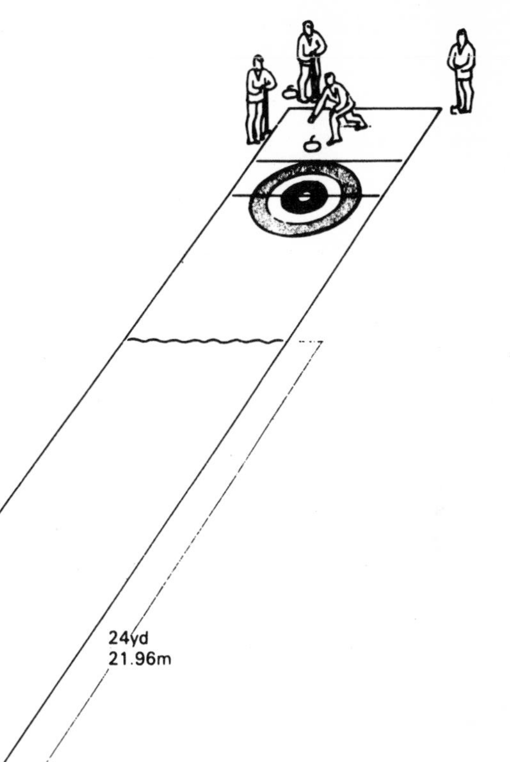

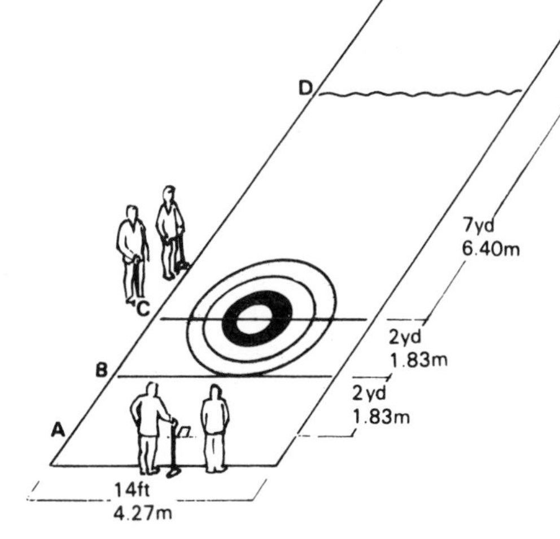

The playing area for curling is 46 yards long with two target circles or houses 38 yards apart.

who use "tee-ringers" – boards with nails which cut circles – and iron pencils to score lines on the three hundred sheets of ice.

The match, started by a cannon, lasts for three hours and is a great sporting occasion. The ice can be smooth and even but is often rough and sometimes heavily biased. As a result, outdoor curling is less precise, more a matter of luck than indoor play but the invigoration of curling on a loch in beautiful surroundings under a red wintry sun has a thrill all its own. The bracing air, the roar of the stones – which is why curling is called the roarin' game – and the feelings of fellowship combine to provide a day to remember.

Experiments with artificial ice rinks were first carried out by John Cairnie, first President of The Royal Caledonian Curling Club, who published his findings in *Essay on Curling and Artificial Pond Making* in 1833. Cairnie, who constructed a clay pond with whinstone impounded in the clay, flooded the pond with water to the depth of a quarter of an inch and claimed he could provide ice for curling after one night's frost.

Concrete and asphalt surfaces were tried with varying degrees of success but the biggest advance was made by tarmacadam, which was cheaper to lay and more effective in use. The first tarmacadam rink was laid in Edinburgh in 1902 and the new system was used in many parts of Scotland.

The first indoor ice rinks were the Rusholme Rink in Manchester (1877) and the Southport Glaciarium (1879) but they failed through lack of support and ice rinks did not come to Scotland until 1907 when the Scottish Ice Rink was opened in Glasgow. It lasted until 1917 and the existing Scottish Ice Rink, built on the same site in 1928, is the biggest ice rink in Europe with seventeen sheets of ice for curling.

The oldest existing ice rink in Scotland is the Edinburgh Ice Rink, opened in 1912, and there are now indoor ice rinks for curling in fourteen Scottish cities.

Indoor rinks made their appearance in Canada at roughly the same time, many of the early rinks having roofs and open sides which allowed for natural ice to be formed in the cold Canadian winters.

Artificial ice is now produced by modern ice-making plants which pump brine through miles of pipes under the playing surface.

The preparation of good ice is an art. Ice-makers flood the ice to provide an even surface, and, prior to play, lightly spray it with water. This produces "pebbled ice" – a surface of small pebbles on which the concave base of a curling stone runs easily, the friction being less than on a flooded flat surface of ice. Pebbling provides keen (fast) ice and keen ice is the best surface for accurate play.

RINK MEASUREMENTS

1 The length of the playing area shall be 46 yards (42.06m). It is recommended that the width of the playing area shall be a minimum of 5.2 yards (4.75m) and that, where possible, the ice be continued a further 4 feet (1.22m) or more behind each foot line.

2 The length of the rink from the foot line to the tee shall be 42 yards (38.40m).

3 The tees shall be 38 yards (34.75m) apart and, with the tees as centers, circles having radii of 4 feet (1.22m) and 6 feet (1.83m) shall be drawn.

4 Additional inner circles may also be drawn. Dividing lines may also be drawn or barriers placed between adjoining rinks.

5 In alignment with the tees, lines, to be called center lines, may be drawn from the tees to points 4 yards (3.66m) behind each tee; at these points foot lines 18 inches (45.72cm) in length shall be drawn at right angles, on which, at 3 inches (7.62cm) from the center line, the inside edge of the hack shall be placed. When hack and crampit are both being used in the same rink, the crampit shall be placed immediately behind the hack.

6 Other lines shall be drawn across the rink at right angles to the center lines:

a) a hog line, distant from each tee one-sixth part of the distance between the foot line and the farther tee.

b) a tee line across each outer circle and through each tee.

c) a back line behind and just touching the outside of each outer circle.

Notes:

A skip directs his team. The object used to mark the center of the target is called a dolly.

1 A stone which does not clear the farther hog line is a "hog" and is removed from the ice.
2 A stone which passes the back line is removed from the ice.

RULES

There are only twenty basic playing rules in curling and this is a proud boast of curling administrators who, through the years, have withstood efforts to extend them. It is clearly understood that it is impossible to write rules to cover all contingencies and that there will always be loopholes in any set of rules. The aim, therefore, has been to keep the rules short and simple and leave it to the curlers themselves to interpret them sportingly.

The regulations concerning curling stones are that they must be of a circular shape and that no stone, including handle and bolt, shall be of greater weight than 44 pounds (19.96kg) or of greater circumference than 36 inches (91.44cm) or of less height than 4½ inches (11.43cm).

A number of the other important rules are:

A skip has the exclusive direction of the game for his rink. When it is his turn to play, he shall select one of his players to act as skip.

The rinks opposing each other shall settle by lot the rink that will lead at the first end, after which the winner of the preceding end shall lead.

In the delivery of the stone, the stone shall be released from the hand before the stone reaches the nearer hog line.

If a running stone is touched by any of the rink to which it belongs, the stone shall be removed from play immediately by that rink. If by any of the opposing rink, the stone shall be placed where the skip of the rink to which it belongs considers it would have come to rest.

No player shall use footwear or equipment that may damage the surface of the ice.

Between the tee lines, a running stone, or a stone set in motion by a running stone, may be swept by any one or more of the side to which it belongs. Behind the tee line, the skip or acting skip of each rink is entitled to sweep any stone but neither of them shall start to sweep an opposing stone until it reaches the tee line. The sweeping shall be across the course of the stone and no sweepings shall be left in front of a running stone.

The players, other than the skip and acting skip, shall not stand behind the house but shall place themselves along the sides of the rink between the hog lines, except when sweeping or about to deliver a stone.

Measurements (which cannot be made until the termination of an end) shall be taken from the tee to the nearest part of the stone.

The simplicity of the rules underlines the friendly nature of the game. The umpire is seldom called to adjudicate, except to measure stones, and games start and end with handshakes. The fellowship of curling is the hallmark of the game and is a feature of it which is recognized in all countries.

Curling is called "a slippery game" because of the lucky rubs and swings of fortune which transform victory into defeat and curlers learn to accept adversity as they accept the ice on which they play – and take the rough with the smooth.

WORLD CHAMPIONSHIP

The world curling championship started in 1959 when The Scotch Whisky Association presented the Scotch Whisky Cup for competition between the champion rinks of Canada, the biggest curling country, and Scotland, the home of the game.

The impression made by the Canadian champions, Ernie Richardson and his family rink from Regina, Saskatchewan, is still reverberating in Scotland. The Richardsons won four times in the first five years. The power and accuracy of their play was a revelation and their take-out game, which carried them to easy victories, forced the Scots to rethink their approach to competitive curling.

The United States champions joined the competition in 1961 and the Swedish champions in 1962. The event was played in Scotland for the first five years.

In 1964, when the competition was played in Canada for the first time (in Calgary), Switzerland and Norway joined and France came in two years later. Germany participated in 1967, to become the eighth nation involved.

Having raised the competition to international stature as the official world championship, The Scotch Whisky Association withdrew from sponsorship in 1967. Air Canada became the sponsor and the world event increased in scope and prestige.

Denmark and Italy enlarged the championship to ten rinks in 1973 and the event is now played annually in March in different parts of the world.

The competing countries run national championships, the winners of which qualify for the world championship, and the most noticeable feature in recent years has been the upsurge, in numbers and quality, in the younger curling countries.

Canada dominated world play from 1959 to 1972, only the United States and Scotland breaking the stranglehold in 1965 and 1967. But, since 1972, Canada has failed to reach the winners' rostrum which has been occupied by Sweden, United States and Switzerland in three successive years.

This is a tribute to the success of the world event and proof of its influence in advancing the standard of play and in spreading the interest in the game.

II

EISSCHIESSEN

Eisschiessen or *Eisstockschiessen* can be translated literally as "ice-stick-shooting." In the crudest sense, it is a type of bowls on ice and is played almost exclusively in the German-speaking areas of the Alps, notably Bavaria and the Austrian Tyrol. *Eisschiessen* is a traditional game whose origins are completely unknown, although it has a strong superficial resemblance to curling. Despite this apparent relationship, a closer examination of the history of the two games show that they are entirely unrelated except insofar as they both consist of sliding objects at a given target across an ice surface.

Eisschiessen, unlike curling, has retained an essentially rustic character and is still played mainly in the area where it is thought to have originated. It has a very long tradition. It was well known in the Alps in the Middle Ages and enjoyed a wide popularity at that time. Even then the main centers of interest were undoubtedly in the Tirol and Bavaria, though there is some evidence that a similar game was played in the low countries. Prints of the fifteenth and sixteenth century and a mass of "winter scene" genre paintings of the sixteenth and seventeenth century of the Dutch school, show small groups of men playing a game using implements that are very similar to the present day *Eisschiessen* "stones". The game never reached the popularity in Holland which it enjoyed in Germany and appears to have died out as skating took over.

Long after curling was an established sport with rules and competitions, *Eisschiessen* was still a happy-go-lucky country game where each group of players made up their own rules as the game progressed. Basically it remained bowls on ice where the "dolly" was a small square of wood and the missiles were flat wooden plates with a handle and an iron rim. The aim, as in bowls, was to get as many missiles as close to the dolly as possible and to remove those of your opponent by knocking his or her missiles out of the field of play. The nearest modern land game is the Italian game of *boccia.*

It was not until the beginning of the twentieth century that any attempt was made to formulate standard rules of play, define the tools used and to organize the game into a competitive sport. However it was not until 1951 that the International Eisschiessen Verband (Federation) was formed by Germany, Austria and Italy. Switzerland, Yugoslavia, Luxembourg and East Germany joined that same year under the first president, Alois Schuber, of

Vienna. Since 1951, European championships have been held in the three established forms or disciplines generally recognized: *Eiswettschiessen* (team game), combined *Ring-und-Stockschiessen* (target and placement) and the *Weitschiessen* (long-distance challenge). Men and women compete separately. In addition to the European championship there is also an international competition for the Europa Cup.

RULES

The game is mostly played for recreation on unmarked, natural ice surfaces of lakes or rivers and makes few demands on the equipment commonly used. This is the *Eisstock*, a circular platter about 9¾ inches (25cm) in diameter with a flat base, an iron hoop about the circumference and the upper surface shaped into a flattish cone. At the apex of the cone is the handle, straight or slighly bent, with a wooden shaped grip, giving a total height of 6 to 9 inches (15–20cm). The entire object is customarily made of wood, preferably larch, and stands rather like a squat bottle 12 to 14 inches high (30–35cm).

Competitive play has a strict set of rules governing the three types of matches and the equipment used in them is also defined. The playing area for *Wettschiessen* and *Ring-und-Stockschiessen* must be a level, prepared surface of either natural or manmade ice. The rink, which is used in both directions, must be 45 yards long by 6½ yards wide (41m by 6m). Within this surface area, an actual playing area of 40½ yards by 4½ yards (37m by 4m) is marked out, with a margin of 2¼ yards (2m) at each end and 1.09 yards (1m) on each side. This playing area is subdivided into three parts: the *Startfeld* (starting area) 8.8 yards (8m) long, the center field 23 yards (21m) long, and the *Zielfield* (target area) 8.8 yards (8m) long. As play is carried out from either end, the two short lengths can be either starting or target areas and both are marked with a center point.

For team competition, the most popular of the disciplines, the *Zieldaube* (target block or dolly), a ten centimeter cube of soft wood, is placed on the center spot. The team consists of four players: a captain known as the *Moar* (hence the name of a team – a *Moarschaft*) and three team members.

The aim of the team is to place their *Stöcke* as close as possible to the *Daube* or dolly and, in any case, closer than those of their opponents. (If the *Daube* is displaced it remains in its new location for the "end.") Competitions are organized so that all teams entered play against each other.

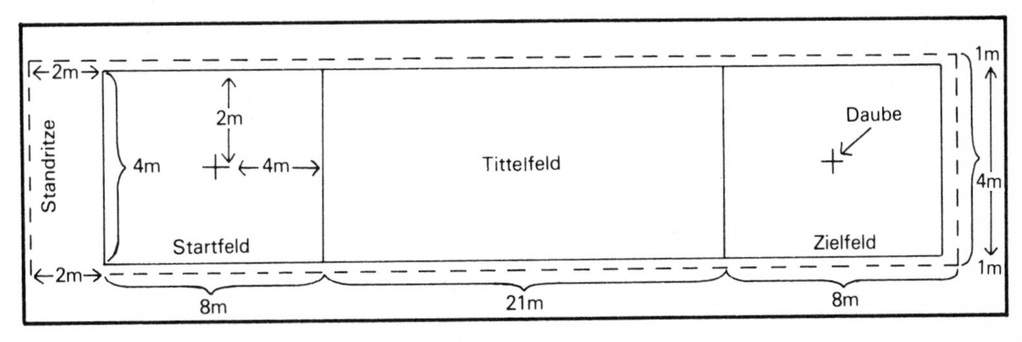

The *Eisschiessen* rink, showing subdivisions of the playing area.

Each individual match consists of six passages, that is to say three passages from each end. Each passage is opened by the *Moar*. He plays, as do all the other team members, from the starting line – the *Standritze* – which is inscribed on the ice, two meters behind and outside each end of the playing surface. The *Moar* aims to throw his *Stock* so that it is in contact with the ice from within the starting area for the entire length of the field. The *Stock* may also be thrown from anywhere inside the starting area. The customary technique is to take two steps, swinging the *Stock* backward on the second step and "bowling" it on the third step in such a way that the base is in full contact with the ice within the starting area. All competitions are controlled by a licensed referee.

Scoring at the end of a passage is recorded in points. Only those *Eisstöcke* score which have come to rest within the target area. A team's first throw is awarded three points if it has come to rest closer to the *Zieldaube* (dolly) than the first throw of the opposing team. For each subsequent throw, if it comes to rest closer to the *Daube* than that of an opponent, a score of two points is made. The team members of the leading team can also score negative (penalty) points which are incurred in the following manner: the winning team in any single pass or "end" may not have used all their *Stöcke* to achieve this and the losing team may have had to play their full complement in an attempt to equal or better the score (for example if the second team to play has won with *Stöcke* in hand). The winning team can then play out their remaining *Stöcke–Nachschiessen*. Any of these which either fail to reach or go beyond the target area are penalized – minus three points for the first and minus two for the subsequent throws. A *Stock* which fails to reach the target area is said to have been starved – *verhungert*. The winning team is the one whose aggregate score has the highest plus points.

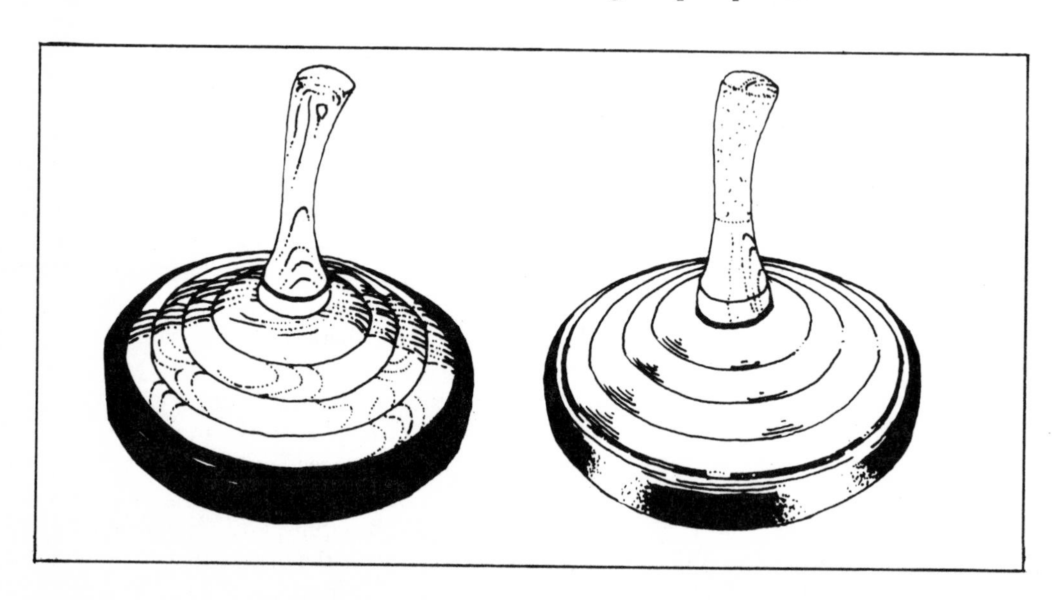

Two types of *Eisstock* for competitive use.

EQUIPMENT

The design of the *Eisstock* for competitive use basically does not differ from those used for popular recreation; in other words it consists of a handle, a body fitted with a metal rim, and a base. However this base can be made interchangeable and recently the entire *Stock* has also been made of an artificial polymer – high density polyurethane – a modernization viewed askance by traditionalists. The competition *Stock* may not exceed a total height of 13.8 inches (35cm) and a diameter of 10½ to 11 inches (27–29cm). The metal band may be between 1 to 1½ inches wide (30–45cm) and the body can be anything from 2¼ to 5 inches high (6–13cm). These variations are important since the team members are attempting to achieve different purposes. While the *Moar* needs only to place his *Stock* in the target area, the team members may have to knock the opposing *Stöcke* away. The *Moarstock* has a bell-shaped body which, if hit, is not easily pushed aside, while the team's *Stöcke* have flat heavy bodies in order to transmit the greatest part of their momentum to an opposing *Stock* and so push it farther away from the *Daube*. This design variation is however no longer permitted in national and international tournaments.

All competition *Stöcke* now have interchangeable bases. This is essential as the rules forbid the preparation of the sliding surface of a *Stock* with waxes or any other form of lubrication. Since the consistency of the ice may change during the course of a competition and will vary from location to location, not to mention from day to day, the interchangeable base – either of different design or made of different materials – enables the competitors to obtain the best possible sliding surface for all foreseeable conditions.

RING-UND-STOCKSCHIESSEN

The *Ring-und-Stockschiessen* competitions emphasize the basic difference of this game from curling, for this particular discipline is an individual competition. As in the normal team competition, both *Ring* and *Stock* games depend upon the placing and knocking out of the *Stock*. The *Ring* competition is a test of placing skill and each competitor demonstrates his ability to play as a *Moar*. The *Daube* is placed in the center of a circular target of 1.4 yards (1.30m) in diameter. A standard size rink is used. The aim is to place the *Stock* as close as possible to the *Daube* or, at the very least, to land within the circular target. One trial shot and five competitive shots are permitted in this discipline. The score is determined by the location of the *Stöcke* within the target rings which count from the outside inward – 1, 3, 5, 7, and 9 points.

Stockschiessen consists of aiming at a number of markers which are *Eisstöcke* placed in a pattern within marked circles. These circles have a diameter of 12 inches (30cm) and the scoring is the number of markers displaced with five shots. *Ring-und-Stockschiessen* are always treated as a combined discipline and the winner of the competition is the competitor who, with a total of ten shots, achieves the highest score.

WEITSCHIESSEN

The last of the *Eisschiessen* disciplines is the distance competition – *Weitschiessen*. It is the most athletic of the games and requires great strength as well as technique, though it is less dependent upon accurate placing. This discipline requires a larger area than is provided by artificial rinks and is consequently always held on frozen lakes. The full playing area must be at least 985 feet (300m) long and the throwing end is marked with a 4.4 yard (4m) circle, in the center of which is the standing line. In front of this circle, at an agreed distance from the standing line, is a marked base line, and from the center of this base line, running at right angles to it down the length of the field, there is a guide line which serves as a direction indicator. This guide line is marked, after the first hundred meters, by small markers at ten-meter intervals and every fifty meters by a large marker. These are used as the basis for the adjudication of the length of throw by an official referee and several unbiased judges.

As competitors in this discipline are concerned with length of throw rather than achieving the kind of accuracy customary in the other games, the rink increases in width from the hundred meter marker onwards. Here it is four meters wide on either side of the center guideline and is widened by one meter on each side every fifty meters. At three hundred meters the field is sixteen meters wide.

A single *Eisstock* is used for the whole competition, by all competitors. It is chosen by the organizers and the referee. Each competitor has five attempts and the winner is the one who achieves the single greatest length without penalties. Such penalties can be incurred by overstepping the standing line, over-throwing the *Stock* beyond the base line or throwing so far off line that the *Stock* slides outside the marked rink.

Since 1965 there has been a notable development in this sport thanks to the chemical industry. Following the development of a number of substances with very low coefficients of friction, notably polyfluorides such as Teflon, it has been possible to develop indoor, all-year rinks of asphalt covered with one of these low-friction films. Rules and equipment remain the same but to avoid confusion with the real thing, the game is referred to as *Asphaltschiessen*.

It is estimated that there are now about one hundred and twenty thousand players in Europe organized into two thousand clubs. The total number of casual players is certainly many times this figure. As yet there are no national or international league tables but the international matches are attracting increasing attention and interest. *Eisschiessen* is essentially a participant sport and receives only minimal press or television coverage. It has no professional qualifications and attracts no sponsorship. The growth in popularity is a direct result of the increasing number of wintersports visitors to mountain villages where they have seen the game being played as a local pastime and have been sufficiently interested to join in. Moderately skilled and definitely less serious than curling, it has remained an island of traditional village calm in a sea of commercial tourism.

12

BANDY

The game of bandy is, fundamentally, field hockey played on ice by two teams of eleven players, including a goalkeeper. The playing area is, to all intents and purposes, that of a contemporary field hockey pitch though slightly longer and wider. The rules of play are more loosely related to field hockey than ice hockey. A solid ball is used and the hockey sticks have the short curved end of field hockey and the long "handle" of ice hockey.

Largely because it is a skating game, bandy is often thought to have been the ancestor of modern ice hockey. This opinion ignores the history of the game shown in prints and paintings dating back to the early sixteenth century. Judging from these illustrations of skating games of the time, some form of ball game, employing a wooden ball and short sticks with a curved end, was such a normal skating pastime as to require no particular comment, though what the game was called is not known. In any event this ice game probably dates from a much earlier age and could even be considered contemporary with the development of skating – at the beginning of the first millennium.

The date when bandy was recognized as an organized team game seems to be generally agreed to be late in the eighteenth century (according to the *Oxford Companion of Sports* between 1790 and 1820) in eastern England, Cambridgeshire and the Fens of Lincolnshire, where speed skating had become an established winter sport.

How far the Gaelic game of shinty was the precursor of bandy cannot be determined, but it is highly probable that this very ancient team game was the precursor of both field hockey and ice hockey and probably should be considered to be the inspiration for bandy. In any case, the game flourished in eastern and northern England and the first record of any bandy club is that of the Nottingham Forest Football and Bandy Club, founded in 1865.

The game emigrated to Canada where it became ice hockey and promptly vanished from the list of games, summer or winter. At the turn of the nineteenth century following the succession of disastrous winters (from a wintersports point of view), the game appears to have emigrated to the eastern Baltic where it replaced football as a winter team game. At the same time it made its appearance in the area of Leningrad and Moscow in Russia and in Finland. It seems likely that it was introduced by resident merchants from the low countries and Britain and by members of the bored diplomatic staffs of the embassies of Holland and Britain (who also introduced skiing to Moscow in the late nineteenth century).

Since then it has become a regular and moderately popular game played in Sweden, Finland, the Baltic States and the U.S.S.R. It is estimated that in Sweden alone there are about twelve hundred bandy clubs, while in the U.S.S.R. the number is probably very much greater. A "world championship" is played by these three countries every two years. It has disappeared completely from the European and North American scene.

It is not hard to see why this should have happened. The area required for bandy is large, far larger than the usual artificial ice surfaces. The preparation of a natural surface of this area implies not only suitable low temperatures but some certainty that the surface is going to be available for most of the winter. Such large surfaces, frozen for two or more months and which will remain relatively snowfree, are only likely to be found in regions of Russia where the continental winter is cold rather than snowy, and countries like Sweden where large natural water surfaces freeze early and the snow cover is manageable. In addition, as the people of these countries are avid and active football players in the summer, the area used for football can easily be flooded and frozen during winter.

RULES

As a game, bandy is fast, furious and extremely entertaining for the players. It also requires a very high degree of fitness. The modern player dresses very much as does his ice hockey counterpart, wearing ice hockey skates, leg, knee and thigh protectors, elbow and head protection and normal ice hockey gloves. Unlike ice hockey, the trousers are knickerbockers. The goalkeeper wears leg pads and, although wearing skates, does not carry a stick. The ball is plastic or rubber, faceted rather like a golf ball, but must not bounce higher than 11.8 inches (30cm) when dropped from a height of 1.6 yards (1.5m). It weighs between 2–2½ ounces (58–62gm). The stick has a short curved end with a maximum width of 2½ inches (62mm) and the total length must not exceed 47 inches (120cm). The end is usually bound with

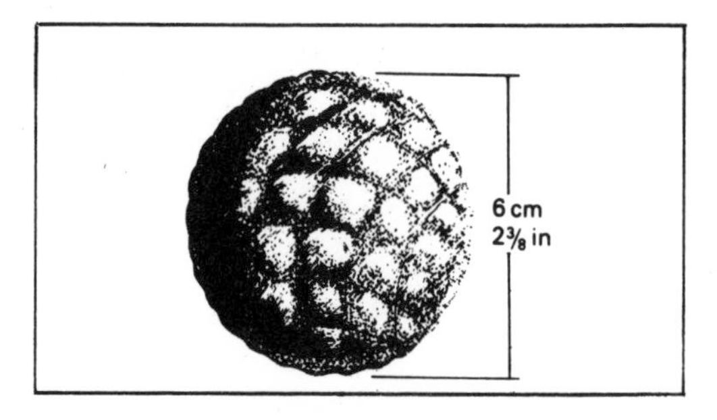

The bandy ball is plastic or rubber and faceted like a golfball.

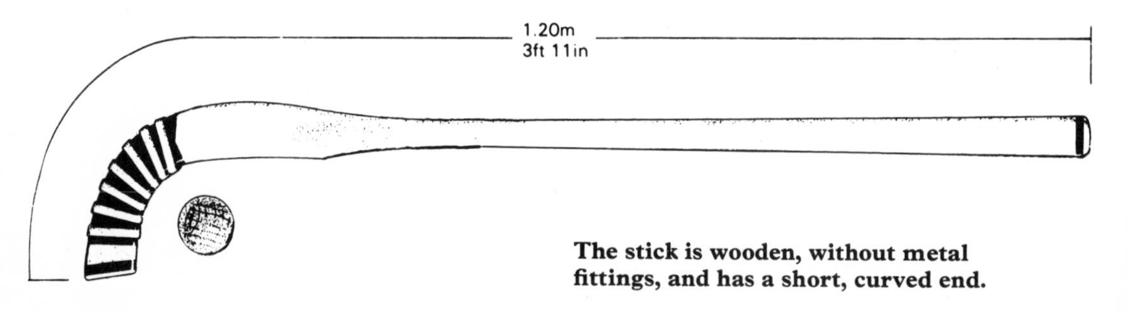

The stick is wooden, without metal fittings, and has a short, curved end.

Bandy players dress like ice hockey players with protective pads, helmets, and gloves. Their skates are similar to ice hockey skates.

tape. The ball may be struck or flicked and air shots are not restricted providing that the height does not exceed the limit of illumination if played under artificial lights. The ball may also be kicked and be stopped or controlled by any part of a player's body, provided that he or she has both skates on the ice. The ball may not be played without a stick or with a broken stick or when the player is lying on the ice, nor may the stick be lifted above shoulder height.

The field is marked off in a manner similar to field hockey and the standard rules of offside apply. Play is controlled by one or a maximum of two officials or

The bandy field is marked out in a similar way to field hockey.

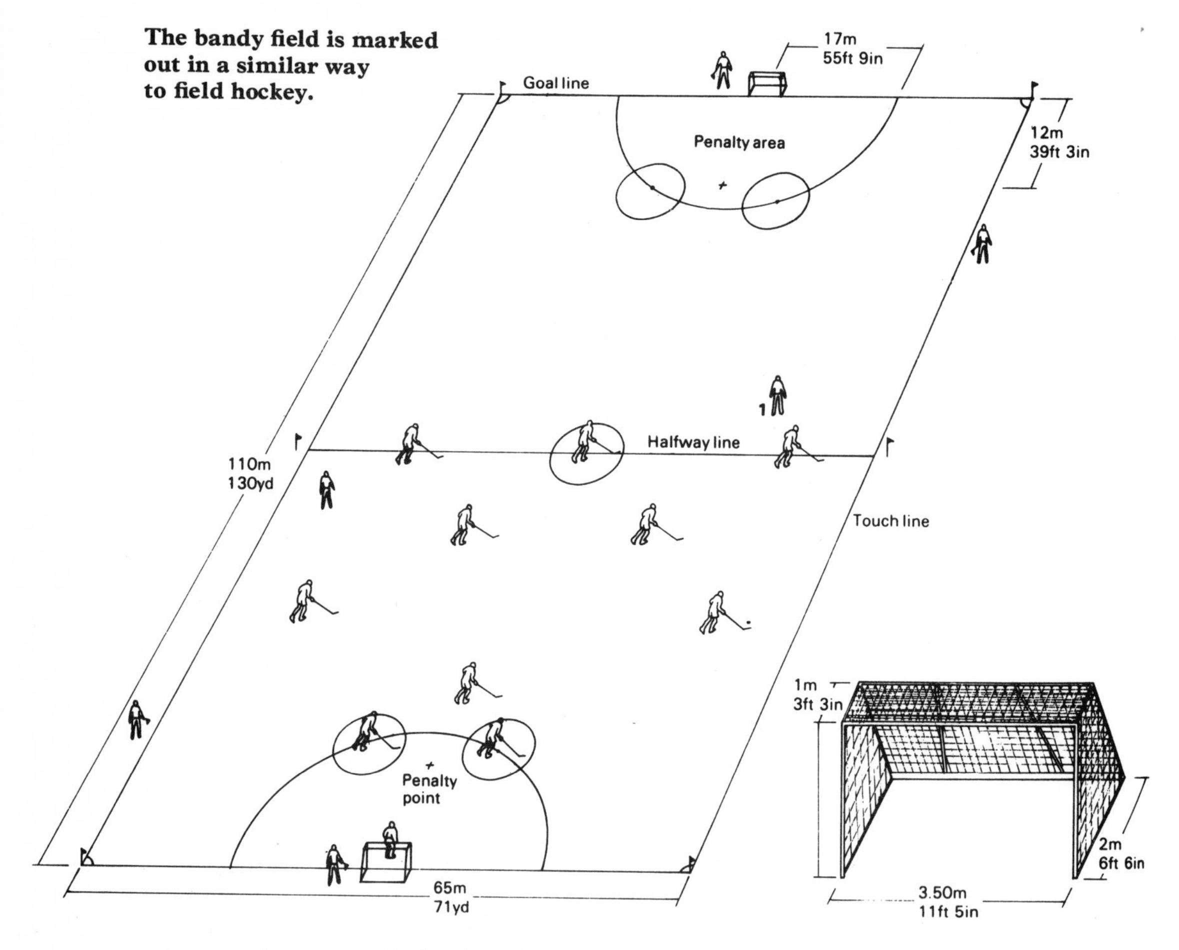

referees who wear distinctive dress. A team consists of fourteen players, including the goalkeeper, but only eleven players are allowed on the ice. Substitution is permitted provided that the substituted player has left the ice before his replacement enters. Playing time is ninety minutes in two forty-five minute halves with a five-minute interval. Ends are changed at the end of a half. Play is started and restarted after every goal with a stroke-off, where the ball is placed on the center spot and is played by the opposing center who hits the ball which must then be played by another player of either side before the center can touch it again. If the ball is played off the field, play is restarted by a stroke-in exactly like a throw-in in football. If the ball crosses the goal line played by an opponent, the goalkeeper is allowed a throw-in. A corner stroke is played if the ball is played over the goal line by a defender. Rule infringements are penalized by a free stroke (if within the penalty area from one of the penalty spots). If play is stopped for any reason other than a penalty, it is restarted by a face-off, as in field hockey.

Tackling is normally stick-to-stick, but body-to-body physical challenge is permitted. Tripping, pushing, holding and physical impeding are not permitted, nor is any other form of play deemed to be dangerous by the referee. Penalties are awarded for infringement of these rules and, in extreme cases, the offender may be sent off. This can be for five, ten minutes or for the duration of the game. No replacement is permitted for a sent-off player.

The goalkeeper defends his goal with hands, legs, feet and body. Within the goal area he may pick up the ball and throw it, provided it touches the ice before it reaches the halfway line. Outside his goal area, the goalkeeper may not use his arms or hands to play the ball but apart from this restriction, he can use any other method of stopping or moving the ball.

In many ways it is a great pity that this game has fallen into disuse. Unlike ice hockey, it can be played and enjoyed by skaters of moderate ability and, what is more, as the rules are simple and familiar to every schoolboy and girl interested in football or field hockey, a game of bandy can be improvised very easily. There is however one serious word of warning to anyone who might be tempted to do this. A bandy ball travels very fast and very far when hit properly and spectators at amateur games must take care. When, some years ago, the lake at Zurich froze over completely for six weeks, the police were quick to stop improvised games of ice hockey and, equally quickly, the skaters substituted their own version of bandy. The fact that this occurred so naturally is a sound pointer to the spontaneous origin of the game. The game of bandy, too, was quickly stopped as it proved to be even more dangerous than ice hockey. However, the lake is very big, the number of policemen who could skate was relatively few, and some novel forms of bandy were played in quiet little backwaters.

It would not be too far fetched to predict that should long icy winters return to Europe, the game of bandy will see a rapid reawakening. Meanwhile, the scholars can continue to debate which game exactly was the ancestor of ice hockey.

13

ICE HOCKEY

There are two separate games of ice hockey played in the world today: the amateur or European game and the professional or North American game. Their differences are so profound and yet so subtle that to attempt to cover both games in a single essay is impossible.

It is for this reason that two separate accounts are included. The first is written by Alan Weeks who has been intimately associated with the European game for more than thirty years both as an administrator and television journalist, and covers the general development and history of the game and the techniques as seen from the European viewpoint. The second, by Doug Gilbert, a Canadian sports journalist for almost the same length of time, covers almost the same ground, but in tempo and style it reflects the differences which separate the two versions of the game. It is a gulf which will not survive much longer now that both sides have begun, in a limited way, to play against each other.

THE AMATEUR GAME

Ice hockey, the world's fastest team game, is far removed from field hockey to which it owes its derivation. It has been suggested that North American Indians played a form of field hockey on frozen ground. Pictorial evidence from the sixteenth century shows Dutch skaters hitting a ball around but there is no doubt that ice hockey as we know it today originated in Canada.

It is recorded that British soldiers, veterans of the Crimean War stationed at Kingston, Ontario in the year 1860, strapped skates to their boots and played field hockey on ice – using a flat wooden disc instead of a ball. Similar games were played at roughly the same time at Montreal, Quebec and Halifax, Nova Scotia. Eventually Montreal became the acknowledged center of the sport.

In 1879, following a visit to England, two students from McGill University, Montreal – W.F. Robertson and R.F. Smith – devised rules for a nine-a-side game using a square puck. One year later McGill University Hockey Club was formed, the first recognized club for the sport Canadians call, quite simply, "hockey." Five years later A.P. Low, a founder member of the McGill Club, took the game to Ottawa, and Canada's national sport was born. In 1880 the first league was formed and in 1893 the first trophy for ice hockey, the Stanley Cup, was presented for the amateur championship of Canada.

The year 1893 also saw the game spread into the United States with matches at Yale and Johns Hopkins Universities, and the United States Amateur Hockey League was formed in 1896.

Ice hockey came to Europe in 1898 when Rhodes scholars – North American students at Oxford University – formed their own team and started to teach the English. By 1903 a five-team league was operating in England, and in 1908 the first match was played at Crossmyloof, Glasgow in Scotland. Within a decade ice hockey had spread to the European mainland with Prague, Berlin, Vienna, Antwerp, Brussels, Davos, and St. Moritz the leading centers.

Under the guidance of a Frenchman, Louis Magnus, the Ligue Internationale de Hockey Sur Glace was founded in 1908. Its four founder members were France, Great Britain, Bohemia and Switzerland, and two years later, in 1910, the first official European championship was played at Les Avants above Montreux in the Swiss Alps. Four countries competed – Great Britain, Germany, Belgium and Switzerland, and the British, thanks in no small part to the expert tuition of their Canadian cousins, became the first-ever European champions.

In Canada the expanding sport was played from coast to coast and there were now professionals as well as amateurs. In 1910 the newly formed National Hockey Association took over the Stanley Cup as a professional prize, with the Allan Cup the symbol of Canada's amateurs.

The most important day in professional ice hockey history was November 22, 1917 when the National Hockey League was formed with four clubs – Montreal Canadiens, Montreal Wanderers, Toronto Arenas and Ottawa. In 1924 the Boston Bruins became the first American club to join the league, and from 1926 onwards only NHL clubs have competed for the Stanley Cup.

European championships continued from 1910 until World War I but it was not until 1920 that the first global competition took place. And, incredibly, that competition was part of the summer Olympic games at Antwerp.

Canada had little difficulty in winning the gold medal; the United States finished second with Czechoslovakia third. Other entrants in this historic tournament were Sweden, Switzerland, Belgium and France. Despite the fact that this 1920 Olympic competition did not constitute a world championship, students of the game regard it as the first, albeit unofficial, championship.

The 1924 and 1928 Olympic winter games were officially recognized as world championships, and in 1930 the first independently organized world championship took place at Chamonix and Davos. Since then it has become an annual event and until 1972 the Olympic games of the year were synonymous with the world championship. From 1972 separate competitions have been held for Olympics and world championships and from 1976 the world championship has been an open tournament to amateurs and professionals.

The three most important years in modern ice hockey are 1946, 1954 and 1969. Although the Soviet Union had dabbled in ice hockey before World War II, the main winter sport was still bandy, which is virtually field hockey played on skates. Played in the open air on a full-sized pitch, the teams consist of eleven players a side who play with curved sticks and a red ball. There is still a championship played annually between the Soviet Union, Sweden, Finland and Norway.

On December 22, 1946 the first-ever ice hockey championship opened with a match between the Central Army Club and the Sverdlosk Army Officers Club which the Central Army Club won 5–1. At the season's end, Moscow Dynamo were the first Soviet champions.

The Soviet Union National team played its first-ever international on January 29, 1954, beating Finland 8–1, and later that year entered for, and won, the 1954 world championship. The Soviet team dropped only one point in seven matches – a draw with Sweden – and beat Canada 7–2. This was the beginning of a new era in amateur international ice hockey.

Canada had invariably been represented in the world championship by their Allan Cup winners, and the last such club was Trail Smoke Eaters in 1961. They won the title but it was to be Canada's last victory in a competition they had won eighteen times previously.

There were five thousand people at the airport to welcome the Czech team in Prague, and every street corner from the airport to St. Wencelas Square was packed with cheering crowds – not because the Czechs had won the title but because they had drawn with the Trail Smoke Eaters (1–1), and beaten the Soviet Union (6–4). I cannot imagine the reception had they won the title and not finished as runners-up.

Canada experimented with a national team but as their dominance faded so the Soviet power increased. 1969 was the turning point when, at the Stockholm world championship, Canada was beaten by the Soviet Union, Sweden and Czechoslovakia. The Canadians had an answer to their decline and it depended on the interpretation of the word "amateur." They considered that the Russians, Swedes and Czechs spent so much time playing, and training for, ice hockey they hardly qualified as amateurs – a view supported by most countries.

Canada's best players are professionals so the Canadian Amateur Hockey Association requested permission to include pros in their team for the 1970 world championship, due to be staged in Canada. Permission was refused, and Canada withdrew from the world championships and Olympic games. Sweden followed suit in 1976. With fourteen of their best players professional in North America and Germany, they withdrew from the Olympic tournament at Innsbruck.

The post-World War II English League, staffed mainly by Canadians of senior amateur status, did much to foster interest in Europe. Brighton Tigers Ice Hockey Club was the first English team to visit Europe, touring Czechoslovakia during the 1946–47 season. I recall discussing British ice hockey with Sven Tumba (Johansson), captain of Sweden's team at the 1964 Olympics. "It is incredible to us that there is no major ice hockey in Britain," he said. "It was those teams that boosted the game; ask any Czech or Russian and he'll tell you the same." That fact was confirmed by Josef Golonka, then captain of Czechoslovakia. Canada, through Britain, had repeated the lesson of 1908.

The professional game in North America has meant a dreadful strain on the source of its talent – Canada. In 1946 the National Hockey League consisted of six clubs – the most famous in the world in the

A Czech team member falls on the ice during the Group A hockey tournament at Innsbruck in 1976. The Czechs won 5–0 playing against the United States.

world's oldest professional league. The six clubs were: Montreal Canadiens, Toronto Maple Leafs, Boston Bruins, New York Rangers, Detroit Red Wings and Chicago Black Hawks. Since 1946 the NHL has expanded four times and its strength is now tripled – to eighteen clubs. The expansion clubs are Cleveland Barons, Los Angeles Kings, Minnesota North Stars, Philadelphia Flyers, Pittsburgh Penguins, St. Louis Blues, Buffalo Sabers, Vancouver Canucks, Atlanta Flames, New York Islanders, Colorado Rockies and Washington Capitals.

The World Hockey Association was founded in 1971 and its fourteen member clubs for the 1975–76 season were Calgary Cowboys, Cincinnati Stingers, Cleveland Crusaders, Denver Spurs, Edmonton Oilers, Houston Aeros, Indianapolis Racers, Minnesota Saints, New England Whalers, Phoenix Road Runners, Quebec Nordiques, San Diego Mariners, Toronto Toros and Winnipeg Jets. By 1977–78 this had been reduced to eight teams.

So, in 1946 Canadian amateur ice hockey was supplying the needs of six major professional clubs. Thirty years later that number had risen to thirty-six major clubs, plus minor pro and domestic amateur leagues. With Canadian talent stretched to the limit, Swedish, Finnish and Czechoslovakian players appeared in major North American pro teams.

With the Russians classified as amateurs and the best Canadians as pros, a head-on confrontation seemed impossible. In 1972 the IIHF accepted the new ruling that amateurs could play against pros without losing their Olympic eligibility, and the long-awaited confrontation took place. Eight matches were played – four in Canada, four in Moscow – between the Soviet National team and a "Team

Canada" made up of an all-star team picked from the NHL. The result – Team Canada four wins; Soviet Union three wins; one draw. In what was probably the most dramatic series of matches in the history of ice hockey, the Canadians won the series by a goal from Paul Henderson, Toronto Maple Leafs, just thirty-four seconds from the end of the last match.

The International Sports Press Association, comprising journalists from seventy countries and numbering twenty thousand members, voted the Soviet Union National Ice Hockey team as the "1973 Team of the Year," ahead of the Italian national soccer team, and Ajax Football Club from Holland.

In 1974 a second Team Canada, this time with pros from the World Hockey Association, played a similar eight-match series with the Soviet national team. Team Canada crashed to defeat, winning just one match.

A series of North American–Soviet ice hockey matches took place during the turn of the year 1975–76 when the Soviet club champions, the Central Army Club, and the Soviet league runners-up, Soviet Wings (Air Force), each played four matches against NHL clubs in North America. The eight-game series ended with five wins for the Russians, two wins to the NHL and one draw.

While this series was in progress, the Canadian Health Minister Marc Lalonde announced that six countries had accepted invitations to an international ice hockey tournament to be played in Canada in September 1976 – Canada, U.S.A., Soviet Union, Czechoslovakia, Sweden and Finland. The tournament would be open and Canada, U.S.A. and Sweden would be able to use players contracted to pro clubs in North America. It was suggested that this would be the forerunner of a world cup.

The tournament was won by Canada, beating Czechoslovakia in the final.

The ultimate in NHL-Soviet Union series occurred in February 1979 when an all-star team played three matches against the Soviet National team at Madison Square Garden in New York. The Russians won the series and took home the NHL Challenge Cup, a magnificent trophy purchased at a London silversmith's by John Ziegler, the president of the NHL and a former director of London Lions.

An extension of professional ice hockey from North America to Europe was actively propagated by Bruce A. Norris, President of the Detroit Red Wings and, at the time, Chairman of the Governors of the NHL. In 1972 he endeavored to bring several European Federations together to form a European Club league, and he showed further faith in the project by introducing London Lions at Wembley in the season 1973–74. This team – all professionals and including Canadian, American and Swedish players – revived the interest that had lain dormant in England for twelve years, but could not convince the European Federations that a league – be it professional or open – would succeed. Thus, Sweden, Finland and Czechoslovakia lost more excellent players to North America, players who might have stayed in their own countries if a league had been in operation, and who would still have been available for their national squads in the world championships.

The governing body of the amateur sport, the International Ice Hockey Federation, has grown from its original four members to thirty countries from all five continents. They are Australia, Austria, Belgium, Bulgaria, Canada, China (Peoples Republic), Czechoslovakia, Denmark, Fin-

A goal is attempted in an outdoor ice hockey game in Switzerland.

land, France, German Democratic Republic, German Federal Republic, Great Britain, Holland, Hungary, Italy, Japan, Korea (Peoples Republic), Korea (South), Luxembourg, Norway, Poland, Rumania, South Africa, Spain, Sweden, Switzerland, U.S.S.R., United States, Yugoslavia.

The president of the IIHF is Doctor Gunther Sabetzki, of the German Federal Republic, who succeeded Britain's John F. Ahearne upon his resignation at the IIHF Congress at Gstaad in Switzerland during July 1975. "Bunny" Ahearne had been the longest serving President having taken up the post in 1954. His twenty-one years of office covered the greatest era of expansion for the game and his shrewdness as a business director is reflected in the Federation finances. When he took over they stood at thirty thousand Swiss francs. On his retirement the figure had risen to two million, which must be the envy of most sports federations. Mr. Ahearne became Honorary Life President.

The IIHF is responsible for organizing the world ice hockey championship and the Olympic Ice Hockey Competition. The world championship is contested by twenty-four countries, split into three groups of eight – A, B and C. The teams play each other on a points basis, with promotion and relegation. One goes down from A, one comes up from B, and two move between B and C.

THE PROFESSIONAL GAME

Ice hockey, as it is known today throughout the world, was almost certainly invented in the Victoria Skating Rink in Montreal on March 3, 1875 – inasmuch as that day saw the first match ever to be brought to public attention in a newspaper. *The Montreal Gazette* said:

> A game of hockey will be played at the Victoria Skating Rink this evening between two nines from among the members. Good fun may be expected, as some of the players are reputed to be exceedingly expert at the game. Some fears have been expressed on the part of the intending spectators that accidents are likely to occur through the ball flying about in a too lively manner, to the imminent danger of lookers-on, but we understand the game will be played with a flat circular piece of wood, thus preventing all danger of it leaving the surface of the ice.

The paper's story went on to note that although the game of hockey was much in vogue in New England and other parts of the United States, "it is not much known here." So much for the early reporter's realizing the significance of what he was viewing – the first game of modern ice hockey ever played.

The game "much in vogue" at the time was an undisciplined form of shinny played by military garrisons and others on open rivers and municipal harbors, massive scrambles featuring as many as fifty men to a side.

The Victoria Skating Rink, on the other hand, measures 200 feet by 85 feet, the exact measurement of today's North American hockey rink.

The driving force behind the game of March 3, 1875 was James George Aylwin Creighton, a railway design engineer and an innovative mind among a group of lacrosse and rugby players in search of a winter fitness activity.

From 1873 onward they experimented with new games, after first trying lacrosse on ice, an idea that never quite worked out because of the continually bouncing ball. Creighton finally suggested the shinny sticks from the massive harbor games, and it was he again who cut off the rounded edges of a ball to form the first rudimentary model of a puck.

Alas, he was also a man who, in true rugby fashion, banned forward passing, insisting that no one could precede the puck carrier, a rule that continued in force for fifty years. Had Creighton been a lacrosse player instead of a rugby player, contemporary thinking goes, the game might have progressed faster than it did.

Later in 1876 the *Gazette* ran another account of a Victoria Rink game, this time between a team of Victoria members and the Montreal Football Club, captained by

Creighton, with both teams wearing club colors and competing under the "Hockey Association Rules."

Still, the rugby rules were causing a lot of problems with off-sides, play-stoppages and an almost continual need for a scrum near the nets. Finally a blue line was permitted three feet from the goal with free defensive movement allowed inside it. In 1905, The Ontario Hockey Association pushed this line out first to ten feet, then twenty and finally thirty to create zones similar to the sixty-foot lines known today.

By 1888 Creighton had formed the Rideau Hall Rebels hockey club and attracted the interest of the two sons of the Governor General, Lord Stanley of Preston. The two boys, William and Arthur, both ended up playing for the Rebels and Lord Stanley went on to donate the Stanley Cup "for the hockey championship of Canada" in 1892. The Stanley Cup today is the most revered trophy in North American professional sport and is awarded annually to the champions of the National Hockey League.

On their return to England following the family's official stay in Canada, Stanley's sons were instrumental in the introduction of ice hockey into Britain.

Hockey spread quickly in Canada in the 1880s and, as more indoor covered skating rinks were built the game increased in popularity and in terms of major teams and spectator interest. It was not long before each town had its own hockey team, playing in league competition with neighboring towns, and towns began to offer financial inducements to top athletes to move to their town to further their hockey careers. The seeds of Canada's future amateur–professional problems were sown early.

The Ontario Hockey Association, the first league based on a provincial organization, was formed in 1890, just three years before the Montreal Amateur Athletic Association won the first Stanley Cup. By this time the teams had been reduced from nine-a-side to seven, just one more than the six of modern times.

The OHA became the model for most other provincial associations in Canada, but the game was not drawn together under one body until the creation of the Canadian Amateur Hockey Association in 1914.

From the beginning, hockey drifted south over the border from Montreal to the United States. Schools quickly became the major cause of the game's growth, just as in all American sport of the day. The first formally recorded game was in 1893 between Yale University and Johns Hopkins. The United States Amateur Hockey League was founded in New York in 1896.

The fact that Canada's cold winter climate favored the game – there was almost no other active winter sports interest at the time other than ice skating – gave hockey a tremendous early impetus. Every town had its team, and every town had a chance to win a major trophy at national level. The top teams battled for the Allan Cup and the juniors (twenty and under) played for the Memorial Cup.

When international hockey came along at the Olympic level in 1920 it was only natural to send the Allan Cup senior champions, who proved to be so much the best it was embarrassing. And yet in some ways these early overpowering Canadian international successes were unfortunate. While the losers went home chastened, the Canadians went home feeling they had absolutely nothing to learn from international hockey, a feeling that persisted right up to 1972 when the Soviet Union's world champions fought the best from the National Hockey League to a virtual standstill in an eight-game series.

Now that Canadians realize that top European hockey is at least on a par with the best at home, there is a great deal of pressure for the development of a true world cup of hockey patterned after the football example. Unfortunately, the game played internationally and the game played in Canada today are far enough apart to come close to two separate sports.

The major professional development of hockey in North America came with the creation of the National Hockey League in 1917, and with the game's spread to the United States in 1926.

These developments paralleled the construction of major arena facilities. The 1917 league included the Montreal Canadiens, Montreal Wanderers, Ottawa and Quebec clubs, and the Toronto Arenas. Quebec did not exercise its franchise in the first year, leaving a four-club league playing a twenty-two-game schedule.

The 1917 league was the first to play a six-man game at professional level (the West Coast Pacific Coast League played seven-a-side until 1922) and by 1918 they had created the center red line to allow forward passing in the center ice area.

By 1926, major arenas had started to sprout in the United States centers as well, such as Madison Square Garden in New York, the Boston Garden, the Chicago Stadium, and the Detroit Olympia. Under

Chips of ice fly around the goalmouth at Moscow's Palace of Sports in a tense moment during a match between Canada and the U.S.S.R.

the direction of Art Ross, the Pacific Coast franchises moved east and created the base for today's National Hockey League, an institution with most of its franchises in more lucrative U.S. cities and Canadian players stocking virtually all the lineups.

In the first year of international operation the league had two divisions: the "Canadian" with the Toronto Maple Leafs, Ottawa Senators, Montreal Canadiens, Montreal Maroons, and New York Americans; and the "American" with the New York Rangers, the Boston Bruins, the Detroit Cougars, the Chicago Black Hawks, and the Pittsburgh Pirates.

There were several franchise shifts between 1926 and 1942, and, at times only the financial wizardry of James Norris Sr. kept the U.S. operation afloat in tough depression years, but by 1842 the NHL functioned as a six-team league with the Montreal Canadiens, Toronto Maple Leafs, Chicago Black Hawks, Detroit Red Wings, New York Rangers and the Boston Bruins.

The post-World War II period launched a twenty-year golden era for franchise owners and the sport boomed in popularity. The schedule was extended to a profitable seventy games. (One knowledgeable expert claimed once that an NHL team of the early sixties reached break-even point after seven or eight of their thirty-five home games). Considering all the teams owned their own real estate right in the middle of the cities' downtown centers, no team was for sale at any price at this time.

But Canadian amateur hockey paid a tremendous price for the professional successes of the 1950s and the 1960s. Since school hockey is underdeveloped in Canada, the pro teams had to turn to junior development programs to stock their teams.

They did this by going from town to town in and near the major population centers and helping the municipalities finance their hockey rinks. In return they took control of all the young players who played in the buildings. This was done through a device called the "C" form, and its effect went all the way back to thirteen-year-old athletes. If a young hockey-player wanted to play in a local arena and continue in the development program, he had to sign the form. And, of course, once the form was signed, the player was the property of the National Hockey League team who held the local sponsorship.

The NHL then went about setting up a super junior league in Ontario as a home for all the top prospects in the country, thus putting an end to the old system where every town had a chance to win a national championship. Now, the scouts went after the outstanding fourteen- and fifteen-year-olds, uprooted them from their home towns, and shipped them to the OHA Junior A League for development as professionals.

Thus the greatest junior hockey teams that ever played on ice, carried the names of the Barrie Flyers (Boston), the Guelph Biltmores (New York), the St. Catherines Teepees (Chicago), the Hamilton Red Wings (Detroit), the Montreal Junior Canadiens (Montreal), and the Toronto Marlboros (Toronto). The two Canadian professional franchises had an edge on the American scouting system. The Toronto Maple Leafs had a tieup with a Catholic school in Toronto, and St. Michael's College fielded a team in the Junior A league, under full Toronto sponsorship, stocked with young Catholic boys from all across English Canada. The Montreal Canadiens already had Quebec locked up solidly through a provision that allowed Montreal annually to draft the two top French

Canadian prospects in Quebec "to protect the French tradition of the Canadien franchise."

The Detroit Red Wings attempted to gain a foothold in Western Canada through strong Edmonton Oil King clubs, but did not have much success. Eventually, in the mid-sixties, the six existing pro clubs had the entire country subdivided.

The system might well have continued ad infinitum if the late 1960s had not brought relentless pressure for expansion. U.S. television would not offer a major contract unless teams were placed on the U.S. West Coast. That was not a big problem, but the threat of a new league of disgruntled cities was serious. So, in 1967 the NHL doubled its size in one swift move jumping from six teams to twelve with the addition of the Philadelphia Flyers, the St. Louis Blues, Minnesota North Stars, Pittsburg Penguins, California Seals and Los Angeles Kings.

That was the end of the "C" form and the farm system throughout Canada. It had to be: there was simply no way that the new clubs could find future talent. What the NHL did was drop the sponsorship of Junior A teams and refuse to allow the signing of any Junior until he had completed his amateur eligibility.

The NHL got some head-to-head competition as well with the formation of the World Hockey Association in 1972. This league has placated Canadian cities left out of the NHL expansion with franchises in Vancouver, Calgary, Edmonton, Winnipeg, and Quebec City, and moved into secondary U.S. markets like Cleveland, Phoenix, Cincinnati, and Indianapolis.

They have also attempted head-to-head competition with the NHL in Toronto, Chicago, New York, Los Angeles, Minnesota, Boston and Vancouver, with disastrous results everywhere but Minnesota and Toronto. In Minnesota it is now a case of which league kills the other first.

The WHA has attempted to lure as many top stars as possible away from the NHL with extravagant salary offers, and the overall effect of inter-league competition has been such that the average hockey player in both leagues today is making $70,000 a year.

Every team in the NHL has four or five players earning beyond, and sometimes well beyond, the $200,000 mark. Suddenly, every team in North American pro hockey is in financial trouble: they are almost all for sale, and several have been sold, a situation which would have been unthinkable in the sixties. Only Chicago and Detroit have continued with the same management they had ten years ago.

Expansion to so many franchises has watered down the product tremendously in comparison with the days of the six-team elite league; has virtually killed off minor professional hockey; and resulted in considerable fan disinterest which has been reflected in tumbling television ratings and season ticket sales.

As a result the North Americans are finally looking back to international hockey as the key to their future – and interestingly enough, Russia's total domination of international hockey has caused the International Ice Hockey Federation to look to North America for its salvation, too.

Canada dropped out of world competition in 1969 due to a continuing dispute over whether or not professional players could be used at the world level. Although that dispute was solved, they steadfastly refused to return to the world championships until 1977/78. If everything remains in the right place, this should signal a new era for hockey at the world level. But there will still be major problems with interpretation of the rules and international officiating as compared to North American officiating.

As far as playing styles are concerned, North American hockey has always rewarded individual excellence at the expense of coordinated teamwork.

As a matter of fact, until the Russians started proving the lesson, year after year, Canadians would not believe their game was one that could be adapted to planned playmaking. "It's too fast," they would chorus, "it's a game strictly of action and reaction, and you have to adapt to what's going on on the ice." Serious conditioning work has always been given short shrift by Canadians too, on the fairly plausible theory that when you play as many as one hundred games a year you can simply play yourself into shape. Two weeks after coaching the Philadelphia Flyers to the Stanley Cup in 1974, Coach Fred Shero went to Moscow where he wound up lecturing Soviet coaches at the Central State Institute for Sports. One of the first questions they asked after giving cursory attention to the lecture, was about off-season training. What, they wanted to know, do the Philadelphia Flyers do in the off-season?

"For two full weeks," said Shero, "they will do nothing but drink and celebrate, both in Philadelphia and back in their home towns. Then they will settle down and play golf until it's time to return for training camp in September."

The Soviet coaches simply smiled. Some day, they seemed to be thinking, the Canadians will tell us the truth.

On the other hand, Alexander Yakushev, whom even Bobby Hull calls the "greatest left winger in the history of hockey," has said he will probably retire at the age of thirty, "because I can't put up with the continual training any longer than that."

But Canada's greatest left winger Gordie Howe (with apologies to the Hull fans) was still playing in the World Hockey Association in 1967 at the age of forty-eight. Mr. Howe has not extended himself unduly in a training session since he was thirty. But then again, he never put in a training camp to equal the off-season work of Yakushev.

Canada's individualism down through the years has produced some incredible hockey players and led to impossible comparisons of stars of one era against another.

From the early days we have names like Fred (Cyclone) Taylor, who is still alive at the age of ninety-one and an invaluable aid to present-day hockey historians. Taylor talks of the Patricks, Frank and Lester, "who played the game the way the Russians play it today, stickhandle and pass until you have a good shot."

Oldtimers talk of the boys who came out of Ottawa in the old days, Frank Neighbor, Frank Boucher, and Frank (King) Clancy.

Anyone who played the game in those days considers Howie Morenz, who died at the age of thirty-five in 1937 after a tragic on-ice collision, the greatest hockey player of all time. Hockey fans go misty-eyed at the mention of his name. Syndicated columnist Jim Coleman was brought up short by his son a few years ago and wrote:

> "Who was Morenz? Don't they teach you anything at school today? Morenz was a dark-visaged dashing knight. He was finely tempered Toledo steel. When he picked up the puck, circled his own net and started for the opposing goal, he lifted you right out of your seat; his step was so light he appeared to fly about two inches above the surface of the ice . . ."

"Was he really as good as you say?" asked the little boy. "He was better. He could skate faster than Davey Keon, he could shoot as hard as Bobby Hull, and he was as strong as Gordie Howe."

The fans of the last decade would say all the same things about Bobby Orr, the "Pele" of post-war hockey. Bobby Orr was so good at thirteen that the Boston Bruins took control of the hockey rink in his home town of Parry Sound just to protect their rights over him. At fourteen he was playing Junior "A" in a twenty and underage group. By sixteen he was being described as the greatest defenseman in the history of that league. And, when he came to the National League at eighteen he stabilized the Boston franchise and sent them on to a decade of total hockey dominance.

Montreal had the legendary goal scorer Rocket Richard in the forties and fifties, a man with a gleam in his eye and a burst of speed from the blue line to the goal that was without equal. And then they had Jean Beliveau in the 1960s, the most classic player in the game. Detroit, Montreal's great rival of the fifties, had Howe, and his linemates Ted Lindsay, Alex Delvecchio, and Syd Abel.

The Chicago Black Hawks of the late 1940s had the Bentley brothers, Doug and Max, and an irrepressible center named Billy Mosienko, the greatest line of their day – and no defense. The press gave nicknames to the great forward line combinations as in Toronto's Kid line of the thirties, Charlie Connacher, Joe Primeau and Busher Jackson. Coming from the motor city of Detroit, Howe, Lindsay and Abel had to be known as the Production Line. Boston came along with the Kraut Line, Milt Schmidt, Bobby Bauer, and Woody Dumart, and Montreal countered with the Elmer Lach, Toe Blake, Richard combination, the Punch Line. Today it's the Buffalo Sabers' French Connection of Gilbert Perrault, Richard Martin, and Rene Robert, probably the top offensive line in the game.

All pointed toward the cult of the individual star. On defense the star goalkeepers, starting with the now legendary Georges Verzina, namesake of the Verzina trophy awarded annually to the NHL's top net-minder, are George Hainswarth, Charlie Gardiner, Frank Brimsek, Bill Durnan, Terry Sawchuck, Turk Brods, Glenn Hall. There are so many superstars today it would be unfair to list them, but Montreal's Ken Dryden has the most élan.

In the last ten years some of the most promising developments in North America have come from a constantly expanding U.S. college game, now strong enough to indicate a potentially powerful U.S. team for future international competition as long as it is open to both amateurs and pros.

Canadian college hockey is starting to draw more attention too, as college-level coaches grapple to try and pick up innovations from the European styled games. "That," says Philadelphia's Shero, "is where the eventual leadership is going to come from. The current coaches in our professional hockey are not going to change their ways or their approach to the sport – in spite of the fact their approach is completely outdated.

"The future of North American hockey lies in the colleges with new approaches and new ideas."

Probably so, but there are some who will never forget the good old days, before the world got complicated, when Canada was the best in the world at its own game and everyone knew it.

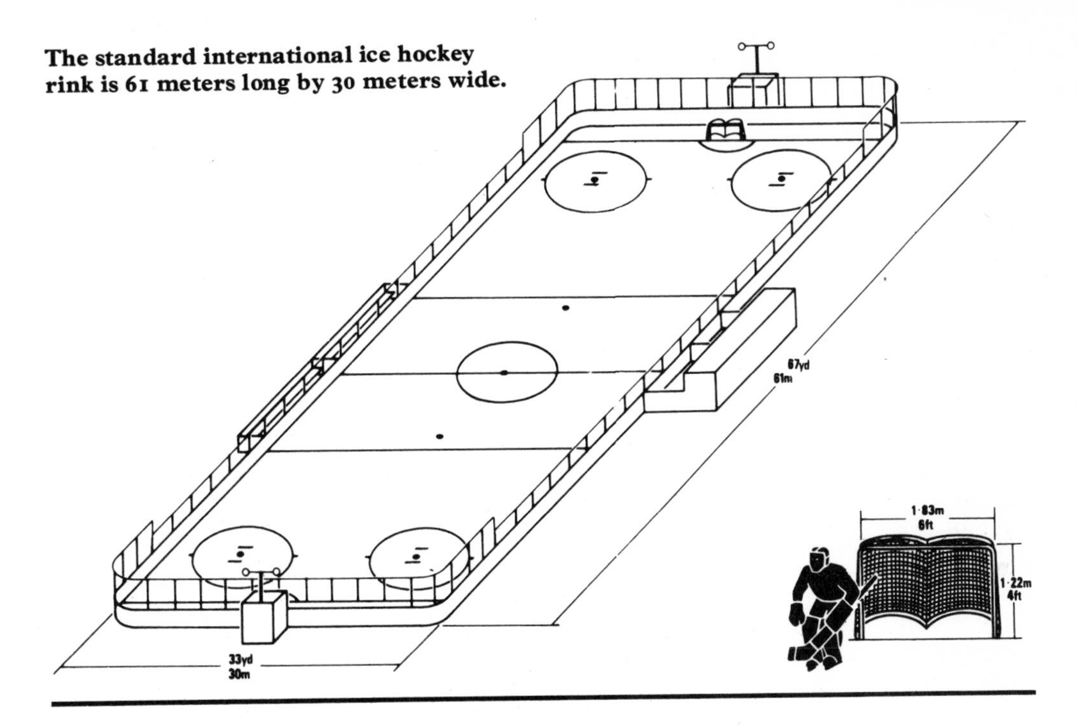

The standard international ice hockey rink is 61 meters long by 30 meters wide.

ICE HOCKEY RULES

PLAYING SURFACE

IIHF rules allow ice hockey to be played on rinks with a maximum size of 200 feet 2 inches long, by 98 feet 5 inches wide (61m by 30m), and a minimum size of 183 feet 9 inches long, by 85 feet 4 inches wide (56m by 26m). The recommended size is 196 feet 10 inches by 98 feet 5 inches (60m by 30m). The rink is surrounded by boards 3 to 4 feet high (1.15m to 1.22m). The NHL recommended size for a rink is 200 feet by 85 feet, considerably narrower than the recommended international size.

At a distance of 13 feet 1 inch (4m) from the end boards a red line is drawn parallel to them and completely across the ice. This is called the "goal line." The ice surface between the goal lines is divided into three equal zones, marked by two blue lines drawn completely across the rink and continuing up the boards. The portion nearest the goal is called the "defensive zone," the center portion is called the "neutral zone" and the portion farthest from the defended goal, the "attacking zone." Midway between each goal line and extending completely across the rink and up the boards is a red line, known as the "center line." Introduced to hockey in 1943 by Frank Boucher of the New York Rangers, its intention was to speed up the game. Prior to the red line, the puck could not be passed out from the defensive zone so a player was obliged to skate over the defensive blue line before passing. Now, with the pass from defense up to the red line, the switch from defense to attack is facilitated and exciting breakaways occur more often.

The "center ice spot" is located at the middle of the center line and surrounded by a circle 14 feet 5 inches (4.5m) in diameter. The center ice face-off circle has a diameter of 13 feet in Canada. Four similar spots and circles are located in the corners of the rinks, 23 feet 7 inches (7m) from the center of the goal line and 19 feet 8¾ inches (6m) out from the goal line. During face-offs no players except those taking the face-off are allowed inside the circles, and all must be nearer their own goal when the puck is dropped. There are two face-off spots in the neutral zone, midway between the side boards and 4 feet 1 inch (1.5m) from the blue line.

The protected goal crease in front of the net is rectangular in North America, 4 feet (1.22m) deep and 8 feet (2.44m) wide. Internationally it is a semi-circle with a 6 foot (1.83m) radius.

TIME

The time allowed for each match is sixty minutes actual playing time divided into three periods of twenty minutes with time added for stoppages. Every time the play stops, the clock stops. The intervals between periods last ten minutes. In IIHF matches the teams change over for the final ten minutes of the last period, a throwback to open air rinks when sunlight and wind could have been effective. NHL teams do not make this change.

The time played or to be played according to the local system, is displayed on a large electric clock so that game officials, players and spectators are never in doubt as to the time element. Behind each goal are two lights. When playing time has expired a green light appears. When a goal is scored a red light appears, operated by the goal judge. Once the green light signifies expiration of playing time, the red light is automatically cut out.

OFFICIALS

The game is controlled by two referees, or one referee and two linesmen. When two referees are used both have equal authority and in matters of doubt the one nearest play has the final decision. When one referee and two linesmen are used, the referee has full authority and the linesmen determine offsides and ice-the-puck rules. All move with the play, but the linesmen work the blue lines to make sure the puck carrier is the first attacker across the line.

The goal judges, one behind each goal, signify by flashing the red light when the puck has completely crossed the goal line between the goal posts. The goal judge's opinions can be sought by the referee in the case of disputed goals.

The game timekeeper is responsible for timing, from start to finish, and for signifying the end of each period by sounding a bell or klaxon. He also instructs the public address people to announce when one minute is remaining of the first and second periods and when two minutes remain of the final period, or overtime.

The penalty timekeeper records the time served, and when, for all penalized players; signals the referee if a player leaves the penalty box before expiration of penalty, and instructs public address to announce the nature of offence and penalty imposed.

The official scorer records on an official form all goalscorers, assists, penalties, and the time in the game of such occurences. He instructs the public address to announce the name of goal scorers and players credited with assists.

A player receives one point for scoring a

goal, and one point for an assist, namely passing the puck to the player who scores. A maximum of two assists may be awarded on any one goal. In competitions a scoring table is kept showing exactly how many games a player has played; how many goals, assists and penalty minutes he has served. The total points from goals and assists determines the position in the table, but the top goalscorer does not have to be the top point scorer. Fifteen goals plus ten assists would give the player twenty-five points. Ten goals plus sixteen assists would give the player twenty-six points and a higher position in the scoring table. So in ice hockey, an assist is as important to a player's scoring record as a goal.

TEAMS

Each team is permitted to have a maximum of twenty players in uniform of which two shall be goalkeepers. In the NHL the rule is seventeen players, exclusive of goalkeepers. Of these players in uniform, six are allowed on the ice at any one time – goalkeeper, two defencemen and three forwards, a center, a left wing and a right wing. Each player is numbered, and the Captain, or Alternate Captain is marked with a "C" or "A" on the front of his sweater. They are the only players allowed to discuss interpretation of rules with the referee. No goalkeeper or playing coach is allowed to be either Captain or Alternate Captain.

Players not on the ice are accommodated on team benches, immediately adjacent to the ice in the neutral zone, to which only players and team officials are admitted.

Most teams in North America have three forward lines, two sets of defensemen, two goalkeepers, and three spares on the bench who can fill in for injuries or form a fourth line when necessary. Match-ups here are important with coaches attempting to put a top checking defensive line on the ice when the other side has their best attackers on the ice. The home team has the advantage here, since they have the right to the final change before the puck is put in play. Once it is in play a team can change its personnel with play in progress as long as the player coming off is within a few feet of the bench and well out of play.

EQUIPMENT

Hockey equipment has continually been changing over the years, but mainly through improvements in manufacturing techniques. The IIHF specifies equipment as clothing (sweaters, pants, stockings, underwear), boots, pads (shoulder, elbow, leg), gloves, helmets, goalkeepers' face masks, skates and sticks.

In the early days the sticks were simply shinty sticks, similar in shape and style to those used in field hockey or bandy. Today, sticks are tailored as much as possible to the individual. They are made of wood, or another approved material and should be no longer than 53 inches (135cm) from the end of the shaft to the heel, and 15 inches (37cm) from the heel to the end of the blade. In the NHL the upward limits are 55 inches for the handle, 12 inches for the length of the blade, 3 inches for the height, and not more than a half-inch blade curve measured through a straight plane from heel to tip.

The angle between blade and shaft can be varied with the playing style of each player and is referred to as the "lie" of the stick. The greater the angle of the blade away from the shaft the lower the lie on a number chart from one to ten. Defensemen who like to skate with a stick well in front of their body will often use a number three or number four lie, while centermen

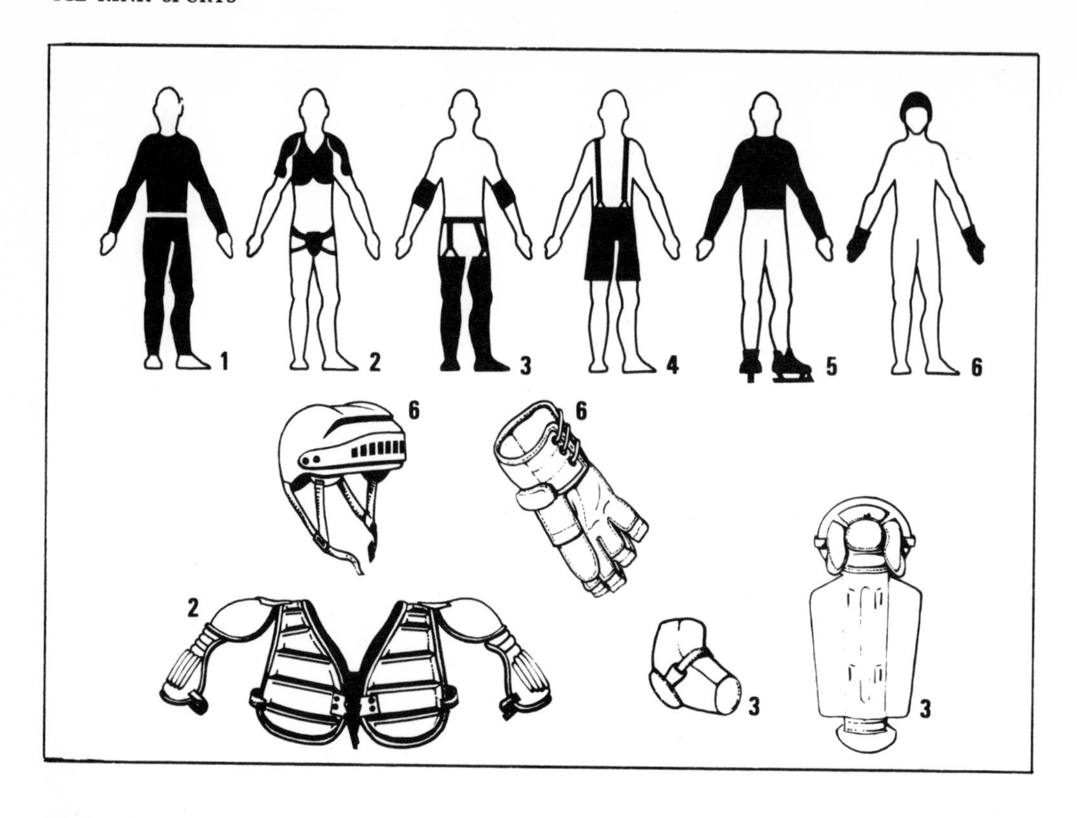

Ice hockey clothing: (1) long underwear, (2) protective cup, shoulder and chest pads, (3) shin pads covered with stockings, elbow pads, (4) pants, (5) shirt and skates, (6) helmet and gloves.

and forwards who keep the puck closer to their feet will use a number six or number seven, or even as high as a number nine. The blade of the stick is almost always taped to help control a wet puck, and the tip of the handle is taped as well to stop the stick from slipping out of a players' hands.

The curved stick was the innovation of Stan Mikita, a Czechoslovakian-born centerman from the Chicago Black Hawks in the mid-1960s. The story goes that Mikita broke a stick in practice one day and took a shot anyway, rather than dropping the stick as the rules require. The puck took a noticeable dip in flight and eluded goalkeeper Glenn Hall who asked the shooter how he made the puck change direction in flight. Mikita could only stare at his broken stick. Later he took some new sticks, soaked the blades and bent them under a hotel room door for an experiment.

The curved stick was effective and was immediately copied by the legendary Bobby Hull and other Black Hawk teammates, eventually leading to the rule limitation on the degree of the curve.

Many people today remain opposed to curved hockey sticks, arguing that they limit the stickhandling skill of a puck carrier, and make the backhand shot almost ineffective. Still, they are popular, a horror for goalkeepers, and the most important recent innovation in the game.

The goalkeeper's stick is much different. The blade is much wider – $3\frac{1}{2}$ inches (9cm) at the tip and $4\frac{1}{2}$ inches (11cm) where it joins the shaft. The shaft may be up to 3 inches wide for the first 24 inches (61cm) of the shaft, or 26 inches in the NHL rules.

Hockey skates are of approved design with slightly rounded steel blades, $\frac{1}{8}$–inch (3mm) thick, sharpened two or three times a week for a biting edge. Goalkeepers wear a flat-blade skate to permit better balance.

Ice hockey skates are specially designed and must have heel guards.

Hockey sticks come in a range of sizes, but the goalkeeper's stick (b) is always larger than the ordinary player's stick (a).

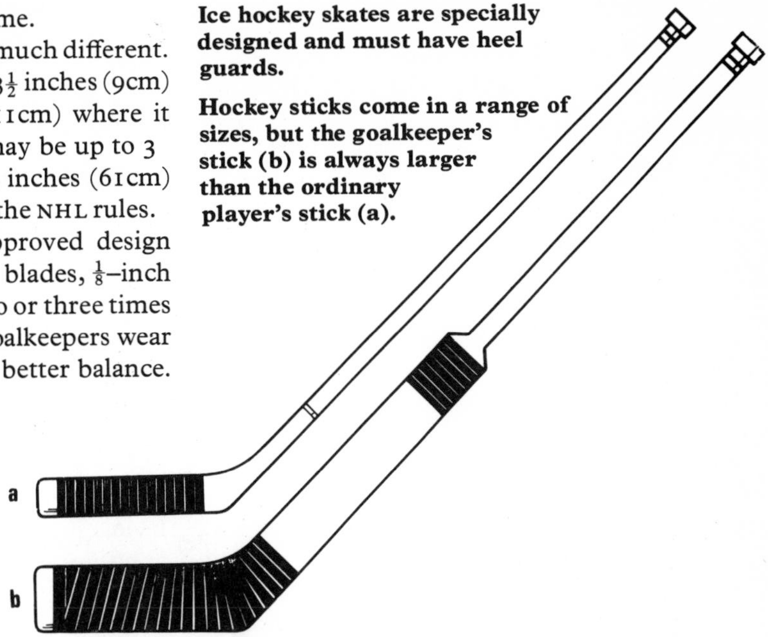

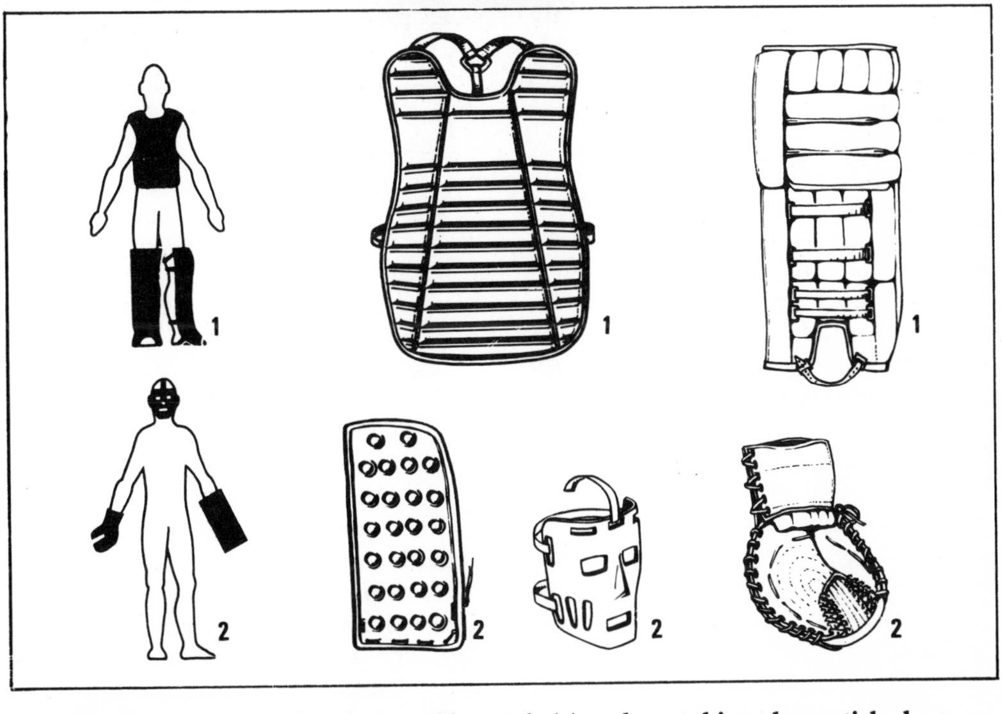

A goalkeeper wears massive chest and leg pads (1) and a catching glove, stick glove and mask (2).

The blades vary in length according to boot size but are approximately 12 inches (30cm) long. The boots are tight-fitting, worn over one pair of socks, and in some case made out of hard plastic similar to an alpine ski boot. The heel of the skate must be covered to avoid injury.

A Brighton Tigers player, Lennie Baker, tripped while chasing an opponent in a British League match. He fell onto the heel of his opponent's skate and it dug into his face about an inch from his right eye. One inch more to the left and he would have lost his eye. That incident occurred before heel guards were mandatory.

Regular players wear thigh-length socks over their shin pads. The socks are held up by a garter belt. They also wear heavy, padded mid-thigh-length pants with braces, elbow pads, shoulder pads and a sweater. Gloves are heavy and protective. Helmets are optional at professional level in the NHL, but required equipment everywhere else.

The goalkeeper face mask was invented by Jacques Plante of the Montreal Canadiens in the late 1950s. At first all but he resisted its use because of a buildup of sweat and a certain limitation of vision, but eventually more and more goalies switched over, until today almost no professional netminders are without them. The IIHF also recommends that goalies wear helmets.

The goalkeeper's glove on his catching hand is similar to a first baseman's glove in baseball. It has broad webbing between the thumb and forefinger.

In addition goalies wear shin pads, which must be no wider than 10 inches (25cm), a chest protector, shoulder pads and elbow pads.

The puck is made of vulcanized rubber and is 1 inch (2.54cm) thick, 3 inches (7.63cm) in diameter and weighs 5½ ounces (156gm). Pucks are often frozen before a match because ice-cold pucks slide more freely over the ice. A puck shot from the playing surface is not returned and as many as twenty pucks have been used in one match.

RULES

In both the IIHF and NHL systems the rules of the game are similar, but handled quite differently in application.

The game is started, and restarted after scoring of goals or stoppages, by a face-off. The puck is dropped by the referee or linesman between the sticks of facing players who must stand squarely opposite each other, about one sticks' length from the face-off spot, and with the blades of their sticks fully on the ice. No other player is allowed nearer to the face-off than 14 feet 9 inches (4.5m) and all players must be nearer their own goal than that of the opposing side.

The puck stays in play until

a) an infraction takes place
b) a goal is scored
c) the puck is trapped against the boards by two or more players
d) the puck is caught and held by the goalkeeper
e) the puck is knocked out of play over the boards that surround the rink.

A goal has to be scored with the impetus of the stick. A shot can strike a player in front of the net and bounce in for a goal, but it cannot be kicked across the line, or pushed with the glove. A player may stop the puck with his hand, but he cannot push it forward, having instead to drop it at his feet immediately on catching it. Nor can he hit the puck with a stick raised above shoulder height.

When bringing the puck up the ice a

In a face-off, the linesman drops the puck between two opposing players.

The goalkeeper stands with knees bent, leaning slightly forward.

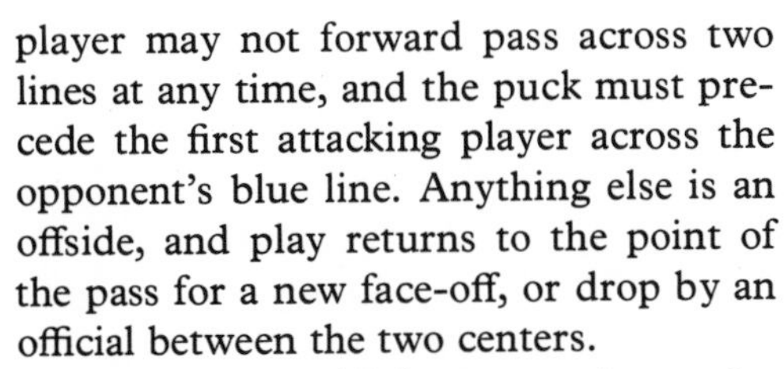

player may not forward pass across two lines at any time, and the puck must precede the first attacking player across the opponent's blue line. Anything else is an offside, and play returns to the point of the pass for a new face-off, or drop by an official between the two centers.

"Icing the puck" happens when a defender shoots the puck from behind the red center line over his opponent's goal line. Should this occur, the game is stopped and a face-off takes place back alongside the defending team's goal. There are three instances when the referee will not call "icing": when the offending team is shorthanded through penalties; if the puck touches an opponent on the way down the ice; or if the referee considers that a player of the opposing team, other than the goalie, could have played the puck.

PENALTIES

Minor penalties last for two minutes, measured in playing time. A player who incurs such a penalty spends this time in the penalty box (or "sin bin") and no substitute is allowed on the ice. The offending player is allowed to return to the game immediately if his team allows a goal while he is off.

Minor penalties are given for adjusting equipment on the ice; boarding (any manner of check that causes an opponent to be thrown violently against the boards); playing with a broken stick; butt-ending

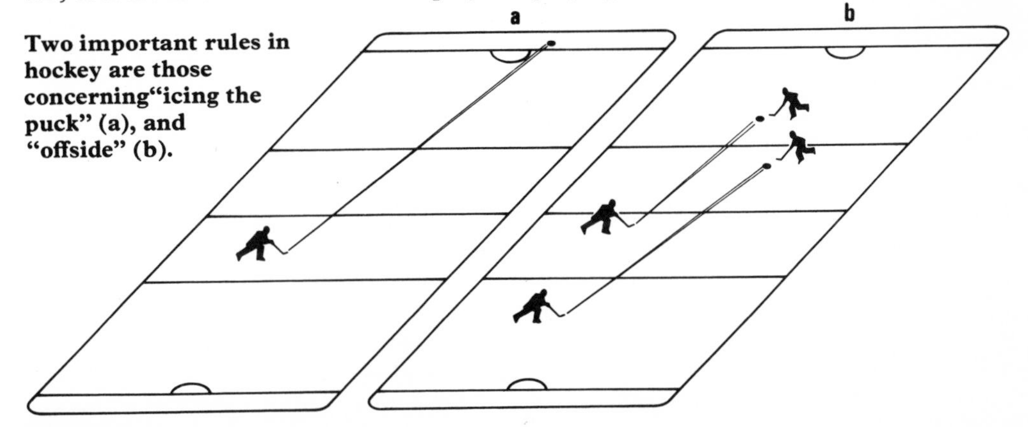

Two important rules in hockey are those concerning "icing the puck" (a), and "offside" (b).

Fouls (left to right): cross checking, charging, holding, high sticking, hooking, and butt-ending.

(jabbing an opponent with the top end of the shaft of the stick); cross-checking (a check delivered with the stick, with both hands on the stick and no part of the stick on the ice); spearing (poking an opponent with the end of the blade); clipping (falling or sliding across the ice causing a puck carrier to loose possession); elbowing; kneeing; high sticks (sticks carried above shoulder height); falling on the puck; closing hand on puck; hooking (impeding progress with blade of stick); interference; tripping; excessive roughness and deliberately shooting the puck out of the playing area.

A bench minor penalty is a team offense and requires the removal of one player from the penalized team with no substitute allowed on the ice. Bench minors are given if players do not proceed immediately to the penalty box; if a player, manager, coach or trainer is abusive to any person; for throwing items onto the ice or for delaying the start of the game.

A major penalty lasts for five minutes during which time no substitute is allowed on the ice. For a second major penalty in the same game, the player responsible is ruled off for fifteen minutes with a substitute allowed after five minutes. For a third major in the same game, the player is ruled off the ice for the rest of the match and a substitute allowed after five minutes. Major penalties are given for excessive boarding; injuring a player through cross-checking, butt-ending, spearing, hooking, slashing, charging, or high sticks; throwing a stick; excessive roughness, and fighting back in fisticuffs.

The misconduct penalty involves the removal of the player for ten minutes during which time a substitute is allowed. A second misconduct penalty in the same game automatically becomes a game misconduct penalty and the player is ordered to the dressing room for the remainder of the match. A substitute is allowed. Misconduct penalties are given for obscene, profane or abusive language; leaving the players' bench during an altercation on the ice; molesting officials; banging the boards with stick or throwing the stick outside the playing area.

Game misconduct penalties are given

Referee's signals: cross checking, charging, holding, high sticking, hooking, butt-ending, boarding, kneeing, elbowing, and slashing.

for persistently profane or abusive language; gross misconduct; molesting officials, and fighting off the playing area.

A match penalty sends a player to the dressing room for the remainder of the game and that player cannot be played again until his case has been dealt with by the appropriate disciplinary authority. Match penalties are given for fisticuffs; deliberate action to injure an opponent; kicking, and molesting officials.

A penalty shot is awarded when a player has gone past the defense with only the goalkeeper to beat and is interfered with to prevent him making his shot at the goal. The puck is placed at the center spot and any player of the non-offending team plays the puck from there and, without interruption, attempts to score. He must keep the puck in motion toward the goal and he is only allowed one attempt; there is no rebound. In IIHF the goalie may move out of his crease after the puck has crossed the blue line. In the NHL the goalie may leave his crease as soon as the puck is played at the center spot.

No team may be depleted on the ice by more than two players through penalties. If a third man is penalized while two are already in the penalty box, his penalty does not commence until the first of his teammates' penalties has expired.

Goalkeepers do not serve minor, major or misconduct penalties. Instead a teammate who was on the ice at the time of the goalie's offense serves the penalty. However, a second major, a game misconduct or a match penalty means the goalie's removal from the game and replacement in the net by the substitute goalie.

The major difference between the North American and the European system of play is in the interpretation of offenses like interference and fisticuffs.

Stickhandling is pushing the puck quickly from side to side when the opposition is in the way.

In North America, if a centerman takes a threatening position in front of the opponent's goal, he can expect to stand alone for two or three seconds before being knocked out of his position by a defenseman. NHL officials will almost never call this interference, although technically it is always interference to attempt to hinder a player who does not have the puck. A North American can pick up a penalty for this in Europe, whereas he would not in his own league play at home.

In the same situation, a European player might well slip past the center, or come at him from behind and dig his stick blade into the unprotected calf muscle at the back of the leg. That is his way of letting the other player know that he's there, and it's very painful.

Since this sort of thing is unknown in North America there is every possibility the Canadian player will drop his gloves and start a fist fight on the spot, an offense that can bring a five-minute penalty in the NHL, and a match penalty internationally.

Canadians have always been more than tolerant of fist fighting in ice hockey, based on the claim a man on skates can do no more damage with his fists than a man sitting at the dinner table swinging from his chair.

On ice, so the thinking goes, it is simply not possible to set your feet for a solid swing. Some Canadian fans don't feel they've seen a good game if it doesn't have something approximating a fight. Players hardly ever carry a grudge after the incident.

Internationally, of course, this behavior is not acceptable, and Canadian teams have not been appreciated in Europe when they come on with the rough and tumble style that is just fine with the folks back home.

HOW TO PLAY

The fundamentals of ice hockey are the three "S's" – skating, stickhandling and shooting. Being primarily a game of speed, the ability to perform faster than an opponent is essential. A good hockey skater must be able to cut equally well on skates to either right or left, to stop in a split second and reverse direction immediately. He must be able to move from stop to top speed in a few strides. He must be able to change place and have perfect balance. The fastest hockey skater on record was Bobby Hull who was timed at 29 mph while playing with the Chicago Black Hawks.

The skating standard in both NHL and IIHF international teams is superb and one inclines to forget that the players are actually on such narrow skates. However, after the Soviet-NHL Team Canada series,

Sweep checking is where a defenseman crouches on the ice and attempts to sweep the puck away from the attacker.

Two kinds of body checking – a shoulder check and a hip check – are tactics used by the defense to regain the puck.

the Russians noted that the professionals skated with their feet slightly wider apart, using the inside cutting edge of the blades. They were steadier on their skates and more difficult to knock off balance.

The trend in ice hockey toward speed, power and team play, has diminished the craftsmanship of stickhandling, although when an expert does perform, it is pretty to watch. Stickhandling is manipulation of the puck in such a way as to retain possession, and by feints with the stick, head or body, confuse an opponent so as to get past him. A good stickhandler always keeps his head up and controls the puck by the feel of the rubber on the blade. Once the player looks down he is prime target for a bodycheck.

Goalscoring is a battle of wits between the attacker and the goalkeeper. The man most likely to succeed is the one who gets his shot away accurately and with power – once the goalie has committed himself. There are three types of shot – forehand, backhand wrist shots, and the slapshot. Strength in the wrist shot can be achieved with a slight snap of the wrist at just the right moment, or by bringing the weight of the body into the shot. The backhand wrist shot is the most difficult for a goalie to anticipate. The slapshot is where a player raises the stick to shoulder height and then brings it forward to hit the puck and ice simultaneously. It produces a shot of high speed and is excellent for a defenseman on the blue line shooting at the goal.

With players in front of the net distracting the goalie, the sheer speed of shot can be telling. A good wrist shot is perhaps best used close in, when the goalie has

Four types of shooting (left to right): the slap shot, wrist shot, backhand wrist shot, and flip shot.

made his move and accuracy is vital, but there is no rule. Some players are better at one shot than the other and use them under any circumstance. The hardest known shooter was, once again, Bobby Hull, whose wrist shot was timed at 105mph and his slapshot at 119mph.

Back-checking is the covering of an opponent so that he will never be entirely free to play the puck. In most cases this applies to covering an opponent when skating back toward your own goal. Fore-checking is a direct attempt to rob the player when facing him, and one of the most

Goalkeepers must be alert to cover shots and able to move quickly across the goal.

valuable players on the team is a good two-way winger, up with the attack yet back covering his opposite number when on defense.

Bodychecking, more prevalent in the professional game, is delivered with either hip or shoulder, or a combination of both. It is most effective when the opponent is least expecting it, and attackers keep a wary eye for well-known bodycheckers. It should be remembered that body-checking takes it out of the giver as well as the receiver.

Pokechecking or poking the blade of the stick at the puck, and hookchecking – attempting to hook the puck away from the carrier – are other ways of attempting to rob a puck carrier.

The old adage, "goalies are born not made," is still true to a certain extent. Despite coaching one cannot instil courage or natural ability. Add to that a good catching hand, speed on skates, sharp reflexes, the ability to take charge around the crease, to eliminate rebounds from pads or skates or stick, to cut the angles giving attackers less of the net to shoot at and the ability to split-second decisions. These are a matter of experience developed with constant practice.

In Europe goalkeeping has seen the greatest advance in any playing position. In the Soviet–NHL Team Canada series Ken Dryden of the Montreal Canadiens, and Vladislav Tretiak of the Central Army Club, were on a par. Jiri Holecek of Czechoslovakia is another excellent netman, while two top Swedish internationals – Leif Holmqvist and Christer Abrahamsson – are playing in the WHA.

The center should be a skilful stick-handler and deadly passer, offensive in his play, yet unselfish in character. It is his responsibility to carry the puck up to the defense, either beat them himself or draw them out of position and make the telling pass to a winger. He takes the majority of the face-offs and aims to win them; the team in possession is the team in charge.

Wingers should patrol the flanks – in both directions – helping out the defense and ready for a fast break into attack. A winger must judge his approach to the marking lines so that he does not cross them before the puck, wasting excellent passes by going offside. He should be able to accept a pass without the puck bouncing off his stick, cut in behind the defense and get a good shot away on the net.

The defenseman's first duty is to stop the opposition scoring, yet he can still play an important part in attack. An accurate pass-out from his defence zone is vital to his forwards. He should never leave his goalie unguarded; if one defender goes into the corner, the other should cover the front of the net. He must be able to block shots with legs or body, and have a good shot from the blue line when his team are on attack. A good rushing defenseman – one who breaks out of his own end and can score goals, or make telling passes that place teammates in good scoring positions – is priceless. That is why Bobby Orr of the Boston Bruins was the highest paid player in the NHL. Although a defenseman, he topped the NHL scoring table for the 1974–75 season with 46 goals and 89 assists for 135 points, eight more than Phil Esposito, a center-ice.

Proof of ice hockey's popularity is in the playing. There are 604,000 registered players in the Soviet Union, 250,000 in the United States and 200,000 in Sweden. As a spectator sport it ranks among the world's best, a position that continued co-operation between the IIHF and the NHL should guarantee.

The Illustrated Encyclopedia of
ICE SKATING

REFERENCE

FIGURE SKATING

WORLD CHAMPIONS

MEN

1896	G. Fuchs (Germany)
1897	G. Hügel (Austria)
1898	H. Grenander (Sweden)
1899	G. Hügel (Austria)
1900	G. Hügel (Austria)
1901	U. Salchow (Sweden)
1902	U. Salchow (Sweden)
1903	U. Salchow (Sweden)
1904	U. Salchow (Sweden)
1905	U. Salchow (Sweden)
1906	G. Fuchs (Germany)
1907	U. Salchow (Sweden)
1908	U. Salchow (Sweden)
1909	U. Salchow (Sweden)
1910	U. Salchow (Sweden)
1911	U. Salchow (Sweden)
1912	F. Kachler (Austria)
1913	F. Kachler (Austria)
1914	G. Sandahl (Sweden)
1915–21	*No competition*
1922	G. Grafström (Sweden)
1923	F. Kachler (Austria)
1924	G. Graftström (Sweden)
1925	W. Böckl (Austria)
1926	W. Böckl (Austria)
1927	W. Böckl (Austria)
1928	W. Böckl (Austria)
1929	G. Grafström (Sweden)
1930	K. Schäfer (Austria)
1931	K. Schäfer (Austria)
1932	K. Schäfer (Austria)
1933	K. Schäfer (Austria)
1934	K. Schäfer (Austria)
1935	K. Schäfer (Austria)
1936	K. Schäfer (Austria)
1937	F. Kaspar (Austria)
1938	F. Kaspar (Austria)
1939	G. Sharp (Great Britain)
1940–6	*No competition*
1947	H. Gerschwiler (Switzerland)
1948	R. Button (USA)
1949	R. Button (USA)
1950	R. Button (USA)
1951	R. Button (USA)
1952	R. Button (USA)
1953	H. A. Jenkins (USA)
1954	H. A. Jenkins (USA)
1955	H. A. Jenkins (USA)
1956	H. A. Jenkins (USA)
1957	D. Jenkins (USA)
1958	D. Jenkins (USA)
1959	D. Jenkins (USA)
1960	A. Giletti (France)
1961	*Cancelled because the entire US team died in an air crash at Brussels*
1962	D. Jackson (Canada)
1963	D. McPherson (Canada)
1964	M. Schnelldorfer (Germany)
1965	A. Calmat (France)
1966	E. Danzer (Austria)
1967	E. Danzer (Austria)
1968	E. Danzer (Austria)
1969	T. Wood (USA)
1970	T. Wood (USA)
1971	O. Nepela (Czechoslovakia)
1972	O. Nepela (Czechoslovakia)
1973	O. Nepela (Czechoslovakia)
1974	J. Hoffmann (East Germany)
1975	S. Volkov (USSR)
1976	J. Curry (Great Britain)
1977	V. Kovalev (USSR)
1978	C. Tickner (USA)
1979	V. Kovalev (USSR)

WOMEN

1906 M. Syers-Cave (Great Britain)
1907 M. Syers-Cave (Great Britain)
1908 L. Kronberger (Hungary)
1909 L. Kronberger (Hungary)
1910 L. Kronberger (Hungary)
1911 L. Kronberger (Hungary)
1912 O. von Méray Horvath (Hungary)
1913 O. von Méray Horvath (Hungary)
1914 O. von Méray Horvath (Hungary)
1915–21 *No competition*
1922 H. Plank-Szabo (Austria)
1923 H. Plank-Szabo (Austria)
1924 H. Plank-Szabo (Austria)
1925 H. Jaross-Szabo (Austria)
1926 H. Jaross-Szabo (Austria)
1927 S. Henie (Norway)
1928 S. Henie (Norway)
1929 S. Henie (Norway)
1930 S. Henie (Norway)
1931 S. Henie (Norway)
1932 S. Henie (Norway)
1933 S. Henie (Norway)
1934 S. Henie (Norway)
1935 S. Henie (Norway)
1936 S. Henie (Norway)
1937 C. Colledge (Great Britain)
1938 M. Taylor (Great Britain)
1939 M. Taylor (Great Britain)
1940–6 *No competition*
1947 B. A. Scott (Canada)
1948 B. A. Scott (Canada)
1949 A. Vrzanová (Czechoslovakia)
1950 A. Vrzanová (Czechoslovakia)
1951 J. Altwegg (Great Britain)
1952 J. du Bief (France)
1953 T. Albright (USA)
1954 G. Busch (Germany)
1955 T. Albright (USA)
1956 C. Heiss (USA)
1957 C. Heiss (USA)
1958 C. Heiss (USA)
1959 C. Heiss (USA)
1960 C. Heiss (USA)
1961 *Cancelled because the entire US team died in an air crash at Brussels*
1962 S. Dijkstra (Netherlands)
1963 S. Dijkstra (Netherlands)
1964 S. Dijkstra (Netherlands)
1965 P. Burka (Canada)
1966 P. Fleming (USA)
1967 P. Fleming (USA)
1968 P. Fleming (USA)
1969 G. Seyfert (East Germany)
1970 G. Seyfert (East Germany)
1971 B. Schuba (Austria)
1972 B. Schuba (Austria)
1973 K. Magnussen (Canada)
1974 C. Errath (East Germany)
1975 D. de Leeuw (Netherlands)
1976 D. Hamill (USA)
1977 L. Fratianne (USA)
1978 A. Pötzsch (East Germany)
1979 L. Fratianne (USA)

OLYMPIC GOLD MEDALISTS

MEN

1908 U. Salchow (Sweden)
1920 G. Grafström (Sweden)
1924 G. Graftström (Sweden)
1928 G. Graftström (Sweden)
1932 K. Schäfer (Austria)
1936 K. Schäfer (Austria)
1948 R. Button (USA)
1952 R. Button (USA)
1956 H. A. Jenkins (USA)
1960 D. Jenkins (USA)
1964 M. Schnelldorfer (Germany)
1968 W. Schwartz (Austria)
1972 O. Nepela (Czechoslovakia)
1976 J. Curry (Great Britain)

WOMEN

1908 M. Syers-Cave (Great Britain)
1920 M. Julin-Mauroy (Sweden)
1924 H. Plank-Szabo (Austria)
1928 S. Henie (Norway)
1932 S. Henie (Norway)
1936 S. Henie (Norway)
1948 B. A. Scott (Canada)
1952 J. Altwegg (Great Britain)
1956 T. Albright (USA)
1960 C. Heiss (USA)
1964 S. Dijkstra (Netherlands)
1968 P. Fleming (USA)
1972 B. Schuba (Austria)
1976 D. Hamill (USA)

PAIR SKATING

WORLD CHAMPIONS

1908 A. Hübler and H. Burger (Germany)
1909 P. Johnson and J. H. Johnson (Great Britain)
1910 A. Hübler and H. Burger (Germany)
1911 L. Eilers and W. Jakobsson (Germany and Finland)
1912 P. Johnson and J. H. Johnson (Great Britain)
1913 H. Engelmann and K. Mejstrik (Austria)
1914 L. Jakobsson and W. Jakobsson (Finland)
1915–21 *No competition*
1922 H. Engelmann and A. Berger (Austria)
1923 L. Jakobsson and W. Jakobsson (Finland)
1924 H. Engelmann and A. Berger (Austria)
1925 H. Jaross-Szabo and L. Wrede (Austria)
1926 A. Joly and P. Brunet (France)
1927 H. Jaross-Szabo and L. Wrede (Austria)
1928 A. Joly and P. Brunet (France)
1929 L. Scholz and O. Kaiser (Austria)
1930 A. Brunet (*née* Joly) and P. Brunet (France)
1931 E. Rotter and L. Szollas (Hungary)
1932 A. Brunet and P. Brunet (France)
1933 E. Rotter and L. Szollas (Hungary)
1934 E. Rotter and L. Szollas (Hungary)
1935 E. Rotter and L. Szollas (Hungary)
1936 M. Herber and E. Baier (Germany)
1937 M. Herber and E. Baier (Germany)
1938 M. Herber and E. Baier (Germany)
1939 M. Herber and E. Baier (Germany)
1940–6 *No competition*

1947 M. Lannoy and P. Baugniet (Belgium)
1948 M. Lannoy and P. Baugniet (Belgium)
1949 A. Kékessy and E. Király (Hungary)
1950 K. Kennedy and P. Kennedy (USA)
1951 R. Baran and P. Falk (Germany)
1952 R. Falk and P. Falk (Germany)
1953 J. Nicks and J. Nicks (Great Britain)
1954 F. Dafoe and N. Bowden (Canada)
1955 F. Dafoe and N. Bowden (Canada)
1956 S. Schwartz and K. Oppelt (Austria)
1957 B. Wagner and R. Paul (Canada)
1958 B. Wagner and R. Paul (Canada)
1959 B. Wagner and R. Paul (Canada)
1960 B. Wagner and R. Paul (Canada)
1961 *Cancelled because the entire US team died in an air crash at Brussels*
1962 M. Jelinek and O. Jelinek (Canada)
1963 M. Kilius and H. J. Bäumler (Germany)
1964 M. Kilius and H. J. Bäumler (Germany)
1965 L. Belousova and O. Protopopov (USSR)
1966 L. Belousova and O. Protopopov (USSR)
1967 L. Belousova and O. Protopopov (USSR)
1968 L. Belousova and O. Protopopov (USSR)
1969 I. Rodnina and A. Ulanov (USSR)
1970 I. Rodnina and A. Ulanov (USSR)
1971 I. Rodnina and A. Ulanov (USSR)
1972 I. Rodnina and A. Ulanov (USSR)
1973 I. Rodnina and A. Zaitsev (USSR)
1974 I. Rodnina and A. Zaitsev (USSR)
1975 I. Rodnina and A. Zaitsev (USSR)
1976 I. Rodnina and A. Zaitsev (USSR)
1977 I. Rodnina and A. Zaitsev (USSR)
1978 I. Rodnina and A. Zaitsev (USSR)
1979 T. Babilonia and R. Gardner (USA)

OLYMPIC GOLD MEDALISTS

1908 A. Hübler and H. Burger (Germany)
1920 L. Jakobsson and W. Jakobsson (Finland)
1924 E. Engelmann and A. Berger (Austria)
1928 A. Joly and P. Brunet (France)
1932 A. Brunet and P. Brunet (France)
1936 M. Herber and E. Baier (Germany)
1948 M. Lannoy and P. Baugniet (Belgium)
1952 R. Falk and P. Falk (Germany)

1956 E. Schwartz and K. Oppelt (Austria)
1960 B. Wagner and R. Paul (Canada)
1964 L. Belousova and O. Protopopov (USSR)
1968 L. Belousova and O. Protopopov (USSR)
1972 I. Rodnina and A. Ulanov (USSR)
1976 I. Rodnina and A. Zaitsev (USSR)

ICE DANCING

WORLD CHAMPIONS

1952 J. Westwood and L. Demmy (Great Britain)
1953 J. Westwood and L. Demmy (Great Britain)
1954 J. Westwood and L. Demmy (Great Britain)
1955 J. Westwood and L. Demmy (Great Britain)
1956 P. Weight and P. Thomas (Great Britain)
1957 J. Markham and C. Jones (Great Britain)
1958 J. Markham and C. Jones (Great Britain)
1959 D. Denny and C. Jones (Great Britain)
1960 D. Denny and C. Jones (Great Britain)
1961 *Cancelled because the entire US team died in an air crash at Brussels*
1962 E. Romanova and P. Roman (Czechoslovakia)
1963 E. Romanova and P. Roman (Czechoslovakia)
1964 E. Romanova and P. Roman (Czechoslovakia)
1965 E. Romanova and P. Roman (Czechoslovakia)
1966 D. Towler and B. Ford (Great Britain)
1967 D. Towler and B. Ford (Great Britain)
1968 D. Towler and B. Ford (Great Britain)
1969 D. Towler and B. Ford (Great Britain)
1970 L. Pakhomova and A. Gorschkov (USSR)
1971 L. Pakhomova and A. Gorschkov (USSR)
1972 L. Pakhomova and A. Gorschkov (USSR)
1973 L. Pakhomova and A. Gorschkov (USSR)
1974 L. Pakhomova and A. Gorschkov (USSR)
1975 I. Moiseeva and A. Minenkov (USSR)
1976 L. Pakhomova and A. Gorschkov (USSR)
1977 I. Moiseeva and A. Minenkov (USSR)
1978 N. Linnichuk and G. Karponosov (USSR)
1979 N. Linnichuk and G. Karponosov (USSR)

OLYMPIC GOLD MEDALISTS

1976 L. Pakhomova and A. Gorschkov (USSR)

SPEED SKATING

WORLD CHAMPIONS

MEN

500 METERS

1893 J. Eden (Netherlands)
1894 O. Fredriksen (Norway)
1895 O. Fredriksen (Norway)
1896 J. Eden (Netherlands)
1897 A. Naess (Norway)
1898 J. Seyler (Germany)
1899 P. Oestlund (Norway)
1900 P. Oestlund (Norway)
1901 F. F. Wathèn (Finland)
1902 R. Gundersen (Norway)
1903 F. F. Wathèn (Finland)
1904 R. Gundersen (Norway)
1905 M. Lordahl (Norway)
1906 J. Wikander (Finland)
1907 O. Steen (Norway)
1908 J. Wikander (Finland)
1909 O. Mathisen (Norway)
1910 O. Mathisen (Norway)
1911 N. Strunikov (Russia)
1912 O. Mathisen (Norway)
1913 O. Mathisen (Norway)
1914 O. Mathisen (Norway)
1915–21 *No competition*
1922 R. Larsen (Norway)
1923 C. Thunberg (Finland)
1924 C. Thunberg (Finland)
1925 C. Thunberg (Finland)
1926 R. Larsen (Norway)
1927 C. Thunberg (Finland)
1928 R. Larsen (Norway)
1929 C. Thunberg (Finland)
1930 H. Pedersen (Norway)
1931 C. Thunberg (Finland)
1932 H. Pedersen (Norway)
1933 H. Engnestangen (Norway)
1934 H. Pedersen (Norway)
1935 H. Haraldsen (Norway)
1936 D. Lamb (USA)
1937 G. Krog (Norway)
1938 H. Engnestangen (Norway)
1939 H. Engnestangen (Norway)
1940–6 *No competition*
1947 S. Farstad (Norway)
1948 K. Kudryavtsev (USSR)
1949 K. Henry (USA)
1950 J. Werket (USA)
1951 S. Naito (Japan)
1952 K. Henry (USA)
1953 T. Salonen (Finland)
1954 Y. Grishin (USSR)
1955 T. Salonen (Finland)
1956 Y. Mikhailov (USSR)
1957 Y. Grishin (USSR)
1958 R. Merkulov (USSR)
1959 G. Voronin (USSR)
1960 Y. Grishin (USSR)
1961 Y. Grishin (USSR)
1962 Y. Grishin (USSR)
1963 Y. Grishin (USSR)
1964 K. Suzuki (Japan)
1965 K. Suzuki (Japan)
1966 T. Gray (USA)

1967 K. Suzuki (Japan)
1968 K. Suzuki (Japan)
1969 K. Suzuki (Japan)
1970 M. Thomassen (Norway)
1971 D. Fornaess (Norway)
1972 R. Grønvold (Norway)
1973 W. Lanigan (USA)
1974 M. Suzuki (Japan)
1975 J. E. Storholt (Norway)
1976 E. Heiden (USA)
1977 E. Heiden (USA)
1978 E. Heiden (USA)
1979 E. Heiden (USA)

1,500 METERS

1893 J. Eden (Netherlands)
1894 E. Halvorsen (Norway)
1895 J. Eden (Netherlands)
1896 J. Eden (Netherlands)
1897 J. K. McCulloch (Canada)
1898 P. Oestlund (Norway)
1899 P. Oestlund (Norway)
1900 E. Engelassa (Norway)
1901 F. F. Wathèn (Finland)
1902 R. Gundersen (Norway)
1903 J. Schwartz (Norway)
1904 S. Mathisen (Norway)
1905 C. Coen de Koning (Netherlands)
1906 R. Gundersen (Norway)
1907 A. Wicklund (Finland)
1908 O. Mathisen (Norway)
1909 O. Mathisen (Norway)
1910 O. Mathisen (Norway)
1911 N. Strunnikov (Russia)
1912 O. Mathisen (Norway)
1913 O. Mathisen (Norway)
1914 O. Mathisen (Norway)
1915–21 *No competition*
1922 C. Thunberg (Finland)
1923 R. Larsen (Norway)
1924 R. Larsen (Norway)
1925 C. Thunberg (Finland)
1926 I. Ballangrud (Norway)
1927 C. Thunberg (Finland)
1928 C. Thunberg (Finland)
1929 C. Thunberg (Finland)
1930 M. Stadsrud (Norway)
1931 C. Thunberg (Finland)
1932 I. Ballangrud (Norway)
1933 C. Thunberg (Finland)
1934 B. Evensen (Norway)
1935 I. Ballangrud (Norway)
1936 I. Ballangrud (Norway)
1937 H. Engnestangen (Norway)
1938 H. Engnestangen (Norway)
1939 B. Vasenius (Finland)
1940–6 *No competition*
1947 S. Farstad (Norway)
1948 J. Werket (USA)
1949 J. Werket (USA)
1950 J. Werket (USA)
1951 W. van der Voort (Netherlands)
1952 W. van der Voort (Netherlands)
1953 B. Shilkov (USSR)
1954 B. Shilkov (USSR)
1955 O. Goncharenko (USSR)
1956 B. Shilkov (USSR)
1957 B. Shilkov (USSR)
1958 O. Goncharenko (USSR)
1959 T. Salonen (Finland)
1960 B. Stenin (USSR)
1961 H. van der Grift (Netherlands)
1962 B. Stenin (USSR)
1963 L. Chih-huan (People's Republic of China)
1964 N. Aaness (Norway)
1965 P. I. More (Norway)
1966 C. Verkerk (Netherlands)
1967 A. Schenk (Netherlands)
1968 M. Thomassen (Norway)
1969 K. Verkerk (Netherlands)
1970 A. Schenk (Netherlands)
1971 A. Schenk (Netherlands)
1972 A. Schenk (Netherlands)
1973 S. Stensen (Norway)
1974 H. van Helden (Netherlands)
1975 A. Sjöbrend (Norway)
1976 P. Kleine (Netherlands)
1977 A. Sjöbrend (Norway)

1978 E. Heiden (USA)
1979 E. Heiden (USA)

5,000 METERS

1893 J. Eden (Netherlands)
1894 E. Halvorsen (Netherlands)
1895 J. Eden (Netherlands)
1896 J. Eden (Netherlands)
1897 J. K. McCulloch (Canada)
1898 P. Oestlund (Norway)
1899 P. Oestlund (Norway)
1900 E. Engelsaas (Norway)
1901 R. Gundersen (Norway)
1902 J. Wiinikainen (Finland)
1903 G. Kiselev (Russia)
1904 S. Mathisen (Norway)
1905 C. Coen de Koning (Netherlands)
1906 N. Sedov (Russia)
1907 G. Strömsten (Finland)
1908 O. Mathisen (Norway)
1909 E. Burnov (Russia)
1910 M. Johansen (Norway)
1911 N. Strunnikov (Russia)
1912 O. Mathisen (Norway)
1913 V. Ippolitov (Russia)
1914 O. Mathison (Norway)
1915–21 *No competition*
1922 H. Ström (Norway)
1923 Y. Melnikov (USSR)
1924 R. Larsen (Norway)
1925 C. Thunberg (Finland)
1926 I. Ballangrud (Norway)
1927 B. Evensen (Norway)
1928 I. Ballangrud (Norway)
1929 I. Ballangrud (Norway)
1930 M. Straksrud (Norway)
1931 O. Blomqvist (Finland)
1932 I. Ballangrud (Norway)
1933 I. Ballangrud (Norway)
1934 B. Vasenius (Finland)
1935 M. Straksrud (Norway)
1936 I. Ballangrud (Norway)
1937 M. Stiepl (Austria)
1938 I. Ballangrud (Norway)
1939 C. Mathisen (Norway)
1940–6 *No competition*
1947 L. Parkkinen (Finland)
1948 C. Broekman (Netherlands)
1949 K. Pajor (Hungary)
1950 H. Andersen (Norway)
1951 H. Andersen (Norway)
1952 H. Andersen (Norway)
1953 O. Goncharenko (USSR)
1954 O. Goncharenko (USSR)
1955 K. Johannesen (Norway)
1956 O. Goncharenko (USSR)
1957 K. Johannesen (Norway)
1958 V. Shilikouski (USSR)
1959 J. Pesman (Netherlands)
1960 V. Kotov (USSR)
1961 I. Nilsson (Sweden)
1962 I. Nilsson (Sweden)
1963 J. Nilsson (Sweden)
1964 K. Johannesen (Norway)
1965 J. Nilsson (Sweden)
1966 C. Verkerk (Netherlands)
1967 C. Verkerk (Netherlands)
1968 F. A. Maier (Norway)
1969 K. Verkerk (Netherlands)
1970 J. Bols (Netherlands)
1971 A. Schenk (Netherlands)
1972 A. Schenk (Netherlands)
1973 G. Claeson (Sweden)
1974 S. Stensen (Norway)
1975 S. Stensen (Norway)
1976 H. van Helden (Netherlands)
1977 H. van Helden (Netherlands)
1978 E. Heiden (USA)
1979 E. Heiden (USA)

10,000 METERS

1893 O. Fredriksen (Norway)
1894 J. Eden (Netherlands)
1895 J. Eden (Netherlands)
1896 J. Eden (Netherlands)
1897 J. K. McCulloch (Canada)
1898 P. Oestlund (Norway)
1899 J. C. Greve (Netherlands)
1900 E. Engelsaas (Norway)
1901 F. F. Wathèn (Finland)

1902 J. Wiinikainen (Finland)
1903 T. Bönsnaes (Norway)
1904 S. Mathisen (Norway)
1905 C. Coen de Koning (Netherlands)
1906 N. Sedov (Russia)
1907 G. Strömsten (Finland)
1908 O. Mathisen (Norway)
1909 E. Burnov (Russia)
1910 N. Strunnikov (Russia)
1911 N. Strunnikov (Russia)
1912 O. Mathisen (Norway)
1913 V. Ippolitov (Russia)
1914 V. Ippolitov (Russia)
1915–21 *No competition*
1922 H. Ström (Norway)
1923 H. Ström (Norway)
1924 U. Pietilä (Finland)
1925 U. Pietilä (Finland)
1926 I. Ballangrud (Norway)
1927 B. Evensen (Norway)
1928 A. Carlsen (Norway)
1929 M. Staksrud (Norway)
1930 I. Ballangrud (Norway)
1931 O. Blomqvist (Finland)
1932 I. Ballangrud (Norway)
1933 E. Schroeder (USA)
1934 A. Carlsen (Norway)
1935 M. Staksrud (Norway)
1936 B. Vasenius (Finland)
1937 M. Stiepl (Austria)
1938 I. Ballangrund (Norway)
1939 A. Berzins (Latvia)
1940–6 *No competition*
1947 R. Liaklev (Norway)
1948 C. Broekman (Netherlands)
1949 K. Pajor (Hungary)
1950 H. Andersen (Norway)
1951 H. Andersen (Norway)
1952 H. Andersen (Norway)
1953 O. Goncharenko (USSR)
1954 O. Goncharenko (USSR)
1955 S. Ericsson (Sweden)
1956 T. Seiersten (Norway)
1957 K. Johannesen (Norway)
1958 K. Johannesen (Norway)
1959 K. Johannesen (Norway)
1960 J. Pesman (Netherlands)
1961 V. Kosychkin (USSR)
1962 J. Nilsson (Sweden)
1963 J. Nilsson (Sweden)
1964 K. Johannesen (Norway)
1965 J. Nilsson (Sweden)
1966 C. Verkerk (Netherlands)
1967 C. Verkerk (Netherlands)
1968 F. Maier (Norway)
1969 J. Bols (Netherlands)
1970 J. Bols (Netherlands)
1971 A. Schenk (Netherlands)
1972 A. Schenk (Netherlands)
1973 G. Claeson (Sweden)
1974 S. Stensen (Norway)
1975 V. Ivanov (USSR)
1976 P. Kleine (Netherlands)
1977 S. Stensen (Norway)
1978 S. Stensen (Norway)
1979 E. Heiden (USA)

WOMEN

500 METERS

1936 K. Klein (USA)
1937 L. S. Nilsen (Norway)
1938 L. S. Nilsen (Norway)
1939 G. Donker (Netherlands)
1940–6 *No competition*
1947 V. Lesche (Finland)
1948 L. Selikhova (USSR)
1949 M. Isakova (USSR)
M. Valovova (USSR)
1950 M. Isakova (USSR)
1951 R. Thorvaldsen (Norway)
1952 N. Donshenko (USSR)
1953 R. Zhukova (USSR)
1954 S. Kondakova (USSR)
1955 T. Rylova (USSR)
1956 S. Kondakova (USSR)
1957 S. Kondakova (USSR)
1958 T. Rylova (USSR)
1959 T. Rylova (USSR)
S. Kondakova (USSR)

1960 L. Skoblikova (USSR)
1961 V. Stenina (USSR)
1962 E. Seroczynska (Poland)
1963 L. Skoblikova (USSR)
1964 I. Egorova (USSR)
1965 I. Artamonova (USSR)
1966 I. Egorova (USSR)
1967 M. Meyers (USA)
1968 L. Titova (USSR)
1969 K. Biermann (Norway)
1970 L. Titova (USSR)
1971 A. Henning (USA)
1972 D. Holum (USA)
1973 S. Young (USA)
1974 S. Young (USA)
1975 S. Young (USA)
1976 S. Young (USA)
1977 V. Bryndzey (USSR)
1978 V. Golovenkina (USSR)
1979 B. Heiden (USA)

1,000 METERS

1936 V. Lesche (Finland)
1937 L. S. Nilsen (Norway)
1938 L. S. Nilsen (Norway)
1939 V. Lesche (Finland)
1940–6 *No competition*
1947 V. Lesche (Finland)
1948 M. Isakova (USSR)
1949 M. Isakova (USSR)
1950 T. Karelina (USSR)
1951 E. Huttunen (Finland)
1952 L. Selikhova (USSR)
1953 R. Zhukova (USSR)
1954 S. Kondakova (USSR)
1955 S. Kondakova (USSR)
1956 S. Kondakova (USSR)
1957 I. Artamonova (USSR)
1958 S. Kondakova (USSR)
1959 T. Rylova (USSR)
1960 K. Guseva (USSR)
1961 V. Stenina (USSR)
1962 I. Artamonova (USSR)
1963 L. Skoblikova (USSR)
1964 L. Skoblikova (USSR)
1965 I. Artamonova (USSR)
1966 T. Rastopsyina (USSR)
1967 C. Kaiser (Netherlands)
1968 L. Titova (USSR)
1969 L. Kauniste (USSR)
1970 S. Sundby (Norway)
A. Keulen-Deelstra (Netherlands)
L. Titova (USSR)
1971 D. Holum (USA)
1972 A. Keulen-Deelstra (Netherlands)
1973 A. Keulen-Deelstra (Netherlands)
1974 A. Keulen-Deelstra (Netherlands)
1975 S. Young (USA)
1976 S. Young (USA)
1977 V. Bryndzey (USSR)
1978 T. Averina (USSR)
1979 B. Heiden (USA)

1,500 METERS

1956 S. Kondakova (USSR)
1957 I. Artamonova (USSR)
1958 I. Artamonova (USSR)
1959 I. Artamonova (USSR)
1960 V. Stenina (USSR)
1961 V. Stenina (USSR)
1962 I. Artamonova (USSR)
1963 L. Skoblikova (USSR)
1964 L. Skoblikova (USSR)
1965 V. Stenina (USSR)
1966 S. S. Kim (PRK)
1967 C. Kaiser (Netherlands)
1968 S. Kaiser (Netherlands)
1969 S. Kaiser (Netherlands)
1970 A. Schut (Netherlands)
1971 N. Statkevich (USSR)
1972 A. Keulen-Deelstra (Netherlands)
1973 G. Stepanskaya (USSR)
1974 A. Keulen-Deelstra (Netherlands)
1975 K. Kessow (DDR)
1976 S. Burka (Canada)
1977 G. Stepanskaya (USSR)
1978 T. Averina (USSR)
1979 B. Heiden (USA)

3,000 METERS

1936 K. Klein (USA)

1937 L. S. Nilsen (Norway)
1938 V. Lesche (Finland)
1939 V. Lesche (Finland)
1940–6 *No competition*
1947 V. Lesche (Finland)
1948 M. Isakova (USSR)
1949 M. Isakova (USSR)
1950 R. Zhukova (USSR)
1951 E. Huttunen (Finland)
1952 M. Anikanova (USSR)
1953 K. Shegoleeva (USSR)
1954 R. Zhukova (USSR)
1955 R. Zhukova (USSR)
1956 R. Zhukova (USSR)
1957 E. Huttunen (Finland)
1958 I. Artamonova (USSR)
1959 E. Huttunen (Finland)
1960 L. Skoblikova (USSR)
1961 I. Artamonova (USSR)
1962 I. Artamonova (USSR)
1963 L. Skoblikova (USSR)
1964 L. Skoblikova (USSR)
1965 I. Artamonova (USSR)
1966 C. Kaiser (Netherlands)
1967 C. Kaiser (Netherlands)
1968 A. Schut (Netherlands)
1969 A. Schut (Netherlands)
1970 A. Schut (Netherlands)
1971 S. Kaiser (Netherlands)
1972 S. Baas-Kaiser (Netherlands)
1973 S. Tigchelaar (Netherlands)
1974 A. Keulen-Deelstra (Netherlands)
1975 S. Tigchelaar (Netherlands)
1976 K. Kessow (DDR)
1977 G. Stepanskaya (USSR)
1978 M. Dittmann (East Germany)
1979 B. Heiden (USA)

5,000 METERS

1936 V. Lesche (Finland)
1937 L. S. Nilsen (Norway)
1938 V. Lesche (Finland)
1939 V. Lesche (Finland)
1940–6 *No competition*
1947 V. Lesche (Finland)
1948 V. Lesche (Finland)
1949 V. Lesche (Finland)
1950 Z. Krotova (USSR)
1951 E. Huttunen (Finland)
1952 R. Zhukova (USSR)
1953 E. Huttunen (Finland)
1954 E. Huttunen (Finland)
1955 R. Zhukova (USSR)

OLYMPIC GOLD MEDALISTS

MEN

500 METERS

1924 C. Jewtraw (USA)
1928 C. Thunberg and B. Evenson (Finland and Norway)
1932 J. A. Shea (USA)
1936 I. Ballangrud (Norway)
1948 F. Helgesen (Norway)
1952 K. Henry (USA)
1956 Y. Grishin (USSR)
1960 Y. Grishin (USSR)
1964 R. McDermott (USA)
1968 E. Keller (Germany)
1972 E. Keller (Germany)
1976 E. Kulikov (USSR)

1,000 METERS

1976 P. Mueller (USA)

1,500 METERS

1924 C. Thunberg (Finland)
1928 C. Thunberg (Finland)
1932 J. A. Shea (USA)
1936 C. Mathisen (Norway)
1948 S. Farstad (Norway)
1952 H. Andersen (Norway)
1956 Y. Grishin and Y. Mikhailov (USSR)

1960 R. Aas and Y. Grishin (Norway and USSR)
1964 A. Antson (USSR)
1968 C. Verkerk (Netherlands)
1972 A. Schenk (Netherlands)
1976 J. E. Storholt (Norway)

5,000 METERS
1924 C. Thunberg (Finland)
1928 I. Ballangrud (Norway)
1932 I. Jaffee (USA)
1936 I. Ballangrud (Norway)
1948 R. Liakley (Norway)
1952 H. Andersen (Norway)
1956 B. Shilkov (USSR)
1960 V. Kosychkin (USSR)
1964 K. Johannesen (Norway)
1968 F. A. Maier (Norway)
1972 A. Schenk (Netherlands)
1976 S. Stensen (Norway)

10,000 METERS
1924 J. Skutnabb (Finland)
1928 *Event cancelled because of the condition of the ice*
1932 I. Jaffee (USA)
1936 I. Ballangrud (Norway)
1948 Å. Seyffarth (Sweden)
1952 H. Andersen (Norway)
1956 S. Ericsson (Sweden)
1960 K. Johannesen (Norway)
1964 J. Nilsson (Sweden)
1968 J. Höglin (Sweden)
1972 A. Schenk (Netherlands)
1976 P. Kleine (Netherlands)

WOMEN

500 METERS
1960 H. Haase (Germany)
1964 L. Skoblikova (USSR)
1968 L. Titova (USSR)
1972 A. Henning (USA)
1976 S. Young (USA)

1,000 METERS
1960 K. Guseva (USSR)
1964 L. Skoblikova (USSR)
1968 C. Geijssen (Netherlands)
1972 M. Pflug (Germany)
1976 T. Averina (USSR)

1,500 METERS
1960 L. Skoblikova (USSR)
1964 L. Skoblikova (USSR)
1968 K. Mustonen (Finland)
1972 D. Holum (USA)
1976 G. Stepanskaya (USSR)

3,000 METERS
1960 L. Skoblikova (USSR)
1964 L. Skoblikova (USSR)
1968 J. Schut (Netherlands)
1972 C. Baas-Kaiser (Netherlands)
1976 T. Averina (USSR)

CURLING

WORLD CHAMPIONS

1959 Canada
1960 Canada
1961 Canada
1962 Canada

1963 Canada
1964 Canada
1965 United States
1966 Canada
1967 Scotland
1968 Canada
1969 Canada
1970 Canada
1971 Canada
1972 Canada
1973 Sweden
1974 United States
1975 Switzerland
1976 United States
1977 Sweden
1978 United States
1979 Norway

ICE HOCKEY

WORLD CHAMPIONS

1920 Canada
1924 Canada
1928 Canada
1930 Canada
1931 Canada
1932 Canada
1933 United States
1934 Canada
1935 Canada
1936 Great Britain
1937 Canada
1938 Canada
1939 Canada
1947 Czechoslovakia
1948 Canada
1949 Czechoslovakia
1950 Canada
1951 Canada
1952 Canada
1953 Sweden
1954 USSR
1955 Canada
1956 USSR
1957 Sweden
1958 Canada
1959 Canada
1960 United States
1961 Canada
1962 Sweden
1963 USSR
1964 USSR
1965 USSR
1966 USSR
1967 USSR
1968 USSR
1969 USSR
1970 USSR
1971 USSR
1972 Czechoslovakia
1973 USSR
1974 USSR
1975 USSR
1976 Czechoslovakia
1977 Czechoslovakia
1978 USSR

EUROPEAN CHAMPIONS

1910 Great Britain
1911 Bohemia
1913 Belgium
1914 Bohemia
1921 Sweden
1922 Czechoslovakia
1923 Sweden
1924 France
1925 Czechoslovakia
1926 Switzerland
1927 Austria
1928 Sweden
1929 Czechoslovakia
1930 Germany
1931 Austria
1932 Sweden
1933 Czechoslovakia
1934 Germany
1935 Switzerland
1936 Great Britain
1937 Great Britain
1938 Great Britain
1939 Switzerland
1947 Czechoslovakia
1948 Czechoslovakia
1949 Czechoslovakia
1950 Switzerland
1951 Sweden
1952 Sweden
1953 Sweden
1954 USSR
1955 USSR
1956 USSR
1957 Sweden
1958 USSR
1959 USSR
1960 USSR
1961 Czechoslovakia
1962 Sweden
1963 Sweden
1964 USSR
1965 USSR
1966 USSR
1967 USSR
1968 Czechoslovakia
1969 USSR
1970 USSR
1971 Czechoslovakia
1972 Czechoslovakia
1973 USSR
1974 USSR
1975 USSR
1976 Czechoslovakia
1977 Czechoslovakia
1978 USSR

OLYMPIC GOLD MEDALISTS

1920 Canada
1924 Canada
1928 Canada
1932 Canada
1936 Great Britain
1948 Canada
1952 Canada
1960 United States
1964 USSR
1968 USSR
1972 USSR
1976 USSR

STANLEY CUP WINNERS

1893 Montreal A.A.A.
1894 Montreal A.A.A.
1895 Montreal A.A.A.
1896 Winnipeg Victorias (Feb)
1896 Montreal Victorias (Dec)
1897 Montreal Victorias
1898 Montreal Victorias
1899 Montreal Shamrocks
1900 Montreal Shamrocks
1901 Montreal Victorias
1902 Montreal A.A.A.
1903 Ottawa Silver Seven
1904 Ottawa Silver Seven
1905 Ottawa Silver Seven
1906 Montreal Wanderers
1907 Kenora Thistles (Jan)
1907 Montreal Wanderers (Mar)
1908 Montreal Wanderers
1909 Ottawa Senators
1910 Montreal Wanderers
1911 Ottawa Senators
1912 Quebec Bulldogs
1913 Quebec Bulldogs
1914 Toronto Blueshorts
1915 Vancouver Millionaires
1916 Montreal Canadiens
1917 Seattle Metropolitans
1918 Toronto Arenas
1919 *No decision*
1920 Ottawa Senators
1921 Ottawa Senators
1922 Toronto St Pats
1923 Ottawa Senators
1924 Montreal Canadiens
1925 Victoria Cougars
1926 Montreal Maroons
1927 Ottawa Senators
1928 New York Rangers
1929 Boston Bruins
1930 Montreal Canadiens
1931 Montreal Canadiens
1932 Toronto Maple Leafs
1933 New York Rangers
1934 Chicago Black Hawks
1935 Montreal Maroons
1936 Detroit Red Wings
1937 Detroit Red Wings
1938 Chicago Black Hawks
1939 Boston Bruins
1940 New York Rangers
1941 Boston Bruins
1942 Toronto Maple Leafs
1943 Detroit Red Wings
1944 Montreal Canadiens
1945 Toronto Maple Leafs
1946 Montreal Canadiens
1947 Toronto Maple Leafs
1948 Toronto Maple Leafs
1949 Toronto Maple Leafs
1950 Detroit Red Wings
1951 Toronto Maple Leafs
1952 Detroit Red Wings
1953 Montreal Canadiens
1954 Detroit Red Wings
1955 Detroit Red Wings
1956 Montreal Canadiens
1957 Montreal Canadiens
1958 Montreal Canadiens
1959 Montreal Canadiens
1960 Montreal Canadiens
1961 Chicago Black Hawks
1962 Toronto Maple Leafs
1963 Toronto Maple Leafs
1964 Toronto Maple Leafs
1965 Montreal Canadiens
1966 Montreal Canadiens
1967 Toronto Maple Leafs
1968 Montreal Canadiens
1969 Montreal Canadiens
1970 Boston Bruins
1971 Montreal Canadiens
1972 Boston Bruins
1973 Montreal Canadiens
1974 Philadelphia Flyers

1975 Philadelphia Flyers
1976 Montreal Canadiens
1977 Montreal Canadiens
1978 Montreal Canadiens

GLOSSARY

Note: French or German language translation of a technical term is given only where this is an official or internationally accepted translation.

The official language for curling is English and there are no generally accepted foreign language versions of the terms used in this game.

Ice hockey presents a special problem due to the two differing sets of rules and to the fact that the French-Canadian terminology is not fully understood in the European French-speaking countries.

Eisschiessen, only played in the German-speaking countries, has no acceptable translation for the technical terms used.

Allan Cup (Ice hockey)
Canadian amateur club championship cup. Traditionally the winner of the Allan Cup represented Canada in the world championships until 1961.

Ahearne, John F. (Ice hockey)
British President of the IIHF from 1954 to 1975. Now Honorary Life President, he will go into hockey history for his brilliant financial management of the IIHF whose capital he increased from 30,000 Swiss francs to 2,000,000 Swiss francs.

Asphaltschiessen (Eisschiessen)
Summer or dryland version of *Eisschiessen* played on an asphalt court coated with a Teflon film.

Axel Paulsen (Skating)
a) Norwegian speed skater, winner of the first international championship in Hamburg in 1885 and who subsequently became world famous as an exhibition and trick skater.
b) Skating jump named after Axel Paulsen, more commonly known as an "Axel," requiring a 540° rotation (one and a half turns) from a forward outside edge to a backward outside edge on the other foot. It is performed in a number of variations, including double and triple versions such as the one-foot Axel, also known as an Oppacher.

Back line (Curling)
A line drawn at right angles to the rink touching the farthest point of the outer circle of the tee. A stone which passes this line is out of play and is removed from the ice.

Back-ring weight (Curling)
Strength required to hit another stone to the back of the circles.

Bandy
A team game played on skates with a hockey-like stick and a round ball. Generally accepted as the ancestor of the modern game of ice hockey, it is still actively played in the U.S.S.R., Finland, Sweden and the Baltic States but is rapidly losing ground to ice hockey.

Bench minor penalty (Ice hockey)
A team offense for players and other members of the team not immediately engaged in play on the ice, given for abusive language, delayed start, throwing objects onto the ice, etc. One player from the team on the ice is removed from the ice and no substitute is allowed.

Biting (Curling)
A stone is biting when it touches the outside circle.

Boarding (Ice hockey)
A body check which causes the opponent to be thrown violently against the boards.

Body check (Ice hockey)
A tackle delivered with either the hip or the shoulder or both.

Bonspiel (Curling)
From the Flemish *bonne*, a district or village, and *spel*, to play, and meaning any large gathering of curlers.

Bracket (Skating) Fr. *Accolade* G. *Gegenwende*
A form of three-turn in which the skater turns counter to the normal rotational flow.

Broom (Curling)
A form of domestic brush or broom used to "sweep" the ice in front of a moving stone. To "stack brooms" means to stop play before going for refreshment.

Burn (Curling)
To derange a game by improper interference: hence "to burn a stone" is to touch it accidentally.

Bushnell, E.V. (Skating)
American inventor of the all-metal skate in the mid-nineteenth century. Before this date only the blade was metal, set into a wooden platform or clog.

Butt-ending (Ice hockey)
Jabbing an opponent with the top shaft end of a stick.

Button (Curling)
North American term for the tee.

Caledonian Curling Club
The mother club of the game of curling, founded in 1838, located in Edinburgh, Scotland.

Camel spin (Skating) Fr. *Pirouette arabesque* G. *Waage-pirouette*
Figure skating spin so-called on account of the hump which novices to the move always adopt. Also known as the "parallel" spin, it is performed in arabesque position with one leg parallel to the ice, behind the skater.

Change (Skating) Fr *Changement de carré* G *Schlangenbogen*
School figure in the shape of three joined circles in which, after half of one circle has been completed, the skater changes edge without interrupting the movement to complete an "S" figure, changes foot with a fresh push-off, completes a further half-circle, changes edges and completes three joined circles.

Clipping (Ice hockey)
Falling or sliding across the ice to cause a puck carrier to loose possession.

Combined *Ring-and-Stockschiessen*
Target and placement competitions, one of the three *Eisschiessen* disciplines.

Counter (Skating) Fr *Contre-trois* G *Gegendreier*
A three-figure skated against the natural flow.

Creighton, James George Aylwin (Ice hockey)
A Canadian railway design engineer generally credited with the invention of the modern game of ice hockey in 1873. His game used shinny sticks and a shinny ball with two rounded sides cut off to reduce bouncing. Robertson, W.F. and Smith, R.F. of McGill University devised the rules for

the modern nine-a-side game in 1879.

Cross-checking (Ice hockey)
Checking an opponent with both hands on the stick and no part of the stick on the ice.

Curling
A game similar to bowls played on ice with fashioned granite "stones" of supposed Scottish origin. Terminology worldwide is in English and there are no other language equivalents.

Stone (Curling)
A circular, highly polished granite or gneiss implement with a concave cup and running rims, a striking band and a countersunk square hole on the top to take the handle. A curling stone may not weigh more than 44 pounds (19.96kg) with a circumference not more than 36 inches (91.44cm) or lower than 4½ inches (11.43cm).

Curling world championship
First staged in 1959 between Canada and Scotland. The first five championships were played in Scotland and the first Canadian venue in 1964 was Calgary. The event is now played annually in different venues all over the world in March.

Death spiral (Skating) Fr *Spirale de la mort* G *Todesspirale*
Basic pair skating movement in which the man swings his partner in a spiral about his own pivot. The partner has one skate resting on the ice on a backward outside edge. It is a hand-held move and the woman leans out and back until her head nearly touches the ice. It was first demonstrated in 1911 by a young German skater (who also made the very first skating films) known only as "Charlotte."

Double (Skating) Fr *Double* G *Doppel*
A prefix used with skating terms to denote the repetition of a move – thus a double three. The most common use of this term is in defining jumps in which "double" refers to the number of complete revolutions – i.e. a double jump is one in which the skater revolves 720° (two complete turns) in the air. The term "triple" is used similarly to denote a three-fold repeat.

Double take-out (Curling)
A fast stone which removes two opposing stones.

Draw (Curling)
A stone with just enough strength to reach the "house."

Dutch roll (Skating) Fr *Roulis Hollandais* G *Holländer Schritt*
Earliest known skating technique, originating in Holland. It involves skating forward on alternate feet using an outside edge.

Edges (Skating) Fr *Carré* G *Kante*
As figure skates are hollow-ground and curved it is possible to draw a distinction between skating with either the outside or the inside edge of the blade in contact with the ice. All skating figures are defined as being skated on the one or the other edge, irrespective whether forward or backward. The terms "inner" and "outer" refer to the location of the edges in relation to the skater's foot.

Eights (Skating) Fr *Huites* G *Achter*
The set of school figures in which from one to four circles are skated, each on alternate feet.

Eisschiessen
A game similar to curling, of Central European origin, played mainly in Bavaria and Austria.

Eisstock (plural *Eisstöcke*)
The missile used in *Eisschiessen*, hence *Eisstockschiessen*.

End (Curling)
An end is the play of all sixteen stones in one direction on a rink.

English school (Skating)
The original, formal figure skating practice which concentrated on the performance of set figures, known as "figuring."

Figure skating Fr *Patinage de figure, Patinage artistique* G *Schaulaufen, Kunstschaulaufen, Pflichtfiguren*
a) General term for all forms of singles, pair and ice dance skating, as compared with speed skating or ice hockey skating.
b) The performance of set figures such as threes, eights, brackets and the like.

Fisticuffs (Ice hockey)
The term employed to denote a person-to-person fight. In the amateur (IIHF) rules this results in an automatic match penalty (the player is sent off for the duration of the match), but in the professional game (NHL rules) it is only a major, double minor or minor penalty.

Foot line (Curling)
The foot line marks the throwing point on a curling rink, 42 yards (38.40m) from the tee.

Freestyle (Skating) Fr *Patinage libre, Style libre* G *Kür, Freistil*
A choreographed program of skating moves of the skater's choice lasting not longer than five minutes for men and four minutes for women. It is skated to music and marked for artistic impression and technical difficulty. The moves must include single, double and triple jumps, spins and fast repetitive step sequences.

Freeze (Curling)
To freeze is to play a slow stone with just enough weight to stop alongside another stone, touching it. This is also called "to crack an egg."

Full draw (Curling)
A stone with sufficient weight to reach the center of the circle.

Garcin, J.
Author of *Le Vrai Patineur*, published in 1813. Garcin was a member of the *Cercle des Patineurs de Paris* and was the first to attempt to name the various skating movements.

Grafstrom spin (Skating) Fr *Pirouette arabesque Grafstrom* G *Grafstrom Pirouette*
A skating spin which is a variation of the camel spin. The skater does not reach full arabesque position.

Grand match (Curling)
Traditional mass match meeting organized by the Royal Caledonian Curling Club on Loch Leven, Lake of Monteith or Lindores Loch, whichever freezes first.

Guard (Curling)
To place a short stone in front of another so that the opposition cannot hit it.

Haines, Jackson
American ballet master who adapted ballet movements to skating and demonstrated the new technique in Europe in 1868. His technique is generally thought to be the origin of modern figure skating to music. Haines also invented the sitting spin.

Hand or handle (Curling)
The turn imparted to the handle of a stone which makes it draw (curl) to one side or another.

Heavy (Curling)
A stone played too fast. Heavy ice is a slow or dull surface.

Henie, Sonja
Henie was a Norwegian champion figure skater who won ten world titles, six

European titles and three Olympic gold medals. She subsequently created the professional "ice spectacular" in the United States. She is credited with the development of a new image of women's figure skating, introducing athletic elements previously restricted to male competitors and also started a fashion movement with her brilliantly designed and unconventional skating attire, notably the short skirt.

Hog line (Curling)
A line one-sixteenth of the distance between the tee and the foot line.
A hog is a stone which does not reach beyond the hog line and is out of play. It is removed from the ice.

House (Curling)
The area within the circles drawn about the tee.

Ice dancing (Skating) Fr *La danse (sur glace)* G *Eistanzen*
Ice dancing is pair skating restricted to formal dance rhythms. It was first practiced in Vienna in the 1880s, and not accepted as a world championship discipline until 1952. It was first admitted to Olympic competition in 1976 at Innsbruck. There are now eighteen compulsory dance patterns.
A championship consists of a compulsory dance, an original set-pattern dance and the free dancing section.
The performances are based very loosely on ballroom dancing practice.

Ice hockey Fr *Hockey sur glace* G *Eishockey*
A team game originally of Canadian origin, similar to and possibly derived from bandy and shinty, and played on skates.

Ice hockey rink
Two sizes of rink (IIHF and NHL) are standardized. The markings in both are similar, consisting of two goal lines, two blue defense lines and a red center line. There are five face-off circles: one in the center and two in the two defensive zones. The sides and ends of the rink are boarded off to a height of between 3 and 4 feet (1 and 1.22m).

Icing the puck (Ice hockey)
The puck, in and out of play position, shot by the defense from behind the red line (center-line) to beyond the goal line without being touched by another player.

International Curling Federation
The international curling body founded in Perth, Scotland, in 1965 with twelve member nations.

International Eisschiessen Verband
The international governing body of *Eisschiessen*, founded in 1949.

International Ice Hockey Federation (IIHF)
The governing body of amateur ice hockey, the direct successor to the original *Ligue Internationale de Hockey sur Glace*. At present thirty member countries from five continents are federated.

International Skating Union (ISU)
The ISU was founded in July 1892 by Holland, Britain, Germany and Austria together, Sweden and Hungary to promote the interests of speed skating. In 1896 they organized the first world championships in figure skating at St. Petersburg (Leningrad).

Jones, Robert
Scottish author of the first book on skating, *A Treatise on Skating*, published in 1772.

Jubilee Stone (Curling)
Biggest known curling stone weighing 117 pounds (53.5kg), at present in the museum at Perth Ice Rink.

Jump (Skating) Fr *Saut* G *Sprung*
A skating move in which the skater leaves the ice completely with both feet. A jump

may or may not include a rotation in the air. The ISU lists forty-five different jumps. Many of these are named after their originator, e.g. Salchow, Lutz, Axel.

Kenn (Curling)
A kenn is an enthusiastic player. "Keen" ice is fast ice.

Kiggle-caggle (Curling)
Kiggle-caggle is the rocking movement of a stone not properly "soled" on the ice.

Lead (Curling)
First player on a rink.

Liedwi
Liedwi, a Dutch girl born in 1380, is pictured in a contemporary engraving being knocked down while skating and breaking a rib. She subsequently became the patron saint of skating.

Lifts (Skating) Fr *Levées* G *Hebungen*
Lifts are a group of skating moves used by pair skaters in which the man lifts his partner in a number of defined moves, so that the partner is clear of the ice.

Ligue Internationale de Hockey sur glace
First European ice hockey federation, founded in 1908 by Louis Magnus of France with four nation members – France, Great Britain, Bohemia and Switzerland.

Loop (Skating) Fr *Boucle* G *Schlinge*
A loop is the name of a tracing in which a loop is performed within the circle.

Lutz (Skating) Fr *Lutz* G *Lutz*
A skating jump from the backward outside edge, followed by a 360° turn in a counter-rotational direction, with a toe-assist takeoff, and a landing on the back outside edge of the other foot.

Macdonald Brier
Major Canadian curling championship started in 1927 and competed annually.

Minor penalty (Ice hockey) Fr *Pénalité de deux minutes G Kleine Strafe*
A two-minute penalty served by any offender except the goalkeeper. The list of offenses is defined in the detailed rules.

Moar (Eisschiessen)
The name given to the captain of an *Eisschiessen* team, hence *Moarschaft*, the name of a team.

Major penalty (Ice hockey) Fr *Pénalité de cinq minutes* G *Grosse Strafe*
A five-minute penalty for major offenses. These penalties are most often given for persistent or excessive breaches which normally incur a minor penalty.

Misconduct penalty (Ice hockey)
Removal of a player for ten minutes during which time a substitute is allowed. These penalties are normally awarded for obscene or foul language, molesting officials and similar offenses.

Narrow (Curling)
A stone is narrow when it is thrown inside the skip's broom which is used to indicate where the stone should come to rest.

National Hockey Association
Canadian Amateur Ice Hockey Association founded in 1910.

National Hockey League
First four-club professional hockey league formed in 1917 in Canada.

National Skating Association of Great Britain
The first skating association in the world, founded in 1879 in Cambridge. It was originally intended for speed skaters. Figure skating was included two years later.

Pair skating Fr *Patinage en couple* G *Paarlaufen*
Two figure skaters, normally a woman and a man, skating together, either touching or in separate harmonized movements. First

performed in Vienna in 1888, pair skating is now considered the highest form of skating art.

Paragraph (Skating) Fr *Paragraphe*
G *Paragraph*
Part of an advanced school figure officially listed as "change double three."

Pebbled ice (Curling)
Special ice surface prepared by spraying a prepared ice surface lightly with water to produce a surface which is faster than conventional flat, flooded surfaces.

Peels (Curling)
To be equal in shots, from a Lothian word meaning to equal or to match, also from the Teuton *pey-len*, to measure.

Penalties (Ice Hockey) Fr *Pénalité*
G *Strafbare Handlung*
Ice hockey penalties are extremely numerous and are exhaustively listed in the official handbooks. All have specific names, though many are referred to in slang terms which vary according to the area where the game is played.

Penalty box (Ice hockey) Fr *Banc des Pénalités*
G *Sündenbank*
Also called "sin bin," the penalty box is located by the side of the rink where players sit while serving the period of their penalty.

Port (Curling)
The space between two stones.

Promote (Curling)
To promote a stone is to hit forward.

Puck (Ice hockey) Fr *Rondelle, Palet*
G *Scheibe*
A circular, flat-sided vulcanized rubber disc, 1 inch (2.5cm) thick and 3 inches (7.6cm) in diameter which is the standard ice hockey playing object.

Referee (Ice hockey) Fr *Arbitre*
G *Schiedsrichter*
Ice hockey referees (two under IIHF rules and one and two linesmen under NHL rules) wear distinctive black and white longitudinally striped vests and indicate the nature of the stoppage or penalty by means of an internationally agreed series of hand and arm signals.

Rink (Curling)
A team of four curlers. The sheet of ice used for the game of curling is also called a rink.

Rocker (Skating) Fr *Contre accolade* G *Wende*
One-foot turns with an edge change combined with direction change.

Royal Montreal Curling Club
First Canadian club founded by Scotsmen in 1807.

Rub (Curling)
A light "wick" or touch off another stone.

Salchow, Ulrich
a) Swedish skater, winner of the first Olympic skating competition, ten world championships, nine titles and thirty-eight gold medals.
b) Freestyle skating jump invented by

Salchow: takeoff on right backward inner edge, one complete turn, landing on left backward outer edge.

School figures (Skating) Fr *Figures Imposées*
G *Pflichtfiguren*
The basic patterns or school figures make up the entire on-ice vocabulary of skating and are based on the fundamental natural circle cut by a skate traveling on one edge which has a radius of about 7 feet (2.1m). There are forty-one different official ISU figures, all of which are variants of circles made on the eight basic edges: right forward outside (**rfo**), and inside (**rfi**); left

forward outside and inside (**lfo** and **lfi**) and the same two skated backward on both edges (**rbo**, **rbi**, **lbo** and **lbi**).

Shinty
Also called shinny, shinty is a team game of gaelic origin played with a hockey-like stick and a hard ball. It may have been the ancestor of bandy and subsequently ice hockey.

Short program (Skating) Fr *Style libre court* G *Pflichtkür*
The compulsory freestyle singles program in international competitions consists of seven moves laid down by the ISU officials (known as the "required elements"). Both men and women skate the same required elements.

Short-track racing (Speed skating)
The official ISU term for racing over indoor, refrigerated courses. Short-track racing is known as "indoor racing" in North America.

Singles skating Fr *Patinage Individual* G *Einzellaufen*
The official name for "figure skating" by a single skater.

Skating disciplines
Six forms of skating are recognized as separate disciplines: singles skating, comprising figure skating and freestyle, pairs skating, ice dancing, touring skating, and speed skating.

Skip (Curling)
The captain of a team of four who directs where he wishes a player's stone to come to rest.

Slapshot (Ice hockey)
One of two methods of making a goal shot. A slapshot is reminiscent of a golf or land hockey stroke and the puck can achieve a speed of over 100 mph (161 kph).

Sole (Curling)
To lay a stone squarely on the ice when delivering or throwing it.

Spearing (Ice hockey)
Poking an opponent with the end of the stick blade.

Speed skating Fr *Patinage de vitesse* G *Eisschnellaufen*
The skating discipline concerned solely with speed over set distances on an oval course. Speed skating is the direct successor to the canal races in Holland and the precursor of figure skating.

Spin (Skating) Fr *Pirouette* G *Pirouette*
A freestyle move in which the skater revolves rapidly about his or her own axis without moving along the ice. A spin must have at least six revolutions (except in the case of the Grafstrom spin, when only five are required). They are carried out by using the master toe and the front part of the blade flat on the ice or on the backward outside edge. Spins are known by their position, i.e., sit spin, upright spin, change-foot spin, cross-foot spin. Some are named after their inventor, i.e., Grafstrom, Jackson Haines etc.

Stanley, Lord Frederick Arthur of Preston
Son of Lord Derby, Governor-General of Canada, Lord Stanley was encouraged by his sons William and Arthur, who played hockey for Rideau Hall Rebels, to donate the "Stanley Cup" for the championship of Canada in 1892. The Stanley cup is now the premier championship of the National Hockey League (Professional).

Stirling Stone (Curling)
Curling stone, dated 1511, with rough finger grips for throwing. This type of stone is known as a "loofie" (Scottish term for the palm of the hand). It is on view at the Smith Institute, Sterling, Scotland.

Sweep (Curling)
Vigorous brushing, "sweeping" or "souping" ("sooping") of the ice which can increase the length of the slide of a stone very considerably. A sweep can be used by either side to improve or to spoil the intended resting place of a stone.

Tee (Curling)
The center of the aiming point and the center of two circles 4 feet (1.22m) and 6 feet (1.83m) in radius.

Three-turn (Skating) Fr *Un trois* G *Dreier*
A school figure in which the tracing resembles the figure three. It is carried out in eight different forms. The basic figure consists of a rapid change of edge and simultaneous change from forward to backward using the natural rotational flow.

Toe (Skating) Fr *Pince* G *Zacken*
The toes are the spikes or teeth on the front underside of a skate for figure skating, together known as the toe rake. For advanced figure skating, the lowest toe is much larger and is known as the "master" toe.

Toe-assist (Skating) Fr *Piqué* G *Getupft*
All jumps can be either with or without toe-assist. In other words, the unoccupied foot can assist in the jump by using the prominent front spike or the specialist figure skating skates to give additional purchase.

Toe loop (Skating) Fr *Demi boucle*
G *Euler Thoren*
The toe loop is the simplest skating jump from the backward outside edge with the assistance of the free toe, a 360° turn to backward inside edge of the same foot. It is also known as a "cherry flip."

Touring skating Fr *Patinage de randonnée*
G *Schlittschuhlanglaufen*
A now almost archaic form of distance skating, touring skating is still carried out in Holland, its place of origin. Skaters travel from town to town by means of the frozen canals.

Triple (Skating)
See "Double."

Walley (Skating) Fr *Lutz en dedans sans piqué*
G *Einwarts Lutz ohne abtupfen*
A walley skating jump from the backward inside edge with 360° counter-rotation, landing on back outside edge of the takeoff foot. These jumps and their variations are usually performed as a succession of single jumps.

Wick (Curling)
A stone which hits another and rebounds at an angle.

Wide (Curling)
A stone is wide when it is thrown outside the skip's broom.

Windmill spin (Skating) Fr *Pirouette arabesque*
G *Himmelspirouette*
A windmill spin skating spin which is a variation of the camel spin. The skater moves his or her arms first upward and then down toward the ice.

World Hockey Association
A professional ice hockey association on formed in 1971 to cover North America. It rivals the National Hockey League.

Wrist shot (Ice hockey)
A flick shot where the stick is not raised backward off the ice and the puck is flicked forward. It is not quite as fast as a slapshot but it is more difficult to field and much more difficult to perform.

Zieldaube (Eisschiessen)
The target "dolly" used in all *Eisschiessen* disciplines, also known simply as the *Daube*.

PICTURE CREDITS

The authors and publishers thank the following for permission to reproduce the illustrations on the pages indicated:

AUSTRIAN NATIONAL TOURIST OFFICE: 35. THE BETTMANN ARCHIVE: 17, 19, 20, 22 (left and right), 26, 27, 36, 42, 49, 83. THE CANADIAN HIGH COMMISSION: 60, 64. CAMERA PRESS: 99. KEYSTONE PRESS AGENCY: 85. KUNSTHISTORISCHES MUSEUM, VIENNA: 31. NATIONAL GALLERY OF SCOTLAND: 32. NETHERLANDS NATIONAL TOURIST OFFICE: 106, 107, 109, 110. NOVOSTI PRESS AGENCY: 164. POPPERFOTO: 103. SWISS NATIONAL TOURIST OFFICE: 21, 44–5, 67, 93, 113, 119, 130–1, 133, 136, 138, 143, 161, 185. WIDE WORLD PHOTOS: 14–15, 24, 47, 80, 86, 88, 120, 124, 159.

Diagrams on pages 37, 38, 39, 100, 147 by Eileen Batterberry. All other diagrams by The Diagram Group.

BIBLIOGRAPHY

Brown, Nigel. *Ice Skating : A History.* Kaye, London, 1959.

Diagram Group, The. *Enjoying Skating.* Paddington Press, New York and London, 1978.

Diagram Group, The. *Rules of the Game.* Paddington Press, New York and London, 1974.

Foxe, Arthur N. *Skating for Everyone.* Deerhill Press, New York, 1966.

Horne, Peri. *A Step-by-step Book of Ice Skating.* Museum Press, 1968.

National Skating Association of Great Britain. *Ice Dances : Official Steps, Diagrams and Glossary of Terms.* N.S.A., 1968.

Noel, John. *Figure Skating for Beginners.* Nelson, 1964.

Ogilvie, Robert S. *Basic Ice Skating Skills : An Official Handbook Prepared for the United States Figure Skating Association.* Lippincott, Philadelphia. Pa., 1968.

Readhead, Monty. *Ice Dancing.* Pelham Books, 1968.

Richardson, Thomas Dow. *The Art of Figure Skating.* Kaye, London, 1962.

Richardson, Thomas Dow. *Your Book of Skating.* Faber, 1963.

Welsh, Robin. *Beginner's Guide to Curling.* Pelham Books, 1969.

INDEX

Page numbers in *italic* refer to the illustrations

The Illustrated encyclopedia of ice skating

DATE			

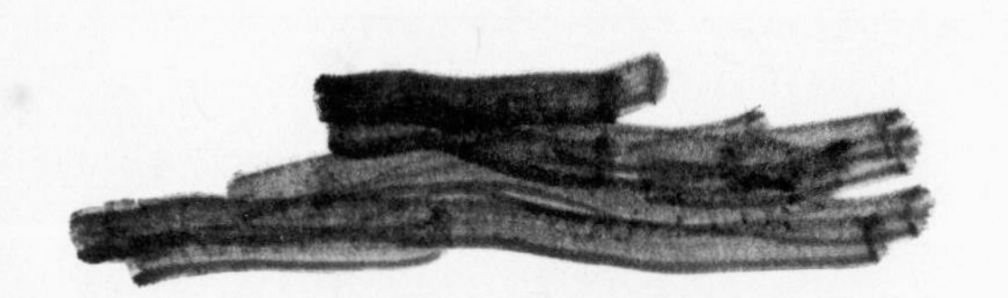